ANTHOLOGY OF NOONOMY: FOURTH TECHNOLOGICAL REVOLUTION AND ITS ECONOMIC, SOCIAL AND HUMANITARIAN CONSEQUENCES

Studies in Critical Social Sciences Book Series

Haymarket Books is proud to be working with Brill Academic Publishers (www.brill.nl) to republish the *Studies in Critical Social Sciences* book series in paperback editions. This peer-reviewed book series offers insights into our current reality by exploring the content and consequences of power relationships under capitalism, and by considering the spaces of opposition and resistance to these changes that have been defining our new age. Our full catalog of *SCSS* volumes can be viewed at https://www.haymarketbooks .org/series_collections/4-studies-in-critical-social-sciences.

Anthology of Noonomy: Fourth Technological Revolution and Its Economic, Social and Humanitarian Consequences

Technology and Socio-economic Progress:
Traps and Opportunities for the Future

Edited by
Sergey D. Bodrunov

Haymarket Books
Chicago, IL

First published in 2022 by Brill Academic Publishers, The Netherlands
© 2022 Koninklijke Brill NV, Leiden, The Netherlands

Published in paperback in 2023 by
Haymarket Books
P.O. Box 180165
Chicago, IL 60618
773-583-7884
www.haymarketbooks.org

ISBN: 979-8-88890-009-3

Distributed to the trade in the US through Consortium Book Sales and
Distribution (www.cbsd.com) and internationally through Ingram Publisher
Services International (www.ingramcontent.com).

This book was published with the generous support of Lannan Foundation,
Wallace Action Fund, and the Marguerite Casey Foundation.

Special discounts are available for bulk purchases by organizations and
institutions. Please call 773-583-7884 or email info@haymarketbooks.org for more
information.

Cover design by Jamie Kerry and Ragina Johnson.

Printed in the United States.

Library of Congress Cataloging-in-Publication data is available.

Contents

Foreword

The collection offered to your attention is the consequence of the scientific community's growing attention to developments in the field of the theory of noonomy. This concept, which was presented in its entirety relatively recently (in 2018), almost immediately attracted the attention of the scientific community both in our country and abroad. This interest is quite understandable: it is not often that detailed theoretical hypotheses appear on the scientific horizon, allowing us to imagine the long-term effects from changes that, at the present time, are just being outlined in the field of production. At the same time, the theory of noonomy does not boil down to just a certain forecast or vision of the future. Such a vision is built as a necessary conclusion from a thorough study of the objective trends in the evolution of the material basis of production, as well as the consequences of this evolution under the current social structure of the economy.

It is no wonder that such a concept has aroused the interest of representatives of various fields in the social sciences. After all, the concept itself is a complex social science theory and largely interdisciplinary in its nature. And there are many reasons to see the interdisciplinary nature of research as one of essential factors determining the potential of scientific achievements. This quite reasonable broad interest in the theory of noonomy is namely reflected in the materials of this collection.

An entire number of major experts representing both Russia and a number of other countries (Austria, Great Britain, Canada, Cuba, the USA, China) enter into a fruitful scientific dialogue with Sergey Bodrunov, the author of the noonomy concept. This dialogue unfolds the ideas of noonomy for further research in various fields of social sciences. All the experts who have contributed to the content of this collection review Bodrunov's ideas from their own experience in scientific research, finding points of interaction and mutual enrichment in the course of deepening the knowledge of social processes.

Among these areas of interaction, one cannot ignore the study of the issues of technological changes with respect to their impact on social relations developing in the world. The collection reviews aspects related to the development and change of technological paradigms, which is the subject of the chapter by a recognized expert in this field and one of the authors of the concept of technological paradigms, Academician of the Russian Academy of Sciences Sergey Glazyev. Alan Freeman, Director of Geopolitical Economy Research Group at the University of Manitoba looks at the development of modern technologies from a slightly different angle. He emphasizes the leading role of the personal factor in technological progress, critically assessing a number of attempts at technological modernization not supported by providing wider opportunities for the development of education and professional growth of employees.

Perceiving the ideas of noonomy, a number of authors pay special attention to those contradictions of the modern social structure that, on the one hand, slow down the progressive socio-economic shifts and, on the other hand, lead to aggravation of urgent problems, which makes shifts in the direction indicated by the theory of noonomy objectively necessary. These matters, in relation to the problems of developing countries, are reviewed in the chapter by Professor Leo Gabriel, Director of the Institute for Intercultural Research and Cooperation (Austria). Professor Oleg Smolin, an Academician of the Russian Academy of Education, also points out the growing inequality and social conflicts, expressing his doubt about the possibility of conflict-free transition of humanity to the new stage of development.

The fact that technological progress is accompanied by the evolution of social relations, which, on the one hand, affect technological changes and, on the other hand, act as their consequence, is also not ignored by the authors of the collection. The chapter by Professor Anatoly Porokhovsky, Head of Political Economy Department at the Lomonosov Moscow State University, examines the influence of modern technological trends as to the subject and method of political economy studying the socio-economic consequences of technological shifts. Jesús Pastor Garcia Brigos, a researcher from the Institute of Philosophy (Cuba), draws attention to the fact that technological development is not neutral, leading to different consequences depending on what socio-economic form it is clothed in. From this point of view, he considers the issue of what are the prospects for the evolution of socialism in Cuba. A similar position is held by Professor Enfu Cheng, Director of the Research Center of Economic and Social Development at the Chinese Academy of Social Sciences, and his colleague, Associate Professor Siyang Gao (China), who draw attention to the development of modern technologies of intellectual production and specific features of its economic implementation under various social systems.

Chapters by well-known experts James Kenneth Galbraith, Professor at the University of Texas (Austin, USA), and Radhika Desai, Professor at the University of Manitoba (Canada), are dedicated to the global or, to be exact, globalization problems of the movement towards noonomy. James Kenneth Galbraith notes how the crisis associated with the COVID-19 pandemic has demonstrated the fragility and unreliability of the modern world economic paradigm based on bare economic calculation and shows the need for a more reasonable structure of production relations, the criteria of which would be more consistent with what is proposed by the theory of noonomy. Radhika

Desai reviews the role of national states in protecting national conditions of reproduction, despite the claims of global financial capital for hegemony, from the standpoint of geopolitical economy. This objectively necessary role of the national state opens up the opportunity for the implementation of development projects that break with the logic of global capital and allow us to take steps towards noonomy.

In the chapter by Professor of the Lomonosov Moscow State University Andrey Kolganov, noonomy is considered as a necessary methodological and theoretical tool that allows implementing strategic development projects, because it contains the necessary predictive potential for understanding trends in both the near and distant future.

Together, the publications presented in the collection paint a broad picture of various research fields related to the theory of noonomy and indicate the significant development potential contained in this theory.

Ruslan Grinberg
Corresponding Member of the Russian Academy of Sciences, Dr. Sc. (Econ.), Professor, Scientific Director of the Institute of Economics of the Russian Academy of Sciences, Moscow, Russia

Acknowledgements

The authors would like to express their gratitude to all those whose participation in the discussion of the problems raised in this book, support and constructive criticism allowed us to take one more step forward in the study of the theory and practical aspects of noonomy.

We are grateful to the many colleagues who have shown a genuine interest in the subject presented in this book and actively participated in discussions with the authors at various scientific forums around the world – in Moscow, St. Petersburg, Paris, New York, Beijing, London, Cambridge, Lisbon, Vienna, Mexico City, and many other science centers over the past five years. Among them, we would like to mention Professor A. Buzgalin from the Lomonosov Moscow State University, Professors A. Plotnikov, S. Bodrunova and E. Tkachenko from St. Petersburg, leader of the International Initiative for Promoting Political Economy (IIPPE) Professor A. Campbell (USA), Professors D. Lane and P. Nolan from the University of Cambridge, members of the Russian Academy of Sciences, famous economists from Russia A. Nekipelov, R. Grinberg and V. Kvint, the excellent Moscow culture philosopher professor L. Bulavka, professors M. Voeikov and A. Gorodetsky from the Institute of Economics of the Russian Academy of Sciences, as well as many other colleagues who cannot be listed here due to the length of the list.

We also must say a few words of gratitude to everyone who participated in numerous conversations, seminars, and colloquia of the S.Y. Witte Institute for New Industrial Development (INID)[1] where the theory of noonomy was born and the problems of our book were discussed extensively. And, of course, we cannot help but mention the help in resolving many issues, both during preparing this book for publication and those that arise every time during the preparation of seminars and scientific conferences at INID, highly qualified specialists A. Zolotarev, N. Yakovleva, A. Osipenko, N. Lee, I. Belykh and G. Maslov.

The editor's special thanks go to the Free Economic Society of Russia and the International Union of Economists, members of the Free Economic Society of Russia Board, Presidiums of the Free Economic Society of Russia and the International Union of Economists, as well as the Free Economic Society of Russia Senate, and in particular – Academicians of the Russian Academy of

---

1   The links to the materials from some of these conversations and seminars can be found on the INID website: https://inir.ru/.

Sciences A. Dynkin, B. Porfiryev, A. Aganbegyan, RAS Corresponding Member A. Shirov, professors S. Kalashnikov, S. Ryabukhin, M. Eskindarov, Y. Silin, R. Golov for their support and positivity in joint activities, and to the teams of these organizations and their director M. Ratnikova for their high level of professionalism and independence in work, which allowed the editor and author of this book (the President of the Free Economic Society of Russia and the President of the International Union of Economists) to be "relieved" from time to time from the affairs of the Society and the Union and find the time to work on this difficult project.

Finally, the editor, taking such an excellent opportunity, cannot help but express his gratitude to his colleagues who have agreed to participate as authors in our joint project.

And finally, to the Koninklijke Brill NV publishing house, which has done a lot to make presenting our ideas to the readers possible.

Figures and Tables

Figures

Tables

Contributors

Sergey D. Bodrunov
Director of the S.Y. Witte Institute for New Industrial Development (INID), President of the Free Economic Society (VEO) of Russia, President of the International Union of Economists (St. Petersburg), Expert of the Russian Academy of Sciences, Dr. Sc. (Econ.), Professor (Russia)

Alexander Buzgalin
Dr. Sc. (Econ.), Professor, Head of the Center for Socioeconomics of the Political Economy Department, Faculty of Economics, Lomonosov Moscow State University (Russia)

Enfu Cheng
Director of the Research Center of Economic and Social Development at the Chinese Academy of Social Sciences, Principal Professor of the University of the Chinese Academy of Social Sciences, President of the World Association for Political Economy (China)

Radhika Desai
Professor, Director of Geopolitical Economy Research Group at the University of Manitoba (Canada)

Alan Freeman
Director of Geopolitical Economy Research Group at the University of Manitoba (Canada)

Leo Gabriel
Director of Institute for Intercultural Research and Cooperation (Austria)

James Kenneth Galbraith
Lloyd M. Bentsen Jr. Chair in Government/Business Relations at Lyndon B. Johnson School of Public Affairs and Professor of Government at the University of Texas at Austin (USA)

Siyang Gao
Associate Professor at the School of Marxism, Liaoning University (China)

Jesús Pastor García Brigos
Senior Researcher at the Institute of Philosophy (Cuba)

Sergey Y. Glazyev
Minister in Charge of Integration and Macroeconomics of the Eurasian Economic Commission, Dr. Sc. (Econ.), Academician of the Russian Academy of Sciences, Professor (Russia)

Andrey I. Kolganov
Head of the Laboratory for Comparative Research of Socio-economic Systems at the Faculty of Economics of Lomonosov Moscow State University; Chief Researcher at the Institute of Economics of the Russian Academy of Sciences, Dr. Sc. (Econ.), Professor (Russia)

Anatoly A. Porokhovsky
Chair of Political Economy Department, Lomonosov Moscow State University, Dr. Sc. (Econ.), Professor (Russia)

Oleg N. Smolin
First Deputy Chairman of the State Duma Education and Science Committee, Dr. Sc. (Philos.), Academician of the Russian Academy of Education, Professor (Russia)

Introduction

What Is Noonomy?

Sergey D. Bodrunov

1   Civilization Faced with Crisis

We are currently seeing clear signs that the human civilization is experiencing an escalating crisis. All elements of this civilization — its economic system, social structure and core characteristics of modern humans' existence — have deeply eroded.

Production relations and economic institutions that serve as the foundation of our production activity increasingly make us question their ability to ensure stable development of the human society, and that primarily pertains to market self-regulatory mechanisms. The proverbial 'invisible hand' of the market is still setting the direction — towards rampant financial speculation that undermines the stability of the very market system and towards continuous predatory consumption of resources, as opposed to harmonious development of human potential and elimination of lingering social ills.

Global social polarization is on the rise, and institutions of political democracy are increasingly focused on political manipulation of voters instead of identifying actual social desires of the general population. Political and ideological technologies that rely on information and digital technologies and mass media's ability to influence people's minds are used not for the sake of progress, but to avoid the resolution of urgent issues while upholding the political status.

Global social and economic relations (which Professor Radhika Desai refers to as the "geopolitical economy" (Desai, 2013)) are also experiencing a period of increasing turbulence. The fight for global hegemony clashes with the trend towards deglobalization, and some countries' exceptionalism is met with resistance from states that seek to protect their national interests. This leads to profound changes in the global geopolitical configuration, and the consequences of such changes are hard to predict.

The most disturbing thing is that all these processes result in the destruction of people's moral and spiritual health. Simultaneously, the loss of cultural and moral markers is being all but justified in the rejection of 'grand narratives" (i.e., essentially rejecting a holistic view of reality from a certain standpoint) and in declaring that criteria of Truth, Progress, Kindness and Beauty have questionable value.

The economy also exhibits multiple clear signs of the escalating crisis. We are experiencing the second destructive financial and economic crisis over the course of fifteen years. And these crises are definitely deeper than the ones encountered by the world economy in the last quarter of the twentieth century. Of course, we can write off the 2020 crisis as a consequence of the COVID-19 pandemic, but, in fact, economists had been anticipating both the economic recession and the stock market crash since 2018, and by the beginning of 2020, the signs of the upcoming crisis had become perfectly clear. The pandemic only triggered the crisis and factored in to modify it dramatically, but did not cause it. Such trigger (one or another) just had to emerge. The development of the economy and society has such periods when, in Nassim Taleb's terms, a Black Swan event (an unpredictable event that changes the current state of affairs (Taleb, 2007)) is sure to occur. The shape that it will take is a secondary matter.

2   Change the Development Model

We have long been pointing out the warped nature of the current model of human development. Under this model, excessive significance is attributed to market criteria that underpin not just the economy; market approach is imposed on all spheres of public life, and commercial criteria start to apply to all aspects of our existence, including the creative spirit of culture and arts, caring about upbringing and education, fighting for people's health, intellectual curiosity, legal protection, etc.

Economic relations comprise production, which is a core dimension of the human society, as it generates material foundations of the human existence. But does it imply that the economy has the right to project principles of economic relations onto all other spheres of public life? Such approach prioritizes economic and particularly financial results, even in areas where commercialization is clearly pernicious. Consequently, commercialization becomes a medium for segregating access to generally significant social benefits and introduces competition where it does not ensure higher efficiency, but stirs up social strife that deforms people's minds, their values and cultural beliefs.

The acuteness of contradictions that are accumulating at the modern stage in the development of the human civilization has long been noted. As early as in the 1990s, public figures, scientists and politicians with a strategic vision agreed on the need to resolve a wide range of urgent issues whose escalation creates major threats. Consequently, the year 2000 saw the adoption of the Millennium Declaration, which formulated goals pertaining to social development and poverty eradication, as well as protection of the environment (United Nations Millennium Summit, 2000). Following partial implementation of the program's goals, in 2015 the UN General Assembly adopted the resolution which set up seventeen sustainable development goals (UN General Assembly, 2015). But we can accurately set relevant goals and comprehend paths required for their achievement only subject to scientifically attuned study of reasons behind issues that stand before our civilization.

It is impossible to resolve these matters by discussing whether current problems stem from excessive interference into market self-regulatory mechanisms, as neoliberal economists believe, or, on the contrary, whether the key to the resolution of present issues lies in the development and improvement of mechanisms for state regulation of the economy (and various Keynesian trends and some other heterodox theories are leaning towards this opinion).

This dispute could be relevant 50–80 years ago. To an extent, it has maintained its relevance. But it is no longer sufficient, for over the past decades the world has changed and continues to change rapidly. And in order to obtain the right answers in the face of aggravating threats and escalating contradictions, we have to start asking different questions.

First of all, we should agree that the answer to the question of 'what model of capitalism (more liberal or more regulated) we should adhere to' is not our primary concern. Nor should we prioritize the question whether capitalism has exhausted its potential for development.

We are actually facing a much more fundamental question: are we witnessing the exhaustion of the entire prior paradigm of human civilizational development reliant on principles of the economic society? A lot points to that. And the pursuit of this development paradigm is rife with not just acceleration of the aforementioned problems, but with a catastrophe that is quite real.

But we should not sink into alarmism. Humans are certainly not intent on rampantly destroying all and everything, including themselves. They are capable of comprehending pending issues and practically resolving them while moving forward and subsequently going beyond the limits of their present-day abilities. That is why the key to resolving issues of the brewing civilizational crisis lies in the plane of studying and understanding this crisis and in the plane of finding practical solutions based both on such understanding and perceiving our own capabilities.

We need socially responsible and theoretically substantiated solutions. They are particularly necessary because our civilization is nearing a choice point: we will either cross the line beyond which the threat to our civilization's existence will become irreversible (the threat may take the shape of an environmental disaster, deployment of weapons of mass destruction, human degradation resulting from injudicious interference with human nature, etc.); or we will find opportunities for overcoming the escalating civilizational crisis and progress to a qualitatively new stage in our development.

So far, neither the neoclassical economic theory nor Marxist political economy has disclosed these opportunities, in spite of their seeking to find theoretical answers to the most pressing modern issues. Other social sciences have also fallen short in this regard. In reality, scholars' and public figures' response often amounts to paying more attention to social, humanitarian and environmental issues without addressing the fundamental causes of these problems. That can be deduced from the ideas of sustainable development which served as the foundation of UN resolutions.

But it is impossible to shape qualitatively new opportunities for overcoming the civilizational crisis without transitioning to a qualitatively new state of society. The path of transitioning to such qualitatively new state and its definition have been described in our work that has been underway for a number of years. That is the path that leads through the New Industrial Society of the Second Generation (NIS.2) to noonomy.

The theory of noonomy, which was created by the author of these lines and has been discussed for many years at academic seminars organized by St. Petersburg-based S.Y. Witte Institute for New Industrial Development (INID), has emerged as a logical result of original extensive research targeting issues related to technological progress, reindustrialization of the economy, trends in the development of industrial production (Bodrunov, 2013, 2016) and its effect on the social structure. Over this period of time, the author has produced a few publications on the matter enunciating obtained results (Bodrunov 2017, 2018a, 2018b).

These results were also regularly presented in publications of INID materials dedicated to various specific aspects of the noonomy (Bodrunov, 2019. See also similar volumes: Bodrunov, 2020, 2021). Ideas and various elements of this concept are being further developed in articles, at seminars, various conferences, congresses and scientific colloquiums of the INID with the participation of its partners from the Russian Academy of Sciences and foreign colleagues. Besides, the publication of the author's core findings on the New Industrial Society of the Second Generation and noonomy was followed by numerous discussions of the proposed theory and multiple colloquiums at various universities, dissertation councils, diverse expert communities — including international expert groups — and research labs (several Russian universities incorporated the theory of noonomy into their curriculum). All this has also contributed to the development and refinement of the noonomy's theoretical platform.

The main site for presenting and discussing the principles of noonomy has been one of Russia's major events, the St. Petersburg International Economic Congress (SPEC) organized annually by the INID specifically with that purpose; moreover, noonomy issues have lately been discussed at various high-profile forums in Moscow, other Russian cities and abroad. The theory of noonomy has been tested by sophisticated and perceptive representatives of the international scholarly community in Cambridge, Lille, Mexico City, Vienna, Lisbon, New York, Beijing, etc.

In general, the work that has been carried out to develop and deepen the theory of noonomy now allows for a clearer, more precise and substantiated explication of its core aspects.

3   Research Methodology: Critical Role of Material Production

It is important to rely on correct methodological approaches and distinct ideas on the role of material production, its product, industrial production and their place in the socioeconomic structure of the society. The starting point for understanding the prospects for the evolution of the social structure is to understand that material production lies at the core of human society's livelihood and, accordingly, changes in material production determine the development of the society.

In this regard, it is important to consider all components of production: specific characteristics of the technological process, the nature of the product of production, the nature of labor, formats for production organization. Only combined, these elements allow for the development of a holistic understanding of the shifts that occur in production.

In its historical development, the material and technological foundation of the economy goes through two main stages: pre-industrial and industrial production. Of course, we can delineate various steps within these two stages, but, fundamentally, no other options (except for these two stages) can be identified in the development of material production. Hypothetical 'post-industrial' production has not yet come to pass. The modern economy rests firmly on its industrial material production, despite the prevailing share of the service sector, which — often wrongfully — is taken to include many modern effects of industrial activity.

In particular, industrial production has characteristics that set it apart from pre-industrial production. Some of these characteristics are as follows:

- use of complex means of production rather than hand tools;
- reliance on universal man-made energy sources (various steam engines, internal combustion engines, electrical motors, jet engines, etc.) rather than on natural energy sources (human and animal muscle strength, natural water and wind power);
- use of technologies primarily based on scientific knowledge that makes it possible to transform various natural processes into human-controlled and human-directed technological processes rather than on empirical production experience;
- facilities allowing both for mass production of standardized products and their adaptation to the needs of individual consumers.

Therefore, the stance that is clearly pursued in the theory of noonomy is the recognition of the fact that industry definitely constitutes the production and technological core in the modern economy. Industrial production provides the necessary economic conditions for the development of all other sectors of the economy – construction, the agricultural sector and the service industries in aggregate – by supplying them with various materials, machinery and equipment and by developing technological processes. Indeed, over the past 250 years industrial evolution has, to a great extent, determined shifts in the society's socioeconomic formation. This development transpires by transitioning from one technological mode to another.

4   Technological Modes

The concept of technological modes emerged as a logical extension of global research trends. It is known that Joseph Schumpeter saw innovative activities of entrepreneurs leading to technological updating of production as a factor in acquiring competitive advantages and the main economic development driver (Schumpeter, 1983). At the same time, Schumpeter came to the conclusion that the distribution of innovative activity was chronologically uneven. Schumpeter referred to new technology complexes that developed during spikes in innovations as 'clusters' (bunches) (Men'shikov and Klimenko, 2014: 192), but the English term 'waves of innovation' came to be used more frequently (Blaug, 2008: 333).

In 1975, Gerhard Mensch, a scholar from West Germany, studied patterns in the shift from technological stagnation – characterized by the prevalence of incremental or even pseudo-innovations – and the periods of implementation of revolutionary (baseline) technological solutions (Mensch, 1975). Like Schumpeter, he wrote on the clusters of basic innovations that lead to industrial metamorphoses. In 1970–1980, English economist Christopher Freeman formulated the concepts of a 'technological system' and 'techno-economic paradigm', which were further developed by his student Carlota Perez (Perez, 2011). The term 'technological mode', which is used in the Russian economic science, is, in a sense, a symbiotic analog to the concepts of the 'waves of innovation', 'techno-economic paradigm' and 'technological system'. This term was first suggested in 1986 by D. S. Lvov and S. Y. Glazyev (Lvov and Glazyev, 1986).

According to the definition given by S. Y. Glazyev, the technological mode is a sustainable holistic structure which comprises a full cycle from the extraction and processing of primary resources to the production of end products that correspond to the type of public consumption.

Now the world is starting to transition from the fifth technological mode, which was formed in the 1950s–1980s and currently constitutes the dominant mode (but only in the most developed countries), to the sixth mode. Research-related premises for the sixth technological mode began to form in the 1980s–1990s, whereas the first applied technologies started to spread in the early twenty-first century and still have not gained much ground. Thus, modern economy's progress towards the sixth technological mode prepares us not only for a change in technological modes, but brings us to the threshold of a new technological revolution.

What is the sixth technological mode? It is Industry 4.0 (Germany Trade & Invest, 2018) based on the creation of so-called smart factories. An integral part of Industry 4.0 is the Internet of Things, or, rather, the Industrial Internet of Things (Boyes et al, 2018), which allows for the interaction of autonomous technical devices with each other and human control over them. In order to ensure such control, we are widely implementing built-in sensors and systems for processing big data obtained from them.

As for production technologies, they are beginning the transition from subtractive technologies based on trimming, grinding and cutting to additive technologies[1] based on the addition or layering of base materials. An additive technology that is rapidly gaining popularity, 3D printing constitutes building from primary materials layer by layer using three-dimensional computer models of an end product. In 2017, worldwide sales of 3D printers exceeded 400 thousand units (Adams, 2018). In 2018, the number of sold 3D printers decreased by several percent, but the sales value increased by 27%, and suppliers' profits went up by 44%. That demonstrates the development of

---

1   For a review of additive technologies' capabilities, see (Prosvirnov, 2012; The Construction of Europe's, 2017; 3D Bioprinting of Organs, 2015).

technology towards greater complexity. The decline was observed in the segment of home desktop 3D printers, whereas sales of industrial and designer units have been growing steadily and now account for about 70% of the market (Greenwood, 2019).

The synthesis of nano-, bio-, information and cognitive technologies (also known as NBIC convergence) also shows a lot of promise (Roco and Bainbridge, 2002; Bainbridge, 2006). Lately, NBIC has grown to include social sciences and transformed into NBICS (Spohrer, 2002: 102). It accurately captures the trend of this process and, in fact, the vector of our civilizational development.

So, what are the most important specific characteristics of the sixth technological mode which allows for an industrial revolution? The main distinctive features of this mode are as follows:
- first, development of new technologies based on fundamental scientific research (which was also typical for the fifth mode, but hardly affected main technologies of material production);
- second, broad development of synergistic interaction of new technologies and the formation of hybrid technologies;
- third, development of information and communication technologies forms the very core that ensures the convergence of various technologies and the formation of hybrid technologies.

It is important to emphasize once again that what we are experiencing now is not just a transition to the next stage of technological development, not just a transition from the fifth technological mode to the sixth.

The fact of the matter is that a spike in the application of new knowledge is becoming a distinctive feature of the new technological revolution. The share of knowledge intensive costs is rising, whereas the relative share of costs associated with material resources is decreasing. If we continue with this trend, we can expect to see what is described in the author's books *The Coming of New Industrial Society: Reloaded* and *Noonomy*, i.e., we will shift to the level of production where knowledge will account for the largest share in the structure of costs in any scenario, regardless of the method of calculation or unit used. Knowledge is assuming the role of the main manufacturing resource of the next development stage, and nowadays this is already the case in many industries.

In particular, if we consider any modern gadget, up to 80–95% of costs in its market price (according to the INID estimates) come from expenses related to the receipt and implementation of knowledge, i.e., the intellectual element, and the remaining costs cover material resources. This is but one example of a knowledge-intensive product at the modern stage. But the same is true of numerous other products manufactured by the modern industry.

Another point which is necessary to emphasize is that achieving this new quality of production requires not only a technological breakthrough, but also an improvement in all components of modern material production because production contains not one, but four components. Apart from technology, production also comprises labor, means of production (simply put, all material resources used in production – from raw materials to equipment), and forms of production engineering.

Usually, a technological breakthrough is primarily perceived as technologies. This is, however, far from true. The entire material production is changing, and at the same time – if we interpret the concept of 'technologies' in a broad sense – labor and industrial engineering technologies, for example, are changing, too. From this point of view, we can speak of a technological revolution. But if we draw on our understanding of the content of production, then we should assess a large, complex industrial revolution.

5   Upcoming Industrial Revolution: Transition to NIS.2

What will be the outcome of this upcoming industrial revolution? If we refer to qualitative changes in all aspects of industrial production, this should mean a transition of the industrial society to a new stage of its development. Thus, this very revolution will bring about a new state of the industrial society. If the previous industrial era, as it unraveled in the times and terms of J.K. Galbraith, is perceived as a new industrial society of the first generation, then we are nearing the transition to the second generation. And this will be a new generation of precisely the industrial society: the society will remain industrial at its core because it will still be based on industrial activity. We refer to such society as the New Industrial Society of the Second Generation (NIS.2).

A change in the main economic resource serves as the core distinction of this generation of industrial production. The role of the main resource and source of development is passing on to knowledge, i.e., humans' scientific cognition of the world around them. The nature of material production is largely determined by where we get our resources. In the old days, we used to get them directly from nature by hunting, foraging and mining. And now we will 'mine' knowledge because it is the main resource that will engender opportunities for the satisfaction of our needs in their significant, basic aspect.

The new industrial mode of production has extremely high knowledge intensity that it will sideline material and labor costs, thus creating knowledge-intensive product. But it does not imply that production ceases to be material. It acquires a new quality by turning into knowledge-intensive material production. Indeed, knowledge (like any resource, let us point out) does not replace the process of material production per se, although it is becoming its core resource. Besides, knowledge is of economic significance only when applied technologically in production, not in isolation.

The growth in knowledge intensity of production and the transformation of the production process into technology-based application of science, into "experimental science, materially creative and objectifying science" (in Marx's words, see (Marx, 1969: 221)) underlies another important trend when humans step to the side of the immediate production process, and the worker assumes the role of a "watchman and regulator" to the production process that is transformed "from the simple labor process into a scientific process, which subjugates the forces of nature and compels them to work in the service of human needs", as Marx put it (Marx, 1969: 208).

And we are seeing that the sixth technological mode leads, to say the least, to a sharp decrease in humans' immediate involvement in material conversion of primary resources. Humans are increasingly assuming the functions of goal setting and control, while immediate handling of natural matter is performed by autonomous technetic beings. Widespread implementation of industrial robots is but the first step on this path. Surgical robots are no longer uncommon; robot drivers cruise the roads; artificial intelligence is increasingly replacing human interaction with clients of commercial and banking firms; and the list of examples may be continued.

Let us consider one example of a robotic center that comprises modern information and telecommunication technologies, robotics itself and 3D printing – the new product Olli.[2] It is marketed by Local Motors, a U.S. company which introduced an unmanned passenger bus manufactured by an integrating information system, made from parts that were almost completely produced on a 3D printer and assembled by an automatic production line (Tess, 2017). Material costs (compared against the use of traditional materials) and the cost of labor were reduced manifold. The breakdown of the full production cycle is as follows: production of all parts took 10 hours; automatic assembly was completed in 1 hour; software download and testing of separate systems and the finished product also took 1 hour, so the overall production time constituted just half a day of continuous work that required virtually no human involvement. For passenger comfort, makers of this unusual (initially) product reached out to IBM, which suggested to add its IBM-Watson system (IBM,

---

2   See Meet Olli presentation on Local Motors website: Local Motors (2021). Mobility for today's communities: Meet Olli. Available (consulted 25 August, 2021) at: https://localmotors.com/products/.

2018). Figuratively speaking, it is a talking guide that can answer any queries (in a number of widely used languages) it hears on the bus, such as: travel time, bus stop closest to destination, expected delay time due to traffic jams, emergency numbers, etc. Thus, Local Motors presented a robot-bus. Will passengers have the same experience compared to riding a regular bus driven by an attentive driver? No! Passengers will have an even better experience (otherwise the new product will not be popular in the competitive market!) because multimedia services installed on the bus will provide them with an opportunity to chat, get a consultation, obtain travel information, use Wi-Fi, watch TV, work, learn, have fun, etc. This example comprises all three paradigmatic technology components (which change the paradigm of the traditional industry and all its elements) of the upcoming new industrial revolution, i.e., digitalization, additive printing and robotization.

The Internet of Things and similar technologies entail essential changes in approaches to many traditional areas of economic activity ranging from retail and the service industry to construction (on a side note: in turn, they serve as a strong foundation for future innovations). At the same time, synergistic potential inherent in modern technologies does not decrease, but increases upon implementation: one striking example is the development of information technologies, where the efficiency of hardware enhances software efficiency, while the improvement of software increases hardware capacity.

Application of knowledge intensive technologies results in fundamental changes that also occur in such component of the industrial process as industrial engineering. These changes include the improvement of production management systems, conversion of product design to 3D modeling, optimization of transportation/material/information/etc. flows, and automation/internetization of management solutions, etc. – when systems administrators become factory administrators! – and much more.

The use of self-learning artificial intelligence (AI) systems leads to cognitive technologies penetrating, under the sixth technological mode, into areas which used to have no alternative to human labor. Nowadays, AI systems are capable of searching, accumulating, sorting and comparing information that provide the foundation for decision-making. *It is cognitive technologies that, thanks to the use of advances in biotechnology and information and communication technologies, allow for direct human interaction with the unmanned technological processes* (human-machine interfaces, human-machine systems, human-machine networks – for discussion on this topic, see (Tsvetkova et al., 2015)). This foundation gives a fresh impetus to the production of robotics, which becomes more flexible, more adaptable and more productive.

6   Civilisational Crossroads

The next major point is as follows: the growth of technological capabilities for the satisfaction of wants presents us with a dilemma of civilizational development. We often say that an environmental crisis is looming since we littered the whole world with plastic, mutant animals are born, dozens and hundreds of species disappear every day, and we see the emergence of technetic creatures that spawn much faster than nature, which created this world. The reason is that the number of the so-called technetic beings (if we use the terminology of geobiocenosis to refer to creatures inhabiting the technological cenoses) is growing quickly.

Those elements of technocenosis that we label the 'technetic beings', which certainly exist and occupy a certain place in our space, are increasingly gaining ground. They are driving out natural beings, and nowadays their creators – humans – have already (if we follow Vernadsky, as early as in his day and time) become a significant geological, not to mention biological, force. According to geologists, the total volume of everything that humans have created over five thousand years of their existence, also known as *the weight of the techno-sphere*, i.e., everything created by humans over their history with the help of technology, *constitutes 30 trillion tons* (Zalasiewicz et al, 2017: 12). According to biologists, *over 4.5 billion years of the Earth's existence, the weight of biome*, i.e., everything created by nature, *constitutes approximately about 2.5 trillion tons* (Korogodin and Korogodina, 2000: 106).

This being said, we are facing an ever-increasing loss of biodiversity. Every hour, three species disappear from the face of the earth. Every day, at least 72 species are lost. Of course, the process of extinction has always been going on as a natural process, with no human involvement. This natural extinction process is estimated at about one out of a million species per year. Still, "current estimates of the number of species can vary from, let's say, two million species to over 30 or even 100 million species," this is how Dr. Braulio Dias, Executive Secretary of the Convention on Biological Diversity, describes the problem (Skobeeva, 2016).[3] Even if we take the highest estimate, we can easily calculate that the rate of extinction will be 262 species out of one million per year, which is definitely above the natural norm.

---

3   Based on sequenation and comparison of the DNA of microorganisms, some studies estimate the number of species on our planet to be approximately 1 trillion. However, this increase in the estimated number of species has occurred only thanks to microorganisms (Locey and Lennon, 2016).

And at the same time, humans have created about one billion technetic species – a lot more than the number of species created by nature (Zalasiewicz et al, 2017). Thus, technodiversity has not only surpassed biodiversity, but is also suppressing it.

So, if we consider the biological aspect of the issue, then humans, out of all living beings, turn out to be the most destructive towards living nature. This leads to a major crisis in many areas: for example, biological crisis, or genomic crisis, when people can both interfere with their own nature and create creatures beyond their control – and much more.

These are no longer ideas out of sci-fi movies. For example, the Massachusetts Institute of Technology (USA) is already editing genes within a human embryo by removing (disabling) some genes and adding other genes on their stead! Another American institute (The Scripps Research Institute, TSRI) has gone even further: its researchers complemented four nucleobases that make up the DNA in nature — adenine, thymine, guanine and cytosine (all living creatures in the world – from bacteria to whales! – are made of them) — with two artificial nucleobases that do not exist in nature; they inbuilt artificial nucleobases into the DNA of living cells and made them reproduce successfully. What is more, acquired (built-in) properties were inherited, and researchers obtained semi-synthetic protein (Medvedev, 2017).[4]

Germany legally introduced the third gender (intersex), but it is quite possible that, due to the interference of technologies that are already available, we will soon be communicating with genderless people (Agaev, 2017) or persons who are only partly human. Still, what if humans want to change their very nature? In this case, do we speak of humans as biosocial creatures or a different species? When we talk about humans, we imply some reasonable restrictions that would not allow such a scenario. This includes different things. Let us make a reference to the idea that Russian writer A. Belyaev described in his novels: if we want to have gills, we must live in the ocean. And vice versa – if we change our habitat, we will have to change ourselves.

It is clear that scientists who are pushing the horizons of scientific knowledge are driven by good intentions, e.g., creation of new medicinal products and correction of genetic disorders. Still, they do not deny that these scientific achievements may very well be used to create new life forms and 'edit' humans' biological nature.

Exactly the same argument can be made regarding numerous modern technologies, for their careless and unlimited application can radically change our

---

4 For more information, see (Kerman, 2017).

habitat, living conditions and, ultimately, ourselves. Is this path unreservedly positive? Or is it rife with fundamental danger for the humanity? The answer appears to be clear. At the very least, we need to heed this escalating challenge pertaining to the uncertainty of development and civilizational risks.

7   Economic Society Deadlocked

What prompts people to travel down this path that is quite likely non-optimal and potentially disastrous? The answer is as follows: people are prompted by the current economic system, which, according to core market principles and foundations, prioritizes profit-making — frankly speaking, more often than not regardless of the cost.

Nowadays, this primarily translates into the promotion of simulative, unnecessary (or fitted with excessive features) products for the sake of this profit. In turn, an increase in the production of these goods pushes us to sense-lessly plunder nature (whereas people's real needs are often not satisfied!), and so on and so forth. It is difficult to talk about reason in this case, even though free-market economists, as well as experts and specialists who cater to them, consider this approach reasonable from the perspective of the econ-omy (take any textbook on economics or other textbooks that verbosely dis-cuss how rational or irrational certain behavior is; they typically discuss the behavior of economic actors in a market environment). S.Y. Witte Institute for New Industrial Development held a colloquium on this issue. Its participants discussed the meaning of 'rationality' and 'reason' and concluded that were not synonymous.

Reason and knowledge correlate in a very complex way. In the criterion basis that is formed on the basis of cognition, our reason is also formed on the basis of cognition. Thus, reason is both a part of knowledge that allows for evaluat-ing some of its conformity with a criterion basis and a part of knowledge which comprises the criterion basis itself. Is something reasonable or unreasonable within a certain criterion basis? 'Noos' also has its criterion basis. However, this 'noo' basis is wider and not utilitarian. Moreover, it changes, as we gain new knowledge.

Criterion basis of reason has been allegorically mentioned from the earliest times. For example, as early as in the eleventh century, Metropolitan Hilarion wrote in *The Sermon on Law and Grace*, "[B]rought us unto the knowledge of the Truth" (Hilarion, 2011: 70), i.e., the criterion basis of reason is the truth as some constant and recognized value; and the 'circle' of knowledge defined by the criterion basis stands for the "light of understanding", while everything else is darkness! This is the fundamental meaning of the Greek word 'noos' that should be perceived. By the way, its translation into Latin as 'ratio' is completely inaccurate because 'ratio' means conformity of something (some knowledge) to any (!) selected criteria, and this something does not necessarily have to be the 'light' and "the knowledge of the Truth".

Where does this framework of rationality come from? The framework is a certain criterion basis built by us. What is it built on? It is based on knowledge in general, proficiency in some areas, relevant awareness and the formation of corresponding boundaries that help to understand where we can and cannot go and at what point we move past the boundaries of rationality.

Please note that rationality is not absolute. This frame of reference or the system of criteria is dynamic. By expanding knowledge, we expand this space, and, therefore, expand our knowledge of the criterion basis. Its borders and criteria expand accordingly. Each stage and every system have their own rationale. In other words, what was rational yesterday may be no longer rational today.

At the heart of all this is the human ability to obtain increasingly more knowledge. Within what framework? Within the framework of wants satisfaction, including the want for new knowledge and specifically the knowledge of what is 'good' and that its boundaries can be 'pushed'. Thus, knowledge is at the heart of this phenomenon, too. This is an extremely important aspect of the problem that helps us understand how the world works and why it is 'going mad' — shifting boundaries is effectively perceived as 'going mad', for it signifies going beyond the boundaries of what used to be deemed rational. And that is why often (particularly nowadays) all those scientific facts and approaches that we have been studying for many years prove completely unfit for analyzing the future, for comprehending the future in general and for cognizing ourselves.

Lately, economic theory started to perceive that humans are not guided by the 'indifference curve' described in economics textbooks, which are time and again trying to apply dry algebraic formulas and graphs in order to fathom the harmony of real trends in — qualitative! — social development. At the same time, we often hear of humans' 'limited rationality'. But that actually betrays a limited approach to the issue: humans are not some mechanical devices with limited rationality, even as it pertains to market rationality; they are more complex and are able to make decisions based on various — including non-market — criteria.

The nature of the new rationality and, consequently, new development objectives come to the fore under the noonomy since it relies on the transition from the paradigm of growth based on economic 'rationality' (targeting an increase in volume cost indices) to the paradigm based on the achievement of specific goals and satisfaction of various human wants shaped on the basis of higher values.

Market economy perceives rationality as the maximization of monetary income. Naturally, the neoclassical economic theory claims that it does not reduce the issue to just money and that it is human nature to maximize the receipt of any benefits — but they are really taken into account only upon their monetary valuation. Pressured by results of behavioral economics research, the neoclassical economic theory only relatively recently has somewhat softened its stance by admitting that humans are not programmed calculators of benefits and losses can be driven by other motives, and their economic decisions can be influenced by non-economic factors. However, all this is interpreted as 'limited rationality' of humans. It means that economics still regards 'true' rationality as the calculation of benefits and losses and thinks that humans are imperfect, their ability to behave rationally limited by various contributing factors.

Let us assume that economy is rational (or at least aspires to rationality), but is it reasonable? Are today's economic agents that are undoubtedly acting rationally (from the perspective of the current economic activity's criterion basis) definitively reasonable as well? Besides, 'rationality', unlike reason, does not engage in the cognition of new knowledge.

In this respect, when we speak of the noonomy, we imply that it constitutes the transition to a fundamentally different criterion basis, to some special, 'noo'-based principles underpinning the formation of means for the satisfaction of human wants. The wants will be definitely growing and changing, but they will still be 'noo'-wants. That is a distinctive method of managing the economy – the noo-method, if you will. Just as the economy stands for a method of management used in an economic society, the noonomy signifies a method of management under the noo-society.

Thus, the noonomy does not prioritize private pursuit of profit or other income resulting from chaotic market activity. Instead, it focuses on the rational aspiration to the satisfaction of specific wants that are deemed reasonable. Therefore, the level of saturation of these reasonable wants sets specific production goals and implies a certain plan of action which keeps market chaos in check by boosting production consistency and making it more structured. Such approach cannot rule out neither chance occurrences nor free individual choices in the absence of relevant regulation. Thus, the issue here is the need to develop a new production program that would be very flexible and adaptable in the face of change and random shocks.

But we are now living in the economic society that has repeatedly proven its ability to bring the human civilization to crisis situations. We should not deny that at certain periods of time economic rationality has been a powerful driver of economic development, but we must also perceive that such development has time and again led to some crises, when human actions went against certain criteria of reasonableness that lay outside the economy.

8   Simulative Needs and Financial Capital

If we consider these issues from the historical and philosophical standpoint, based maybe not only on Marx's theory of socioeconomic formations, but also on other experts that addressed these topics (Spengler, Toynbee), this will lead us to the conclusion that every change of such "civilizations" — as they termed it, but I believe that these are stages in the development of our whole civilization — is likely associated with challenges that the humanity faces in the course of its development.

In our case, these challenges are not geological disasters that happened in the days of old or some natural phenomena (drought, flood, blight, hunger, etc.); the current main challenge is today's scientific, technical and technological progress. More precisely, the challenge certainly is not the progress in and of itself, but the use of technological achievements within the existing social structure, with accepted criteria of rationality which are unable to contain neither the growing disruption of the environmental balance nor the destructive interference into the human nature. All this is unfolding in the context of unrestrained pursuit of increasing the volume of consumed resources that turn into waste for the sake of ethereal satisfaction of false, illusory, simulative wants. In his recent Encyclical Letter "Fratelli tutti" (All Brothers), Pope Francis points out, "Often the voices raised in defence of the environment are silenced or ridiculed, using apparently reasonable arguments that are merely a screen for special interests. In this shallow, short-sighted culture that we have created, bereft of a shared vision, 'it is foreseeable that, once certain resources have been depleted, the scene will be set for new wars, albeit under the guise of noble claims'" (Francis, 2020) — he is quoting his own words from the Encyclical Letter "Laudato Si" (Praise Be to You) (Francis, 2015). He also expresses his concern that after the current pandemic crisis the world will "plunge even more deeply into feverish consumerism and new forms of egotistic self-preservation" (Francis, 2020).

What is the source of this unchecked consumerism race that is gorging increasingly large volumes of natural resources? When a certain market segment is saturated and people are essentially provided for (compared with the previous stage of development), an economic actor starts asking: what can be used to make profit? In this situation, it is necessary to expand markets either by using innovations to offer a completely new product, invest into creating and launching it in the market (which tends to be the most costly and bears higher risks) or by expanding the market with an old product (which is usually cheaper and less risky), which involves capturing new markets through various means, including suppressing any competitors (who may offer a better solution, but are weaker) and domineering at the expense of progress and people's real needs — hence the predatory nature of capital. It seeks to spend as little as possible, absorb as many resources as possible while cutting costs, and has no qualms about making profit using predatory methods. Another predatory and increasingly popular method involves obtrusive imposition of simulative products and goods.

Of course, we do not encounter purely false wants and purely simulative, useless goods all too often. False wants typically 'cling' to real wants, and the simulative component sort of 'envelops' a product that satisfies real wants. Moreover, a product may initially be really useful, its arrival progressive, but then it acquires a simulative addition — and its progressiveness is gone.

What trends will prevail? It depends on the correlation between the pace of two things: pace/speed of production development, technical progress v. pace/speed of humans' cognizance of social consequences associated with the application of various technologies and structures for the satisfaction of human wants, the social superstructure. The social superstructure is changing as well, but its changes follow after changes in material production.

This correlation gives cause for concern because the society must 'mature' in order to resolve these issues, to cognize and choose the path of its further development. Society matures with the accumulation of knowledge, and the element that facilitates this process is the satisfaction of wants, at least the satisfaction of real wants (real wants also change over time, and some that used to be simulative become real at the next stage, but that is a topic for a different discussion).

In this case, we clearly have a very serious problem. Our society has not yet 'matured' enough to use technological progress and its achievements properly. To an extent, the society has not yet matured because the current technological progress, for all its power and perfect ability to resolve all basic human problems at this stage, still has not 'fed' everyone – people still lack basic goods, and their needs are not met. So why, for example, has not it 'fed' everyone, even though nowadays the world produces enough grain to make bread and provide nourishment for all? Why do millions of people starve? Because we still exercise the economic method of goods appropriation. Moreover, this leads to the following situation: technological progress — combined with financial capital that has absorbed the results of the technological progress — allows for the redistribution of income in favor of this very financial capital as opposed to production capital and the satisfaction of people's real wants.

The nature of financial capital is related to the fact that, as it went through certain stages in its development, it became the master and the ruler of the entire public process. It not only took over public production, but also captured the hearts and minds of the people.

Why did financial capital manage to pull it off? Because people *a priori* have vital, natural biological wants that are zoological in their manifestation, etc. These wants are satisfied in a certain way. They require that humans develop those characteristics which, while not inherently negative (for example, creation/accumulation of reserves, etc.), can still be excessive and redundant in a particular context.

This stems from such a factor as the substantial uncertainty of human existence. From the first days of their separating from nature and cognizing themselves as separate from it, humans cannot determine how long they will require some resource and, consequently, cannot gauge the amount of adequate reserves. We cannot be sure that reserves will suffice for a period of time that we also cannot grasp. Thus, this uncertainty serves as the foundation for the formation of corresponding elements within humans' criterion basis. These elements require that humans make expedient decisions, e.g., that it is necessary to increase stock and accumulate a reserve, albeit incommensurable with what can be consumed at the moment.

Remember the fable about the thrifty ant and the careless grasshopper? The moral of this fable is a perfect match with public virtues (behavioral criterion basis) of the socioeconomic mode under which the fable was written. The economic society retains the generic feature of humans' natural existence. Under the noo-society, developed noo-production will allow for the factor of complete non-simulative wants' satisfaction to assume the role of the 'reserve' – and it will bring about a corresponding change in the criterion basis that determines the 'correctitude' of human behavior and, in fact, human behavior itself.

But now we are living under the economic society and in accordance with its laws. One such law stipulates the expansion of reserves, capital (as its certain sublimation) and 'living space'. Thus, we transferred the natural want to provide for our existence in the context of uncertainty into the financial system. Why has it happened? Because the financial system/money at a certain point in time replaced, substituted the element of accumulation. Because money has a certain function and opens certain well-known opportunities in this regard. Money can be easily exchanged. Money is much more flexible. Money can be 'stored' easier (especially under the current technological conditions) and does not go to waste as fast as some time-sensitive goods, figuratively speaking, etc., even though money can also disappear.

The financial system used to ensure the accumulation of resources not only for consumption, but also for production. At some point, the segregation of financial capital from production capital was a step in the right direction because it ensured the concentration of dispersed monetary resources and their effective use for investing in production. But as financial market institutions developed and claimed an increasingly prominent role in ensuring the functioning of the economy, the more significant part came to be attributed to financial capital's own interests, i.e., self-expansion of this financial capital. Financial objectives are starting to replace real goals – that is what is at the core of the process referred to as the financialization.

If production capital encounters market saturation and a drop in demand, which is discussed above, then what action will the financial capital take in order to overcome this problem? Indeed, the functioning of financial capital, unlike production capital, does not have a direct correlation with the saturation of human wants. Clearly, production capital also prioritizes the money flow, but, in order to get it, this capital must satisfy some specific human wants, so, to an extent, it depends on consumer response, whereas financial capital is interested exclusively in the money flow regardless of its source. Financial capital assesses its consumers from only one perspective – to whom and on what conditions it can allocate money in order to receive the highest return.

As they become dependent on financial capital, its clients also have to heed these criteria. And once the market is saturated with some objects or goods, they become cheaper, so there is no capital gain, and there comes the question: what can be done to ensure further capital gains? Investments in innovations emerge in order to claim new market niches. And since those 'innovations' that are inherently pseudoinnovations (false innovations) are easy, elegant and generate the same, if not higher, revenue, they actually prevail. They are marketed to consumers as something valuable, very important, essential, highly desirable, etc. That requires a change in human values, in what humans perceive as valuable. Let us go back to the starting point: this is the reason why financial capital encourages human corruption; it does not create a 'noo'-human (on a side note: humans develop continuously, from 'zoo' to 'noo', and I wrote about it in my article published in *Voprosy filosofii* (Bodrunov, 2018b)), but instead provokes the formation of zoo-needs.

Financial capital seeks to spread its expansion to the entire world, but this desire has different consequences for various segments of the global economy. Presently, even though the world is global for financial capital, it is still not global enough to ensure globally equal satisfaction of wants. In other words, the capital under the current world order, in spite of globalization, can confine the means for the satisfaction of wants within certain areas. Consequently, some regions, countries and communities are poorer, while others are wealthier. Some satisfy more human wants, some less. Imposed, false wants tend to form in areas where people are more or less well-off. The level of satisfaction of natural, real wants in these areas is higher, and technical progress allows for even higher saturation, but there is not much room for further saturation. It is expensive, so it is economically more feasible to nurture simulative wants.

From this perspective, the use of technological progress by financial capital leads to the latter becoming super-over-measured at the current stage. Imposed, induced wants are being hyped up, accompanied by corresponding consumption of natural and other resources. That is most likely leading to a global catastrophe because, in realizing this process of wants satisfaction, humans consume resources. And there is a finite amount of resources available. The use of limited resources by infinitely growing (inherently) financial capital is a global contradiction. The use of this development paradigm, i.e., unchecked infinite development of the financial capital, has led to a clash between this financial capital's absolutely unbounded lust for development and self-development, on the one hand, and limited capacity for the satisfaction of these financial capital's desires due to limited natural, human, labor resources, etc., on the other.

Hence the link between simulativity and financial capital because the latter, while 'rationally' (from the perspective of the market paradigm) promoting the expansion of simulative consumption, inherently directs its efforts towards increasing the actual financial gain. And that leads us to a civilizational crisis.

Such situation occurs at every stage of the technological progress. Each transition to a new technological mode is accompanied by further expansion and escalation of conflicts, even though it would seem that the satisfaction of a large range of wants should provide for a better life. Why does it happen? Due to obvious disharmony and a gap between social relations and, consequently, public conscience and capabilities offered by the technological progress.

Here is the current dilemma: the society will either waste opportunities provided by the technical revolution, indulge in the pursuit of false goals and values and exacerbate the negative trends of the modern civilization to the point of losing core human characteristics — or the humanity will manage to recalibrate its current civilizational priorities.

9   Through Socialization — to *Homo Culturalis*

So how do these civilizational priorities develop? Gradually, historically, through their personal development, humans progressively acquire the traits of noo-type beings, i.e., humanistic beings who increasingly heed not only their own interests, but also the interests of their environment, society, habitat and other people. This progress from 'zoo' to 'noo' does exist and can be supported by historical evidence.

But there is also another matter: how can we ensure that this progress is a priority, accelerate the movement towards 'noo' and hamper negative processes which reduce humans and the society to 'zoo'? The general layer of behavioral norms and human cognition simultaneously formed on the basis of these norms is what makes up general human and societal culture. We see that the cultural component of the human existence is constantly growing and developing. Of course, history knows examples when the opposite was true, but we still understand that the general cultural level of the modern society is significantly higher than what it was thousands of years ago. At the same time, let us point out, some people who have not sufficiently entered into this very cultural space are still exhibiting many traits of the 'primitive' outlook on life.

This brings up a key point. What do we mean by 'entered'? We understand that people have not entered the cultural space equally: some social strata, some individuals or their communities are more susceptible to the layer of knowledge that is referred to as 'culture' and leads to the development of noo-wants and the formation of noo-outlook on life. We see multiple examples of the modern society's deficiencies in this regard and, in some cases, targeted construction of a system that creates restrictions for humans' entry into a cultural space, prevents them from shaping their personal identity and stultifies them. That is done intentionally, for *limiting people's access to culture creates premises for manipulating them*. It can be easily deduced that these are the doings of the financial capital and its satellites. Its satellites are its derivatives, its siblings, children and grandchildren, i.e., poverty, inequality, less access to the consumption of cultural phenomena, education, etc. — in other words, everything that results in humans lacking in the arsenal of knowledge and cultural goods that allow for the formation of noo-humans. All this is also used to justify the well-known theses that humans are beast-like and to substantiate conjectures that they cannot be rid of the 'zoo'.

The theory of noonomy objects to that. Every person, every individual from the moment of his/her birth has 'noo' potential. Clearly, potential does not determine ability, but provides premises for its formation and development. So what affects the formation of human ability? According to social psychology,

the mechanism behind such formation entails the generalization and incorporation of an entire gamut of psychical processes in an individual's activity. In
turn, these processes (in philosophical terms) serve as the reflection of the outside world and its effect on individuals, shape their outlook by embedding the
'codes' and values in their minds, and allow for their awareness of the world
and the society.

We are living in a world where scientific, technical and technological
progress is combined with the progress of social knowledge, i.e., cognition
of humans, society and their special characteristics. In fact, social studies,
by and large, developed later than scientific, technological and technical
research, even though the first manifestations of such general development
can be found in philosophical treatises and ideas that go back more than two
thousand years. But the study of humans as social beings, i.e., as individuals
within a society, started with the development of psychological sciences and
social studies approximately in the end of the nineteenth century, continued
throughout the twentieth century and obtained some recognition as a large
area of social studies in the second half of the twentieth — early twenty-first
century.

This development bore fruit. The term 'socialization' was introduced in the
end of the nineteenth century by sociologist and philosopher Georg Simmel,
who used it to refer to the formation of social groups. But in the meaning that
is closer to our modern understanding, socialization was explored by sociologists Franklin H. Giddings (Giddings, 1897) and Gabriel Tarde (Tarde, 1890),
who interpreted it as the formation of the human personality under the influence of the social environment.

Nowadays this concept is used in various branches of social sciences, and
it has taken on very different meanings. Economic theory does not perceive
socialization as the process of humans mastering a system of social norms and
stereotypes, but rather defines it as the proclivity for increasing the economy's
orientation on the achievement of social results. Such social focus of the economy relies on wide production of public and patronized goods (Rubinstein,
2011) with mediation and direct involvement of public authorities. It stipulates
the development of state regulation of the economy, social services for the
population and public funding of education, research and healthcare.

But economic theory cannot ignore socialization issues in a sense in which
they are explored from the perspective of sociology. The fact of the matter is
that the role of humans in modern production is changing dramatically. They
are acting predominantly as bearers of knowledge, which is the main resource
for the development of the economy. And the fate of our civilization depends
on our choice of criteria for the application of modern knowledge's colossal

power. Therefore, the level of humans' social responsibility acquires para-mount importance in production.

Progress in science and technologies, decrease in the desire to own prop-erty and the development of creative labor functions — all these phenom-ena actually push humans to become increasingly more responsible, cultured and socially oriented; in other words, push them to prioritize their social mis-sion and public recognition instead of engaging in endless pursuit of material goods and consumption. Thus, as humans gradually move from 'zoo' to 'noo', they are changing not only their behavior, but also core spiritual norms and values that they rely on.

And in this matter it is important to account for the flip side of the process. In the process of socialization, humans do not just passively adopt social con-ventions, public morals and social stereotypes. Indeed, socializing humans are actively affecting values and sociocultural norms developed by the society. In other words, while humans definitely socialize under the influence of the soci-ety, the society also socializes under the impact of vigorous activity of humans who transform conventional cultural and spiritual norms, values and motives, as well as relevant social institutions. If this process comprises people's mea-sured and aligned efforts targeting the society's absorption of the best achieve-ments of human culture, it will ensure the expansion of the social noo-space and lead to the noo-society.

The term 'socialization of society' (suggested by us) allows for the following insight: by combining within the theory of noonomy our approach related to technological development and the idea of humans' advanced acquisition of social knowledge, their formation of a social structure through the mechanism of socialization, we managed to demonstrate that sequential progress towards a new human being ('new' from the perspective of humans' adaptation within a society and adapting the society as they see fit in light of real wants), move-ment towards self-restriction, etc. mark the moment that should be taken into account in *practical* activity of both state and public institutions.

Let us point out that *the idea of humans as social beings formed by the society and simultaneously shaping the society* is hardly new. Neither is the question whether humans make history. It is important to understand that when indi-viduals are in a society, they are 'encoded' by it and in the process of social-ization adopt core morals and values which constitute the social essence of a society at any given moment and are determined by the criterion basis of values endemic to a society at that point in time. Individuals socialize. But in affecting the society, individuals also 'socialize' it by changing its core morals and values, so the objective is to ensure that they change this core in *the direction deter-mined by the noo-criterion basis*. And the discovery, expansion and acquisition of such knowledge, as well as its inclusion in core morals and values, constitute an important aspect of such a task as ensuring socialization of the society, i.e., making it more 'social', non-individualistic (in the negative sense of the word), more comfortable for an individual and more noo-oriented.

If we add to that the process of humans' cognition of their wants, i.e., if we combine the two processes of acquiring one type of knowledge with another type of knowledge into a single whole, then these mechanisms and method-ological practices will provide us with a key to solving the problem of how we should proceed towards a noo-human. That means that we will get a key to 'cre-ating' not just non-economic humans (from the perspective of their not using economic mechanisms to pursue the objectives of satisfying their wants), but humans who will consciously perfect themselves and do what is necessary, both internally and within the society, in order to: achieve a level of social, material, spiritual and mental wellbeing that is recognized and deemed suffi-cient, on the one hand; and, on the other hand, have no need (that is right – a need, an actual need!) to expand the production of goods which, at the current stage in civilizational development, cannot be obtained without doing damage to the society, environment and other people.

That, in our opinion, is the trajectory of the path to gradual reformatting of the current civilizational and sociocultural settings. But what should serve as the foundation and content of such reformatting that is already pushing its way onto the current agenda?

10   Transition to Noonomy

It would have to involve the transition to reasonable management of the economy – to the noo-stage. At this stage, noo-production, while detached from humans and the society, will still have its goals and objectives subju-gated to public interest. The development of the noo-society and the transi-tion to noo-production and noo-needs will be accompanied by the transition from economic rationality to a new one, and this new nature of rationality and, accordingly, a new definition of development goals will gain paramount importance and serve as the basis for changing the nature of public relations.

Thus, the economy will be replaced by the noonomy. The noonomy relies on a non-economic way of satisfying human wants which will be shaped through a new quality of production wherein people will — according to Marx's pre-diction — "step to the side of the production process."

There have been recurrent questions about the term 'noonomy', which is often interpreted quite superficially as the combination of 'noosphere' and 'economy'. This interpretation is reflected in the scientific discourse, for many publications use this combination of terms when they mention the term 'noonomy'. In their opinion, noonomy generally stands for 'noospheric economy', 'reasonable economy' or even 'humane economy'.

Such interpretations, as any scientific point of view, definitely have the right to exist, but when we speak of 'noonomy', we imply a completely different meaning. Our understanding of noonomy is much broader and deeper. We derive the term 'noonomy' directly from Greek words 'noos' (νους) — intellect and 'nomos' (νομός) — law, order. Therefore, it is not our intention to draw on a mechanical combination of 'noosphere' and 'economy', and 'noonomy' should not be perceived as portmanteau of 'economy' and 'noosphere'.

We employ the Greek term 'noos' in the following meaning: 'intellect reliant on the criterion basis of truth as a perceived timeless value'. In the aforementioned *The Sermon on Law and Grace*, Metropolitan Hilarion wrote, "[B]rought us unto the knowledge of the Truth" (Hilarion, 2011: 70). In this sense, it is a big mistake to reduce the Greek 'noos' to its Latin counterpart 'ratio'.

'Rational' means conforming to certain criteria (but are these criteria reasonable in and of themselves?). The economy is always rational, but are actions of rationally operating economic agents necessarily reasonable? Can they transcend the limits of criteria that are imposed by the current economic system?

The noonomy stipulates a different method for assessing economic actions and a different method for assessing wants that is based not on rationality, but on reason, i.e., on 'noo' that stems from understanding true consequences of economic decisions and true value of satisfied wants. Thus, we are not talking about the economy or individuals who are rationally maximizing their pleasures, but about a different method for the formation and satisfaction of wants that can be referred to as *noo-wants*. At some point, e.g., under the gathering society, humans satisfied their wants without any economic calculations. The noonomy constitutes a non-economic way of wants satisfaction which will be formed at a new stage in the development of human knowledge and technologies.

On the other hand, the second part of the term 'noonomy' (derived from the Greek 'nomos', or 'law, order') is an ancient concept used by philosophers in the first third of the twentieth century to signify the basic principle for organizing any space (see: (Shmit, 2008)), an absolute law that governs the existence of all things. Thus, 'nomos' stands for law, order and principle for organizing general management of the economy. Let us once again refer to *The Sermon on Law* (nomos!) *and Grace* (noos!), "Law was the precursor and the servant of Grace and Truth. Grace and Truth were the servants of the future life" (Hilarion, 2011: 41). Thus, the noonomy constitutes a structured paradigm, a method for the satisfaction of wants under the society which has "the light of knowledge"; wherein there are no relations to production and no production relations; which has no relations to possessions and no ownership relations; and wherein there is no economy, and the economy is impossible. *The noonomy stipulates non-economic satisfaction of wants.* That is why discussion of 'noospheric economy' is an oxymoron, like non-economic economy, non-carnivorous predator, etc.

Clearly, movement towards the noonomy is a long historical transition. But it is important to emphasize that in the near future changes which lead to the transition to the NIS.2 *stage and, ultimately, the transition from the economy to the noonomy will bring about changes in economic relations and in the nature of ownership relations endemic to this new generation of the industrial society.*

11   Evolution of Ownership Relations

Even at the modern stage in societal development, before the transition to the NIS.2, we can observe trends in the evolution of ownership relations that lead to their socialization and dilution. Ownership relations, especially as they pertain to private ownership, are supposed to secure owners' uncontested rights to hold, use and allocate economic resources. But the evolution of economic relations has long since led to possessions' encrustation with various encumbrances meant to ensure owner's social accountability.

For example, various easements (right of way, right of access to water sources, right of livestock crossing, right of access to coastal areas, right to lay the service lines, etc.) provide third persons with an opportunity to use, within certain limits, land lots that they do not own or possess. There are numerous restrictions and encumbrances of the rights of ownership that pertain to construction, transportation and industrial activity and are related to ensuring compliance with safety regulations, upholding certain quality standards, observing environmental regulations, etc.

We should pay special attention to the evolution of intellectual property relations because they regulate the economic turnover of knowledge – the main resource of modern production. In this segment, we see the emergence of such phenomena as crowdsourcing, Wikinomics, free software, open source, copyleft, etc. that promote free access to intellectual resources. At the same time, there is rather stiff competition for intellectual property enclosure. This situation correlates to two trends in the development of ownership relations that can be observed in the modern economic system: (1) preservation of existing relations, and (2) dilution of ownership rights to the point of complete disavowal of ownership.

The dilution of ownership rights manifests itself in the development of formats for joint ownership and use of possessions, as well as in the division of functions that pertain to ownership and use. An owner may temporarily relinquish the use of possessions or property and transfer the right of usage to another person through such mechanisms as renting, leasing, coworking and various types of sharing (office sharing, car sharing, kick sharing, bike sharing, time-sharing, food sharing, etc.). The size of the sharing economy market is already hundreds of billions of US dollars per year, and it continues to grow rapidly. In China alone, according to iiMedia Research consultancy report, the market size of the sharing economy reached $1.05 trillion in 2019 and is expected to exceed $1.28 trillion in 2020 (China sharing economy ..., 2019). Thus, the share of the sharing economy came close to accounting for 8% of China's GDP. Even though the sharing economy went mostly unnoticed before 2010, the survey of 30,000 consumers in 60 countries, which was conducted in Q3 2013, demonstrated significant willingness to participate in the sharing economy (see Figure 0.1).

Car sharing holds the largest share in the sharing economy, and the growth of this segment serves as one of the most important indicators of the entire sector's development (see Figure 0.2). The growth of car sharing has exceeded the most optimistic forecasts. A forecast from August 2016 predicted that in

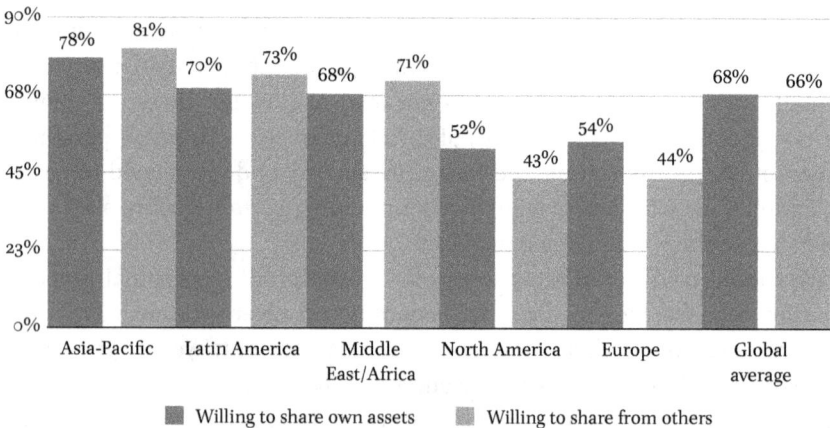

FIGURE 0.1   Percent of online consumers willing to participate in sharing communities
SOURCE: RICHTER, 2014.

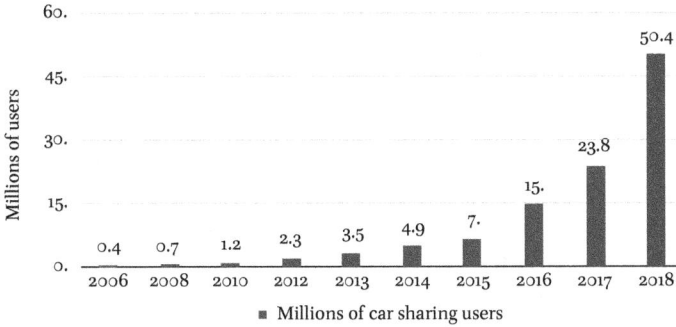

FIGURE 0.2 Number of car sharing users from 2006 to 2018
SOURCES: NUMBER OF CAR SHARING USERS, 2016;
SVEGANDER, 2019; THE CARSHARING TELEMATICS
MARKET, 2018; SHAHEEN ET AL., 2018.

2025, the number of car sharing users would reach 36 million, but it already passed the 50 million mark in 2018 (Number of car sharing users …, 2016).

Such quick rise of the sharing economy is supported by considerable investment. Business perceived people's increasing willingness to use without owning, so investment in the sharing economy has seen rapid growth (see Figure 0.3).

To a great extent, the transition towards temporary use of possessions and property without the need to acquire the right of disposition – and frequently without the need to acquire the right of ownership – is determined by accelerated pace of technological changes. It is not economically feasible to invest in

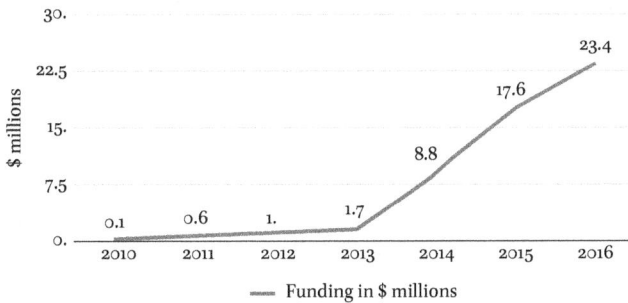

FIGURE 0.3 Cumulative funding for asset-sharing startups, 2010–2016
SOURCE: WALLENSTEIN AND SHELAT, 2017: 5.

obtaining full ownership rights on items that will soon become obsolete. Quite often owners of such items may assume additional obligations to repair and update them for users.

Another trend that is also contributing to the dilution of ownership rights is the fragmentation of capital. Economic theory of ownership rights pays a lot of attention to the issue of fragmentation of rights and dilution of ownership rights – and for good reason. The emergence of stock ownership leads to the fragmentation of ownership rights that is even more complex and goes beyond possession, use and allocation. Stockholders no longer have full ownership rights to the capital. Moreover, the aggregate of their authority depends on the type and number of shares.

Appropriation and allocation functions in the framework of ownership relations have also changed dramatically because the first half of the twentieth century saw these functions split between capital owners and managers. These issues were raised by a number of scholars (Thorstein Veblen (Veblen, 1921), Adolf Berle and Gardiner Means (Berle and Means, 1932), Stuart Chase (Chase, 1932),[5] etc.) long before James Burnham was hailed as the pioneer merely for introducing his flashy term 'the managerial revolution' and stating that the capitalist society would be replaced by the managerial society (Burnham, 1941: 71).

In fact, fragmentation of ownership functions goes even deeper than splitting them between stockholders and managers. J. K. Galbraith showed that actual use of capital was being transferred to a whole army of experts that comprised corporate 'technostructure'. But there is more to the issue because all hired employees serve as end users of capital elements, albeit each employee performs only a small partial function. That does little for an individual employee, but provides grounds for collective action, and the reality of such fragmentation of rights manifests itself, for example, in the signing of collective agreements or in case of strike.

Nowadays, going hand in hand with the technological progress, robots and artificial intelligence systems are replacing blue and white-collar workers. So what happens to ownership relations when humans yield some functions to technetic beings? For example, how should we assess user responsibility if an accident is caused by a self-driving car? The owner may be liable for damages. But who will be held responsible for traffic violations?

Humans are gradually losing use and even allocation functions. In the future, this trend will only accelerate. These processes, along with the aforementioned tendency to a decrease in the value of ownership, lead to changes

---

5   F.D. Roosevelt used the title of the book, *A New Deal*, as a motto during his electoral campaign.

in the system of ownership and changes in the entire public order. The theory of noonomy predicts with a high degree of surety that *the economy of joint ownership, the economy of fragmented and diluted ownership rights will dominate the NIS.2 stage.*

Thus, as we transition to the NIS.2, the system of ownership relations is undergoing dramatic changes, which brings about a change in the entire system of economic relations. The nature of the market is changing; an increasingly larger role is being played not by spontaneous market fluctuations, but by outcomes of complex coordinated actions between persons who hold various and intertwined elements of ownership rights. It is no coincidence that business circles and economy experts are now more and more actively discussing the concept of 'stakeholder capitalism', which reflects higher dependency of company operations on interests of various public groups, such as company employees, members of the local community, consumers, environmentalists, etc.[6] The nature of state regulation is also changing, as it will start to seek consensus in order to achieve a complicated balance of economic interests that stems from a new nature of ownership relations and a new type of market relations.

12   Role of Humans in Noo-production

What will the relation between humans and production (noo-production) be like under the noo-social stage of civilizational development? At the noo-stage, noo-production will be detached from humans and the society, but the goals and objectives of noo-production will still be subjugated to public interest. It is the goal setting, statement of goals and objectives and control over suitable means for the accomplishment of set objectives within the technosphere that will remain in the realm of human relations. Autonomous technobeings that function in the area of noo-production and are capable of self-development will still be dependent on the human society. The society will determine the limits of their self-development by blocking the directions that do not benefit the society and by guiding the functioning and development of noo-production in the directions necessary for humans' own development.

---

6   At the World Economic Forum in Davos, representatives of 120 large corporations even "supported efforts to develop a core set of common metrics and disclosures on non-financial factors for their investors and other stakeholders." See: (Measuring Stakeholder Capitalism ..., 2020).

Human relations pertaining to technosphere regulation will, for the most part, cease to qualify as production relations in so far as humans will be removed from immediate production processes. In this context, working hours will decrease dramatically, as determined by necessity and external viability, and will be replaced with various creative activities predominantly targeting the process of cognition.

But what criteria will humans use to make their decisions regarding the development of a relatively autonomous technosphere? What wants will they concentrate on, what goals will they pursue, and what means will they consider acceptable? In this context, it is about time we expound on an important idea of the theory of noonomy, which warrants a closer look. It should be emphasized that this whole structure provided for in the theory of noonomy can only develop when humans manage to muster and acquire one type of knowledge (in particular, in technologies, science and natural sciences) in parallel to other knowledge. What kind of other knowledge? Knowledge and cognition of the world as a world of culture and as a world of self-restriction, i.e., reasonable self-limitation of wants. At one point, man came out of nature, and there are examples of humans' natural 'zoo'-approach to the satisfaction of their wants. It is often said that humans have a very difficult time going against their instincts and giving up such attitudes as "I want more here and now", etc. That engenders the 'zoo'-approach. This approach serves as the foundation for the emergence of the main public institutions, including the phenomenon of the state.

But, apart from 'zoo', we have our mind, i.e., the 'noo'. Humans are capable of teaching themselves to renounce things that are hazardous to them. Drugs. Gluttony for a diabetic. Millions of people demonstrate this approach on a daily basis at, if you like, the micro-level. Humans should recognize this hazard. They should understand what is bad and what is good for them and for the society, establish the interests of other people and what is bad and what is good for them, and determine what should be done to make things right. There have been many examples of self-sacrifice and of people giving up many things, up to giving up their own life, for humanitarian reasons and in accordance with a different kind of wants that are based on noo-values. Moreover, there definitely are moral values and cultural wants, and they increasingly grow in the process of human development (both development of humans as individuals and human society as a whole). No one would deny that the phenomenon of culture has become a critical factor in a modern human's progress.

It is absolutely wrong to say that man is just a beast. The further humans progress in their development, the more they become noo-humans — as opposed to zoo- or biohumans. Moreover, it is both the natural course of human development and our true and essential need, for if we predominantly follow the zoo path, we will bring about the demise of our planet and the environment and impair our children's future. This is an important realization. It is sacral knowledge for the majority to cognize due to the all-encompassing pressure of the capital and market rationality, but it is already opening up to those who are more or less advanced in understanding true development goals and what our society really needs.

13   Nature of Human Activity and Nature of Wants

The theory of noonomy stipulates that in the foreseeable future the humanity will perceive this the urgent global need to change the trend in its development. Why is that? And why is it becoming increasingly more pertinent right at this very moment? The New Industrial Society of the Second Generation (NIS.2) can already release humans from labor to a great extent and ensure a significant increase in the amount of spare time, but this will not immediately translate into a similar 'increase in happiness' – in order to achieve that, we still have to learn how to use our free time for personal development (boost spiritual needs, culture, etc.).

The skepticism of Hannah Arendt, who doubted that more spare time would contribute to human development, is understandable because, in her opinion, people usually tend to use this time only for mindless consumption. She wrote, "[T]he spare time of the animal laborans is never spent in anything but consumption, and the more time left to him, the greedier and more craving his appetites. That these appetites become more sophisticated, so that consumption is no longer restricted to the necessities but, on the contrary, mainly concentrates on the superfluities of life, does not change the character of this society, but harbors the grave danger that eventually no object of the world will be safe from consumption and annihilation through consumption" (see: (Arendt, 1998: 133)).

This is exactly the case within the current social system, within the so-called capitalism and market because they actually leave humans just enough spare time to consume what they produce during their working time, then earn again and consume again, thus equally encouraging both to consume and produce for the sake of this (increasingly simulative) consumption.

The society can find a way out of this vicious circle, but it certainly does not lie through the ideology of asceticism, forced rationing or reduction of consumption or through purely verbal propaganda of higher ideals. In fact, the problem can be resolved only in case of and through the development of objective prerequisites. Both personal development and understanding of the need for self-restriction can play a part exclusively if these prerequisites are met.

What are they? The first prerequisite is a change in the nature of human activity: the transition to predominantly creative activities changes the structure of human wants by shifting priorities from the consumption of increasingly large volumes of material goods to the pursuit of means that promote personal development and creative potential. The second prerequisite stipulates that, as humans broaden their participation in creative activities, they expand their involvement in the process of cognition and amplify their perception of reasonable boundaries as they pertain to production activity and consumption.

Third, humans enjoy more opportunities for the satisfaction of essential wants to the point of satiation where the fight for the satisfaction of such wants and the danger of underconsumption cease to be critical. All these three factors work together and make self-restriction not only desirable, but also possible.

When using the term 'self-restriction', we emphasize that it is not the most precise definition. We are referring to a broader concept — rather to humans identifying themselves as homo sapiens. And through such self-identification, they set the boundaries of what is reasonable here and now and what falls outside the scope of reasonable. We are definitely not suggesting the imposition of some kind of stereotyped behaviors on people nor their coercion (spiritual or physical) to some kind of asceticism. We imply the creation of conditions in which humans will shift their criteria of rationality towards a more reasonable attitude to consumption, to the natural environment and to themselves.

14   Principle of Solidarism

Unfortunately, we have a gap now: technologies are progressing much faster than what is commonly referred to as an increase in the level of culture, human understanding of 'what is permitted and what is not' and progress towards the resolution of current issues listed in the UN development goals. But objective forces and real challenges demand that we resolve these issues, and there are objective historical events that prove the possibility of finding solutions. Great scholars and engineers who created the atomic bomb realized that it should not be used and took certain widely known steps to prevent it from happening. That is a telling example of humans perceiving the need to restrict the application of technological achievements. Another example is the Cuban Missile

Crisis of 1962. It demonstrated that politicians could come to an agreement and find ways to eliminate emerging threats and dangers.

Due to concurrently escalating risks, the development of modern technologies not only increases the need for public alignment of people's actions, but also creates premises for such alignment. Naturally, such premises cannot be acted on automatically because they are being hampered by conventional interests and social stereotypes. Thus, it is even more important to explore the ideological foundation of the transition to a society that is ridding itself of economic rationality.

The principle of solidarism is a cornerstone of this ideology, for it can provide the foundation for the formation of socio-institutional framework that would ensure conflict-free interaction between individuals and social groups. We are not considering instances of the so-called 'solidarity economy' (e.g., cooperatives or mutual benefit societies) studied by the economic science, even though such instances have a certain connection with the phenomenon of solidarism. We are referring to a much broader phenomenon which encompasses interactions between all social subjects at a qualitatively new level. A key point here is the shift away from social conflicts, clashes, animosity and competition. They are being replaced with other principles of human interaction: finding a common platform of development values and goals, working towards locating mutually acceptable paths for the resolution of issues and organization of relevant joint activity, and seeking compromise even when there is a difference in interests.

Solidarism (from French *solidarisme*) is an ideological construct formulated in the middle and second half of the nineteenth century. It seeks to achieve mutual trust, cooperation and solidarity between different social strata and to join the efforts of various classes, parties and public organizations that lend a voice to a wide range of interests. Ideas of solidarism are implemented through voluntary associations and a system of contractual relations that ensure the promotion of common interests.

Philosopher and economist Pierre Leroux (Leroux, 1840) and statesman Léon Bourgeois (Bourgeois, 1896) laid the foundation for the development of solidarism concepts. They sought to eliminate social discord, facilitate the transition to cooperation and abate social antagonism through the tax system and various social programs. In their opinion, that required adherence to democratic ideals, equal rights and desire to foster rapport between various social groups and strata.

In the twentieth century, various political parties and public initiatives used the ideas of solidarism in their political and ideological practices in order to ensure consolidation of society, organize cooperation between social groups and strata seeking to accomplish common goals, etc. Solidarism was used by the National Alliance of Russian Solidarists established by a group of anticommunist emigres (since 1943, solidarism became the Alliance's official ideology); by Italian and German Christian Democratic Unions after World War II; and by Polish "Solidarity" movement in the 1980s. Far-right movements and even totalitarian regimes also exploited the ideas of solidarism, but more so as an ideological cover for the desire to impose a system of tight top-down hierarchical control on the society.

To be fair, even political forces that were far removed from totalitarian ambitions failed to ensure consistent practical application of solidarism ideas. Perhaps that is inevitable in a society permeated with objectively conditioned misalignment of socioeconomic interests that causes acute conflicts between various social strata and groups. Still, a change in conditions of production creates material foundations for a higher level of essential human needs' satisfaction and, therefore, for overcoming bitter struggle for means of existence; thus, it also creates new, more favorable conditions for implementing the ideas of solidarism.

We have already observed some sprouts of solidarism ideas' practical manifestation in prominently developed formats of the 'solidarity economy' (that we have mentioned earlier). We can forecast further expansion of their application, which will partake in the process of shaping transitional steps in the human civilization's progress towards the noo-society.

It is clear that the modern society still maintains a market, capitalist and economic core. In such society, real solidarism-based links and institutions can, for the most part, function only in a latent (hidden) manner under the dominant system of relations. Solidarism is closely bound to socialization of the society and economy, which creates foundations both for the economic progress and abatement of social contradictions. Since the society remains essentially economic, we should use existing economic means to foster such development. And in this regard, it is well worth the time to turn our attention to opportunities inherent in the application of strategic planning instruments and corroborative active industrial policy. Moreover, we should use the potential that is ingrained in the social orientation of the economy and the development of various formats of joint production, exchange, appropriation, use and consumption.

Our national development strategy should incorporate all these instruments that allow for the formation of an economic and social model which would reject relations stipulating one social subject's dominion over or subjugation to another subject and would put an end to the selfish fight over one-sided benefits and preferences. Conventional socioeconomic institutions (including the institution of property) still perpetuate such approach. But further development and search for ways out of the brewing civilizational crisis already insistently require mutual regard for various subjects' interests, for finding a compromise between them and, ultimately, — for organizing solidary vanquishment of all those contradictions that are escalating in production, environmental and social spheres.

Recognition thereof is reflected in the concepts of 'stakeholder capitalism' (Measuring Stakeholder Capitalism …, 2020) and coopetition, which stipulates the merger of cooperation and competition (Brandenburger and Nalebuff, 1996). Current shift to the study of the increase in the significance of relations pertaining to cooperation and mutual regard for others' interests is another argument in favor of recognizing the concept of solidarism as a promising ideological foundation of progress towards the noo-society.

Russia is also starting to perceive the value of solidarity-based public relations. Recently, the Constitution of the Russian Federation was amended, and Article 75.1 was rewritten as follows, "In the Russian Federation … civil rights and duties shall be balanced and social partnership, economic, political and social solidarity shall be ensured" (The Constitution of …, 2020). In summary, how can we define the trajectory of our transition to the formation of the noo-society, to a qualitatively new state of public existence?

15   Four Vectors of Change

This process of movement, i.e., genesis of the noonomy, develops as the resultant of four main vectors of changes. *Vector 1* determines the creation of *materials foundations* that underpin movement towards the noonomy. Even under the current level of technological development, when the fifth technological mode claims the leading position, but the face of the economy is still, to a great extent, determined by the third and fourth modes, and material production employs 20–25% of the workforce, this workforce manufactures machinery and equipment, produces agricultural goods, mines natural resources and ensures transportation of everything that is manufactured in volumes that are sufficient for domestic consumption and exports. Transition to the sixth technological mode can ensure the satisfaction of all essential (non-simulative) wants.

We are already on the verge of making the technological transition to a qualitatively new industry that will allow for the creation of unmanned production, whereas humans will retain such functions as goal-setting, R&D and production organization. New production is becoming highly knowledge intensive, and, consequently, human knowledge is ultimately assuming the role of a critical productive resource.

Vector 2 determines new foundations for the formation of human wants reliant on new opportunities for their satisfaction. As it departs from economic rationality, the humanity will transition to *non-economic criteria* for the formation and satisfactions of wants. A major shift in this direction that we have been observing for a while is the diffusion of ownership. The latest trends that we can perceive today include such phenomena as the 'disavowal of ownership' and the development of various formats for temporary use and joint consumption.

Such trends indicate that ownership relations, which are based on economic relations, are gradually blurring, dispersing and dissolving (which correlates with the literal meaning of the term 'diffusion'). And that signifies the end of the very economic relations, transition to production, exchange and consumption and corresponding appropriation type reliant on non-economic criteria. Naturally, this transition cannot and should not be imposed. It will mature over time, as we accumulate objective requisite foundations and progress along all vectors of the transition to noonomy.

Vector 3 of such transition shapes social conditions for movement towards the noonomy, i.e., human socialization targeting acquisition of noo-qualities and socialization of the society. This process stipulates an active role of the subject that adopts the most progressive norms, stereotypes, moral and cultural values from the social environment and, in turn, affects the formation of social institutions which facilitate the evolution of the society in the same direction — towards the noo-society. Pursuit of individual gain ceases to serve as the criterion for being a part of the society. Instead, the focus shifts to the development of creative potential and personal self-fulfillment. In turn, social institutions create the platform for such self-fulfillment by supporting conditions for personal development and promoting the rejection of *bellum omnium contra omnes* principle in the pursuit of personal prosperity.

Vector 4 targets the creation of ideological conditions for moving towards the noo-society. The ideology of *solidarism* establishes such conditions. It allows for fostering gradual rejection of the focus on competition in the fight for private appropriation of material goods and facilitates the transition to cooperation and solidarity that promote both general and individual progress. In order to achieve that, we must recognize the fundamental unity of our interests and values and perceive common risks and dangers stemming from thoughtless pursuit of economic success and unchecked consumption.

Implementation of all these four vectors can take us to a qualitatively new stage of public existence and, which is becoming critically important for the humanity, overcome the brewing civilizational crisis. At the same time, we definitely understand that there are many problems, and one of their causes is the economic policy implemented by world powers, which, from our perspective, does not always or necessarily contain the right development measures. It is also clear that the trajectory of progress towards the noonomy and noo-society will not be straight. It will experience multiple lateral and backward movements.

The theory of noonomy is intended to contribute to the resolution of the aforementioned problems by setting goals and pointing to the future that we should aspire to. Progress towards this future will signify overcoming problems that we are facing today. The noonomy suggests the path that lies ahead and establishes priority milestones on this journey.

References

Adams, S. (2018) Half million 3d printers sold in 2017 – on track for 100m sold in 2030. *3D Printing Industry* (April 06). Available (consulted 25 August, 2021) at: https://3dprintingindustry.com/news/half-million-3d-printers-sold-2017-track-100m-sold-2030-131642/.

Agaev, V. (2017) Male, Female, Intersex. *Ogonyok*, 11 December, no. 49. Available (consulted 25 August, 2021) at: https://www.kommersant.ru/doc/3486805.

Arendt, H. (1998). *The Human Condition.* 2nd ed. Chicago: University of Chicago Press.

Bainbridge, W.S. (ed) (2006) *Managing Nano-Bio-Info-Cogno Innovations: Converging Technologies in Society.* Dordrecht, Netherlands: Springer.

Berle, A.A. and Means, G.C. (1932) *The Modern Corporation and Private Property.* New York: Macmillan. Available (consulted 25 August, 2021) at: http://www.unz.org/Pub/BerleAdolf-1932.

Blaug, M. (2008) J. Schumpeter. In: *Great Economists before Keynes: An introduction to the lives & works of one hundred great economists of the past.* Saint Petersburg: Ekonomikus.

Bodrunov, S.D. (2013) *Russia's New Industrial Development Concept.* Moscow, St. Petersburg: S.Y. Witte Institute for New Industrial Development (INID).

Bodrunov, S.D. (2016) *The Coming of New Industrial Society: Reloaded.* St. Petersburg: S.Y. Witte Institute for New Industrial Development (INID).

Bodrunov, S.D. (2017) Return of Industrialization – Galbraith Redeemed. *Ekonomicheskoe vozrozhdenie Rossii* 2: 17–21.

Bodrunov, S.D. (2018a) *Noonomy.* Moscow: Kul'turnaia revoliutsiia.

Bodrunov S.D. (2018b) From ZOO to NOO: Man, Society and Production in the Conditions of a New Technological Revolution. *Voprosy filosofii* 7: 109–118.

Bodrunov, S.D. (ed.) (2019) *New Industrial Society: Sources, Reality, Prospects. Noonomy. (Select materials of Seminars, Publications and Events of S.Y. Witte Institute for New Industrial Development on the Concept of the New Industrial Society of the Second Generation)*. Vol. III. St. Petersburg: S.Y. Witte Institute for New Industrial Development, 561–663.

Bodrunov, S.D. (ed.) (2020) *New Industrial Society: Sources, Reality, Prospects. Noonomy. (Select materials of Seminars, Publications and Events of S.Y. Witte Institute for New Industrial Development on the Concept of the New Industrial Society of the Second Generation)*. Vol. IV. St. Petersburg: S.Y. Witte Institute for New Industrial Development.

Bodrunov, S.D. (ed.) (2021) *New Industrial Society: Sources, Reality, Prospects. Noonomy. (Select materials of Seminars, Publications and Events of S.Y. Witte Institute for New Industrial Development on the Concept of the New Industrial Society of the Second Generation)*. Vol. V. St. Petersburg: S.Y. Witte Institute for New Industrial Development.

Bourgeois, L. (1896) *Solidarité.* Paris: Colin.

Boyes, H., Hallaq, B., Cunningham, J. and Watson, T. (2018) The industrial internet of things (IIoT): An analysis framework. *Computers in Industry.* Vol. 101: 1–12. doi:10.1016/j.compind.2018.04.015.

Brandenburger, A.M., and Nalebuff, B.J. (1996) *Co-opetition.* New York: Doubleday.

Burnham, J. (1941) *The Managerial Revolution. What is happening in the world.* New York: A John Day Book.

The Carsharing Telematics Market – 2nd Edition. Summary. *Berg Insight.* M2M Research Series 2018. Available (consulted 25 August, 2021) at: http://www.berginsight.com/ReportPDF/Summary/bi-carsharing2-sum.pdf.

Chase, S. (1932) *A New Deal.* New York: Macmillan.

China sharing economy market to exceed 9 trln yuan: report (2019). *Xinhua,* 11 February. Available (consulted 25 August, 2021) at: http://www.xinhuanet.com/english/2019-11/02/c_138523206.htm.

The Constitution of the Russian Federation (adopted by nation-wide vote on 12.12.1993 with amendments approved during the all-Russian vote on 01.07.2020) (2020). *Consultant Plus.* Available (consulted 25 August, 2021) at: http://www.consultant.ru/document/cons_doc_LAW_28399/844d980197f23461acb5a6699db6e34227150003/.

The Construction of Europe's First 3d Printed Building Has Begun and is Almost Complete (2017). Available (consulted 25 August, 2021) at https://3dprinthuset.dk/europes-first-3d-printed-building/.

Desai, R. (2013) *Geopolitical Economy: After US Hegemony, Globalization and Empire.* London: Pluto Press.

Francis I. (2015) *Encyclical Letter Laudato Si'.* 24 May. Available (consulted 25 August, 2021) at: http://www.vatican.va/content/francesco/ru/encyclicals/documents/papa-francesco_20150524_enciclica-laudato-si.html.

Francis I. (2020) Encyclical Letter Fratelli Tutti. 3 October. Available (consulted 25 August, 2021) at: http://www.vatican.va/content/francesco/en/encyclicals/docume nts/papa-francesco_20201003_enciclica-fratelli-tutti.html.

Germany Trade & Invest (2018) Industrie 4.0 – Germany Market Report and Outlook. Available (consulted 25 August, 2021) at: https://www.gtai.de/resource/blob/64500/ 8b7afcaa0cce1ebd42b178b4430edc82/industrie4-0-germany-market-outlook-progr ess-report-en-data.pdf.

Giddings, F.H. (1897) *The theory of socialization.* New York: Macmillan Company.

Greenwood, M. (2019) 2018 Was a Strong Year for the Global 3D Printer Market. *engineering.com.* January 21. Available (consulted 25 August, 2021) at: https://www.engi neering.com/AdvancedManufacturing/ArticleID/18279/2018-Was-a-Strong-Year -for-the-Global-3D-Printer-Market.aspx.

Hilarion (2011) *The Sermon on Law and Grace.* Foreword by Metropolitan Ioann (Snychev). Introduction by Deriagin, V.I. Compiled and transl. by Deriagin, V.I. Old Russian text reconstructed by Zhukovskaya, L.P. Comments by Deriagin, V.I., and Svetozarsky, A.K. Managing editor Platonov, O.A. Moscow: Institute of Russian Civilization.

IBM (2018) A Bus That Speaks Sign Language? Meet Olli. January 11. Avaliable (consulted 24 May, 20220 at: https://www.ibm.com/blogs/industries/olli-ai-and-iot-aut onomous-bus/

Kerman, A. (2017) Organism with 6-Letter DNA Created. *XXII vek,* 26 January. Available (consulted 25 August, 2021) at: https://22century.ru/biology-and-biotechnology/ 42655.

Korogodin, V.I. and Korogodina, V.L. (2000) *Information as the Foundation of Life.* Dubna: Phoenix Publishing Center.

Leroux, P. (1840) *De l'humanité, de son principe et de son avenir, où se trouve exposée la vraie définition de la religion, et où l'on explique le sens, la suite et l'enchaînement du Mosaisme et du Christianisme.* Vol. 2. Paris: Perrotin, Éditeur-Libraire.

Local Motors (2021). Mobility for today's communities: Meet Olli. Available (consulted 25 August, 2021) at: https://localmotors.com/products/

Locey, K.J. and Lennon, J.T. (2016) Scaling laws predict global microbial diversity. *Proceedings of the National Academy of Sciences of the United States of America* (PNAS), 113(21): 5970–5975. Available (consulted 25 August, 2021) at: https://doi.org/ 10.1073/pnas.1521291113.

Lvov, D.S. and Glazyev, S.Y. (1986) Theoretic and Practical Aspects of Managing Science and Technology Enterprises. *Ekonomika i matematicheskie metody* 22(5): 793–804.

Marx, K. (1969). Economic Manuscripts of 1857–1859. In: Marx, K. and Engels, F. *Collected Works.* Vol. 46, Part II. Moscow: Politizdat.

Measuring Stakeholder Capitalism: Towards Common Metrics and Consistent Reporting of Sustainable Value Creation (2020). White Paper, September 2020. World

Economic Forum, 22 September. Available (consulted 25 August, 2021) at: https://www.weforum.org/reports/measuring-stakeholder-capitalism-towards-common-metrics-and-consistent-reporting-of-sustainable-value-creation.

Medvedev, Y. (2017) Life of Six Letters. First Bacteria with Synthetic DNA Created. *Rossiiskaia gazeta – Federal Issue*, 12 December, no. 7448(282).

Men'shikov, S.M. and Klimenko, L.A. (2014) *Long Waves in the Economy: When the Society Changes Its Skin*. 2nd ed. Moscow: LENAND.

Mensch, G. (1975) *Das technologische Patt: Innovationen überwinden die Depression*. Frankfurt a.M.: Umschau Verlag Breidenstein.

Number of car sharing users worldwide from 2006 to 2025 (2016) *Statista*, 2 August. Available (consulted 25 August, 2021) at: https://www.statista.com/statistics/415636/car-sharing-number-of-users-worldwide/.

Perez, C. (2011) *Technological Revolutions and Financial Capital: The Dynamics of Bubbles and Golden Ages*. Moscow: Delo.

Prosvirnov, A. (2012) New Technological Revolution Is Sweeping Past Us. *ProAtom Agency*. Available (consulted 25 August, 2021) at: http://www.proatom.ru/modules.php?name=News&file=article&sid=4189.

Richter, F. (2014) The Rise of the Sharing Economy. *Statista*. 3 June 3. Available (consulted 25 August, 2021) at: https://www.statista.com/chart/2323/the-rise-of-the-sharing-economy/.

Roco, M.C. and Bainbridge, W.S. (eds) (2002) *Converging Technologies for Improving Human Performance: Nanotechnology, Biotechnology, Information Technology and Cognitive Science*. Arlington, VA, US: National Science Foundation.

Rubinstein, A. (2011) A Theory of Patronized Goods: Inefficient and Efficient Equilibria. *Voprosy ekonomiki* 3: 65–87. Available (consulted 25 August, 2021) at: https://doi.org/10.32609/0042-8736-2011-3-65-87.

Schumpeter, J.A. (1983) *The Theory of Economic Development*. Moscow.

Shaheen, S., Cohen, A. and Jaffee, M. (2018) Innovative Mobility: Carsharing Outlook. *UC Berkeley: Transportation Sustainability Research Center*. Available (consulted 25 August, 2021) at: http://dx.doi.org/10.7922/G2CC0XVW.

Shmit, K. (2008) *Earth's Nomos in Public Law Jus Publicum Europaeum*. St. Petersburg: Vladimir Dal'.

Skobeeva, V. (2016) Sixth Major Extinction. *Vokrug sveta*. October 29, 2016. Available (consulted 25 August, 2021) at: http://www.vokrugsveta.ru/article/233607/.

Spohrer, J. (2002) NBICS (Nano-Bio-Info-Cogno-Socio) Convergence to Improve Human Performance: Opportunities and Challenges. In: Roco, M.C. and Bainbridge, W.S. (eds) *Converging Technologies for Improving Human Performance: Nanotechnology, Biotechnology, Information Technology and Cognitive Science*. Arlington, VA, US: 101–116. Available (consulted 25 August, 2021) at: https://obamawhitehouse.archives.gov/sites/default/files/microsites/ostp/bioecon-%28%23%20023SUPP%29%20NSF-NBIC.pdf.

Svegander, M. (2019) The Carsharing Telematics Market – 3rd Edition. Product Sheet. *Berg Insight*. M2M Research Series 2019. Available (consulted 25 August, 2021) at: http://www.berginsight.com/ReportPDF/ProductSheet/bi-carsharing3-ps.pdf.

Taleb, N.N. (2007) *The Black Swan: The Impact of the Highly Improbable*. New York: Random House.

Tarde, J.-G. (1890) *Les lois de l'imitation: étude sociologique*. Paris: Félix Alcan.

Tess (2017) Local Motors' self-driving 'Olli' shuttle helped along by Makerbot 3D print-ers. *3D printer and 3D printing news*. August 30, 2017. Available (consulted 25 August, 2021) at: http://www.3ders.org/articles/20170830-local-motors-self-driving-olli-shut tle-helped-along-by-makerbot-3d-printers.html.

Tsvetkova, M., Yasseri, T., Meyer, E.T. et al. (2015) *Understanding Human-Machine Networks: A Cross-Disciplinary Survey*. E-Print. Cornell University Library. Available (consulted 25 August, 2021) at: https://arxiv.org/pdf/1511.05324v1.pdf.

UN General Assembly (2015) *Transforming our world: the 2030 Agenda for Sustainable Development*. New York: United Nations, Dept. of Public Information. Available (consulted 25 August, 2021) at: https://undocs.org/en/A/RES/70/1.

United Nations Millennium Summit (2000) *United Nations Millennium Declaration*. New York: United Nations, Dept. of Public Information. Available (consulted 25 August, 2021) at: https://www.un.org/en/development/desa/population/migrat ion/generalassembly/docs/globalcompact/A_RES_55_2.pdf.

Veblen, T. (1921) *The Engineers and the Price System*. New York: B.W. Huebsch. Available (consulted 25 August, 2021) at: http://socserv2.mcmaster.ca/~econ/ugcm/3ll3/veb len/Engineers.pdf.

Wallenstein, J. and Shelat, U. (2017) Hopping aboard the sharing economy. *Boston Consulting Group, Henderson Institute*, 22 August. Available (consulted 25 August, 2021) at: http://image-src.bcg.com/Images/BCG-Hopping-Aboard-the-Sharing-Econ omy-Aug-2017_tcm104-168558.pdf.

Zalasiewicz, J., Williams, M., Waters, C.N. et al. (2017) Scale and diversity of the phys-ical technosphere: A geological perspective. *The Anthropocene Review* 4(1): 9–22. DOI: https://doi.org/10.1177/2053019616677743.

3D Bioprinting of Organs, How It Works? (2015). Available (consulted 25 August, 2021) at: https://make-3d.ru/articles/biopechat-organov-na-3d-printere/.

PART 1

Global Transformations of the Twenty-First Century and the Genesis of Noonomy

∵

Noonomy as the Core of the Formation of New Technological Mode and Global Economic Order

Sergey Y. Glazyev

The revolutionary technological and institutional changes going on in our world evoke a sense not of the end of history but the end of times. Orthodox fundamentalists see the signs of the Apocalypse in the broad introduction of digital passes as part of quarantine measures; in Israel, rabbis declare the coming of the Messiah (Mashiah),[1] in London, politicians are talking about the formation of a world government.[2] Following the latest financial market crash, capitalists reason upon a new reality, extorting money from the state to save their businesses, and socialists claim the end of capitalism.

This chapter analyzes the essence of what is going on in the framework of the theory of large cycles: technological shifts in the economy – from the standpoint of the theory of long waves and their underlying technological modes; institutional changes – from the perspective of the theory of secular cycles of capital accumulation and the underlying world economic orders. Based on this, a conceptual view of the ongoing transition to a new world order is build up as a formational one – from the economy of commodity production to the economy of knowledge, which is the basis of noonomy.

1 Basic Definitions

Since this report focuses on the formation of new technological, managerial and social structures, it would make sense to give author's definitions of these terms for an accurate interpretation thereof. The *technological mode* is understood as a group of clusters of technologically related industries that are distinguished in the technological structure of the economy, connected to each other by the same type of technological chains and form reproducible integrities. Each such mode represents a holistic and sustainable entity, within which

---

1 Yaakov Litzman, Israeli Minister of Health, stated this in his interview for Chamal News.
2 This was stated by G. Brown, former British Prime Minister (see (Danilov, 2020)).

a complete macro-production cycle is carried out, including the extraction and acquisition of primary resources, all stages of their processing and the production of a set of end products that meet the corresponding type of public consumption (Glazyev, 2018).

The *world economic order* is a system of interconnected international and national institutions that ensure expanded reproduction of the economy and determine the mechanism of global economic relations. The leading country's institutions play a major role. They exercise dominant influence on the international institutions that regulate the world market and international trade, economic and financial relations (Glazyev, 2016a, 2016b).

According to the definition of S. D. Bodrunov, the author of the theory of *noonomy*, the latter term is understood as a non-economic way to arrange the economy for the satisfaction of needs, performed by people who have gone beyond material production. Unlike all previous stages, the essence of noostage in the development of our civilization lies in the fact that it is not individuals who enter into relations with each other in the process of material production but two different areas of civilizational design do – production (nooproduction confined to the technosphere) and human society (Bodrunov, 2018: 171).

The transition to noonomy, according to S. D. Bodrunov, "will be based on natural, knowledge and technological revolution. This transition will be fulfilled through the progress of knowledge, intelligence and mind, directed to more and more complete satisfaction of the growing needs of people. The very possibility of such an increasingly complete satisfaction of needs will serve as the major prerequisite for removing the conflict of transition. At the same time, the structure of the needs will be increasingly dominated by true needs of human beings – education, study of the universe, spiritual development, culture. All aspects of a man's lifestyle will be transformed on the basis of culture – physical culture, culture of relationships, culture of consumption ... The accelerated development of human knowledge will force society to adjust the speed of its spiritual and social development to the pace of technological development ... Therefore, a natural "alignment of shares" of material and spiritual needs should precede an advance in the growth of spiritual needs. It is this – and the only! – basis that will allow the rise noocivilization. And it is noonomy, rather than economy, that will become a knowledge-intensive and "smart" way to meet the needs of individuals – members of the noocommunity, and the noocommunity as a whole" (Bodrunov, 2018: 432).

The theory of noonomy clarifies the concept manifested back in 1917 – that of the post-industrial society,[3] emphasizing the role of technological development and intellectualization of the economy. This concept list should be added by a definition of *knowledge economy* as the "model of development of post-industrial society or a stage of development of a post-industrial economy due to the advancement of ICT, broad application of innovative technologies in the industry, the globalization of markets" (Kuznetsov, 2009: 27).

In contrast to the concepts of post-industrial society and the knowledge economy, which simply reflect changes in the structure and factors of production skipping production relations, the theory of noonomy speaks of a qualitative leap in the development of productive forces, which makes production relations senseless. The logic of this leap is based on the assumption that progress in production automation will make it unnecessary for people to participate in it, thus releasing them from the curse of Adam.[4] Finally, a long-awaited "leap of humanity from the realm of necessity to the realm of freedom" will be made (Engels, 1961: 294–295).

Indeed, the level of productive forces allows us to feed more than 20 billion people yet today (Klyukin and Gutnikov, 2018). The share of people working in the material production sector is currently less than a quarter of the employed and tends downward (Zynovyev, 2000: 97–98). The share of those engaged in routine work in management, social services, construction and infrastructure is decreasing too. They are replaced by robots, algorithms, automated processes. We can assume that this trend will lead to the complete displacement of all non-creative activities in the immediate future. And that industrial relations in this realm of freedom from hard work will be replaced by social relations. This, however, does not mean commonweal and global harmony. Inequality in the possession of property, money and power creates complex contradictory relationships between people that can prove antagonistic.

---

3   The term "post-industrial society" was first used in 1917 by A. Penty, a theorist of English liberal socialism. In 1958, this concept was used in an article "Rest and Work in a Post-Industrial Society" by American sociologist D. Riesman (Riesman, 1958). But the founder of the holistic theory of post-industrial society is deemed to be D. Bell, who described key elements of this theory in his books (Bell, 1973, 1976).

4   "And to Adam He said: "Because you have listened to the voice of your wife and have eaten from the tree of which I commanded you not to eat, cursed is the ground because of you; through toil you will eat of it all the days of your life. Both thorns and thistles it will yield for you, and you will eat the plants of the field. By the sweat of your face you shall eat bread till you return to the ground, for out of it you were taken; for you are dust, and to dust you shall return"." (Old Testament, Genesis, Chapter 3).

The laws of economic reproduction as a single system of technical and socio-economic relations will supposedly cease to apply in the future. But the cessation can only occur as a result of this very application. Below, the laws of long-term economic development are extrapolated to the future in order to identify signs of noonomy in new emerging technological, social and economic structures.

2   World Crisis as a Process of Change of Technological and World Economic Orders

The crisis that has overtaken the world is structural in its nature and caused by fundamental technological and institutional changes. Currently, there is a transition from the fifth to the sixth technological mode, which is based on a complex of nano-, bioengineering and additive technologies which, along with information and communication and cognitive technologies, are a key driver of the new technological mode. Its core is expanding at a rate of about 35 % per year, shaping technological trajectories for a new long wave of economic growth (Glazyev and Kharitonov, 2009).

The transition to the sixth technological mode is effected by another technological revolution, which dramatically increases the efficiency of focal points of economic development. The cost of production and operation of nanotechnology-based computer equipment will decrease by an order, and the volume of its use will increase manifold due to miniaturization and adaptation to specific consumer needs. Nanomaterials exhibit unique consumer properties that are built for a purpose, including that of considerable increase in the durability, wear resistance and reliability of products produced from them. In mechanical engineering, the "nanocomputer – nanomanipulator" system serves as a basis for the creation of automated assembly complexes and 3D printers that can assemble any macroscopic objects according to a pre-taken or developed three-dimensional atomic configuration grid. The development of nanomedical robots, methods of targeted drug delivery to affected areas of the body and cellular technologies enhance the possibilities of preventive treatment and prolongation of human life.[5] Medicine will come into possession

---

5   In 2016, the author of this article registered the scientific discovery "Law of Change of Technological Modes in the Development of World and National Economies" (Certificate of Registration No. 65-S, issued by the International Academy of Authors of Scientific Discoveries and Inventions under the scientific and methodological guidance of the Russian Academy of Natural Sciences).

of technologies to combat diseases at the cellular level, which involve precise delivery of medicines in minimal volumes and with maximum use of the body's regenerability. Transgenic crops repeatedly reduce costs, increase the efficiency and improve consumer properties of pharmaceutical and agricultural production. Genetically modified microorganisms will be used to extract metals and pure materials from mining raw materials, thus revolutionizing the chemical and metallurgical industry.

The technological revolution is accompanied by the socio-political one. There is a transition from the imperial to the integral world economic order occurring. The American century-long cycle of capital accumulation is being replaced by the Asian one.[6] The system of institutions that set the American accumulation cycle to motion does not ensure a more progressive development of productive forces. The global US dominance has been established some quarter-century ago, but the global market is no longer able to provide an expanded reproduction of the institutions of the American accumulation cycle. There is a new center of rapidly expanding reproduction that emerged on the periphery of the American accumulation cycle and surpassed the USA in terms of the production of goods. The failure of the latter to strengthen their competitive advantages by organizing transoceanic free-trade zones give evidence of the transition of the current world economic system to a phase of decline. Progressively as American aggression increases, escalating from a trade war to the use of biological weapons, the countries of the core of the emerging new world economic mode are no longer able to maintain the financial pyramid of American liabilities that form the basis of the American capital accumulation cycle. China's decision to stop building up its dollar reserves marked the limit of conflict-free disentanglement of contradictions between the expanded reproduction of American bonds and global investment opportunities. This process will inevitably become avalanche-like in the near future, which will lead to the destruction of the current world economic mode.

The modern development of productive forces requires new production relations and institutions for organizing the global economy, which would ensure sustainable development and address planet-wide threats, including environmental and space threats. The rise of China and India is the basis for the development of a new world economic order, which entails the reform of the world economic order and international relations. This is also evidenced

---

6   Scientific hypothesis of S. Glazyev "Hypothesis about the periodic alternation of world economic orders" (certificate No. 41-N on registration by the International Academy of Authors of Scientific Discoveries and Inventions under the Scientific and Methodological Guidance of the Russian Academy of Sciences, 2016).

by the re-emergence of institutions that used to be rejected by the Washington consensus for socio-economic development planning and state regulation of global settings for capital reproduction, industrial policy, control of cross-border capital flows and currency restrictions.

By combining state planning and market self-organization, state control over the money flow and private entrepreneurship, by integrating the interests of all social groups around the goal of social well-being, the People's Republic of China (PRC) has led the world in terms of economic growth for more than thirty years, exhibiting record growth rates of investment and innovation activity. While US economy continues to stagnate, despite a five-fold increase in the volume of dollars over the past decade, the PRC combines the maximum levels of monetization of the economy, accumulation and growth rates. Focused on maximizing current profits, the American financial oligarchy is clearly inferior to Chinese communists in terms of economic development managerial efficiency, as the latter use market mechanisms to increase public welfare by increasing production and investment. Moreover, it is inferior to Indian nationalists who created their own version of an integrated system for managing the economic development within a democratic political system.

All countries – from Vietnam to Ethiopia – that follow the path of a convergent model based on a combination of socialist ideology and state planning with market mechanisms and private entrepreneurship, as well as regulate the latter in order to increase the production of material goods, now exhibit advanced sustainable development compared to the stagnation in the leading capitalist countries. The American century-long cycle of capital accumulation is being replaced by the Asian one, and the center of world economy is shifting to South-East Asia.

The new world economic order is based on the principles of non-discrimination, mutual respect for the sovereignty and national interests of cooperating states, directing them not to servicing the international capital, but to raising public welfare. The approach to international policy that is characteristic of countries of the core of the integrated world economic system (refusal from interference in domestic affairs, military intervention and trade embargoes) provides developing countries with a real alternative to building equal and mutually beneficial relations with other states. It radically rejects the use of force, as well as the use of sanctions in foreign policy.

A new, more efficient system of economic reproduction institutions is being formed, and the center of world development is shifting to South-East Asia, which suggests the start of a new Asian century-long cycle of capital accumulation. Such countries as Vietnam, Japan, Singapore, India and South Korea form the core of the new world economic order along with China, although they are fundamentally different from the latter in terms of their political structure and dominant form of ownership. They share a combination of institutions of state planning and market self-organization, state control over the main parameters of economic reproduction and free enterprise, the ideology of commonwealth and private initiative, as well as the priority of public interests over private ones, which is expressed in tough mechanisms of personal responsibility of citizens for their fair play, decent performance of their duties, compliance with laws and serving national goals. The system of socio-economic development management is based on mechanisms of personal responsibility for improving the well-being of society.

The change of world economic orders has always been followed by world wars. They were provoked by a global leader losing its influence and aimed to maintain control over its periphery in the final phase of the life cycle of the corresponding world economic order. And these wars always ended up with the emergence of a new global leader, whose superiority was ensured by the institutional advantages of the new world economic order. Thus, the two world wars of the previous century mediated a transition from the world economic order of colonial empires to the imperial order, which in the final phase of its life cycle took the form of liberal globalization. A driver of this transition was the contradiction between the rapid expansion of production on the American and European periphery that was dominating in world economic relations of Great Britain and the latter's ability to maintain global control.

The current escalation of the world hybrid war merely reflects the desire of the USA to delay the collapse of its financial system as much as possible by any means and tools and to leap over to a new long wave of growth before the collapse occurs. In order to do this, they try to shift the burden of servicing their obligations off to other countries or to write them off altogether. Wars in the Middle and Near East help keep control of petrodollars. Control of the drug money means the control over Afghanistan. A coup d'etat in the Ukraine and the establishment of an anti-Russian Nazi regime is aimed at pitting European NATO countries against Russia and weakening all parties to the conflict for the sake of increase of control over them by the American ruling elite in order to strengthen the latter's chance to weaken China. At the same time, American geopolitics consider control over Russia as the key to maintaining global leadership.

The current situation is characterized by overlapping processes of alternation of technological and world economic orders, which results in a resonant amplification of crisis developments. The arms race (that is typical for the change of technological modes), aggravated by military and political tensions, is turning into a world war, which is a natural phase of the change of world economic orders.

From the historical perspective, the current decade is similar to the Great Depression that preceded the Second World War. Although world currency issuers have managed to mitigate the structural crisis and to avoid a sharp drop in production by means of forcing more money into circulation, the leading economies of the world continue in a state of a longtime stagnation. The loss of potential GDP accumulated over the decade are quite comparable to the damage caused by the decline in production of the 1930s, which was relatively quickly overcome.

The unfolding global crisis is currently aggravating the economic situation, and the GDP loss rate of our times is likely to exceed the collapse of the corresponding period of the last century. While the exit from the Great Depression occurred quickly and abruptly owing to the huge increase in public demand due to the militarization of the economy on the threshold of and during the world war, the hybrid war of today is waged primarily in the are of human technologies and does not need to produce a large number of weapons and military machinery. And, fortunately, it is not accompanied by huge losses of population and material wealth, which eliminates growing costs for its restoration. At the same time, the threats to humanity arising from the profound structural changes in world economy should not be underestimated. Particularly in the situation when an aggressor has crossed the red line, opening the biological front of the war for its hegemony at the cost of threatening the very existence of humanity.

In the past century, the ruling elite of Great Britain tried to maintain its global hegemony by provoking wars between its major competitors: between Japan and Russia; between Germany with Austro-Hungary and Russia and the USSR; between Japan and the USA. In the 30s, in order to restrain the development of the latter, the British Empire even imposed an embargo on American goods. Today, US leaders are trying to do the same with regard to Chinese goods. Similarly, American intelligence agencies are provoking conflicts between their major competitors by pushing Vietnam and Japan to conflict with China and promoting Russo-phobic regimes in the post-Soviet space in order to destroy the historic Russia.

But the laws of global socio-economic development are relentless, and the USA are doomed to defeat in the trade war that have unleashed with China. Notwithstanding this, the American ruling elite will fight for global leadership through every possible means, regardless of international law. But they have already destroyed the latter anyway: by ignoring WTO guidelines in the trade war with China; by violating the UN Charter with armed aggression in the

Balkans and the Near East, as well as by organizing coups d'etat in a number of countries in Europe and South America; they have violated the IMF Charter by imposing financial sanctions against Russia; by developing biological weapons, cyberterrorism and military buildup in other countries and in the space, in contradiction to international conventions; by sponsoring religious extremism and neo-nazism in order to organize and manipulate terrorist organizations; by seizing property and abducting unwanted citizens of other countries. This war is initiated by the ruling elite of the USA to retain their global hegemony in the context of the emergence of a more effective system of economic development in China (Glazyev 2016c), which is fully compliant with the theory. It remains an open question, how far American leaders can go in their crimes against humanity in an effort to maintain their dominance?

World wars differ significantly in terms of the technologies used. The Second World War was a war of engines. It gave a powerful impetus to the development of the automobile industry and the organic chemical industry, which formed the core of the technological mode that was new for that time. By the mid-1970s, this technological mode has reached the limits of its development, and transition to the next technological mode began. The core of the latter was the microelectronic industry and information and communication technologies. The Star Wars Doctrine and the arms race in the rocket and space sphere deployed by the USA gave a powerful impetus to its growth, which continued until the beginning of this century. Today, there is a process of replacing this technological mode with the next one, with the core made up of digital, nano- and bioengineering technologies. Same as before, it is spurred by an arms race. However, primary technologies of the currently new technological mode differ significantly from the previous ones. Their development is well promoted by high-precision missile, targeted biological, cybernetic and informational cognitive weapons that hit strategic targets, control systems, population and consciousness of the enemy.

It is plain to see where these weapons are employed now: high-precision weapons – in armed hostilities; biological weapons – in the form of the coronavirus pandemic; cyber weapons – in cyber-attacks against financial and energy infrastructure; cognitive weapons – in social networks. When it is impossible to use nuclear and chemical weapons, the modern world war takes a hybrid form including the extensive use of financial, trade and diplomatic methods to destroy the enemy. The USA use their superiority in all these areas, seeking to strengthen its advantages in the global economy by weakening the enemy.

The world wars of the last century were fought for the territory. This is true at least for the main aggressors – Germany and Japan, which proclaimed the goals of expanding the living space for their nations wishing to enslave the rest of the humanity. The current hybrid world war is started by the ruling elite of the USA for controlling the world economy, primarily its financial system. The privatization of the function of issuing the world currency allowed the American ruling oligarchy to exploit all of humanity by exchanging the fiducial money it creates for real material goods and assets. Their aggression is aimed to complete the process of liberal globalization, under which all countries ensure the free circulation of the dollar as the world currency and the use of this currency for the exchange of all national goods and assets. Therefore, the hostilities in the current hybrid war are conducted through the targeted use of financial instruments, trade restrictions, cyber-attacks and manipulation of public consciousness, rather than using tanks, ships and aircraft, as it was in the last century. Armed forces are involved in the final phase of combat operations as a punitive means to finally demoralize the defeated enemy. As for biological weapons, they are employed to incite a panic within the population in order to disorganize management and stop economic activity. As the final result – to impair the assets of millions of investors and citizens for the purpose of their subsequent buying up by the global oligarchy.

The collapse of the world system of socialism shall be regarded as the beginning of current transition to a change in world economic orders (Shveytser, 1995). Today, it is entering the final phase, involving the eventual failure of the imperial world economic order that came under the US control after the collapse of the USSR and the transition to a new order. The latter has already taken its shape in China and other countries of the South-East Asia. These countries are opening up the institutions and creating the systems for managing the reproduction of the integral world economic order. They prove their effectiveness not only in terms of macroeconomic factor dynamics, but also in successfully repelling American aggression during the hybrid world war.

There is no doubt that the Chinese system of economic reproduction management will get out of this crisis and become stronger. Its monetary authorities took advantage of the financial market decapitalization in order to consolidate national control over the segments of the Chinese economy that are dependent on foreign shareholders. A drop in energy and commodity prices will make it undoubtedly more efficient and attractive for foreign investment. Although a slump in production due to the shutdown during the epidemic is estimated at 50–70 billion dollars, China will recover quickly compared the USA and the EU that have yet to survive it. Moreover, the PRC managed to avoid the bankruptcy of strategic banks and enterprises owned and supported by the state, which fully controls the country's banking system, its transport, energy and social infrastructure.

The further development of the global financial crisis will reasonably be followed by the PRC strengthening of and the US weakening. Countries on the periphery of the US-centric financial system, including the EU and Russia, will also suffer significantly. The only point is the scale of these changes. At best, the Great Economic Stagnation of Western countries that has been going on for more than a decade will continue for several more years until the funds remaining after the collapse of financial bubbles are invested in the production of the new technological mode. In this case, they will manage to "ride" on a new long Kondratiev wave. At worst, forcing more money into the financial system will result in galloping inflation, which will cause a disorganization of economic reproduction, a drop in the standard of living of the population and a political crisis. The US ruling elite will have two options: wither to accept the loss of global dominance and to contribute to the formation of the new world economic order, or to escalate the world hybrid war they are already waging. Although they will certainly not win this war, the damage they may cause to humanity can be catastrophic, through to mortal.

3   New World Order: Scenarios for Transition to Noonomy

During a similar period of simultaneous change of technological and world economic orders in the last century, the world followed three global political trajectories. The socialist revolution in Russia created a prototype of a new world economic order, with Communist ideology and total state planning. A decade and a half later, in order to overcome the Great Depression, there was the New Deal implemented in the USA. It formed a different type of new world economic order, with the ideology of a welfare state and state-monopolistic regulation of the economy. A little later, there was another order type emerging in Germany, with the Nazi ideology and the private-state corporate economy.

All these changes occurred at the ending period of the British cycle of capital accumulation and the underlying colonial world economic order. Central to the world economic system, the ruling elite of Great Britain was trying to resist changes that undermined its global dominance. They imposed an economic blockade against the USSR, and only grain was allowed to be imported from Russia to provoke mass starvation. They imposed trade embargo on the USA. In Germany, the encouraged anti-Communist Nazi coup, and British special services protected Hitler and supported him to come to power in order to counter the influence of the USSR. With these very intentions and in anticipation of large dividends, American corporations are investing heavily in the modernization of German industry (Higham, 1983).

The British pursued their traditional geopolitics based on the principle "divide et impera", provoking a war between Germany and the USSR. They hoped to replicate their success in unleashing the First World War, which had resulted in the self-destruction of all of Britain's major competitors in Eurasia: The Russian, German, Austro-Hungarian, Ottoman, and, finally, Chinese Empires. But they discovered immediately upon the outbreak of the war, that the Third Reich surpassed over all European countries, including Great Britain, in terms of the effectiveness of economic management and the mobilization of all available resources for military purposes. Although Great Britain, thanks to its friendly relations with the USSR, was among the Winners, it lost the whole of its colonial empire after the Second World War – more than 90 % of its territory and population.

The Soviet system of managing the national economic system proved to be the most effective at that time. The country performed as many as three economic miracles at once: the evacuation of industrial enterprises from the European part to the Urals and Siberia and rebuilding new industrial areas in six months; reaching the fantastic parameters of labor and capital productivity that substantially exceeded the indicators of Europe united around the Nazis; the rapid restoration of cities and production facilities completely destroyed by the invaders in the postwar era.

Roosevelt's New Deal significantly contributed to the mobilization capabilities of the American economy, which allowed the USA to defeat Japan in the Pacific Basin. The USA had no competitors in post-war Western Europe: it was the former colonies of European states that became the area of rivalry between American corporations and Soviet ministries. Subsequent development of the world took the shape of the cold war between two world empires – the Soviet and the American, which had similar technocratic and diametrical political models for managing socio-economic development. Each of them had its own advantages and disadvantages, but nevertheless they were utterly superior to the system of family capitalism with the merciless exploitation of employees and slaves in terms of mass production efficiency and resource deployment capacities.

Now we see a similar picture. The emerging new world economic order has three possible forms too. The first of them has already been built in China under the leadership of the Communist Party of China. It is characterized by a combination of institutions of state planning and market self-organization, state control over key parameters of economic reproduction and free enterprise, the ideology of commonwealth and private initiative. It shows an amazing efficiency in managing its economic development which is superior to the American system by an order. This has been clearly manifested in manifold higher rates of development of advanced industrial sectors over the past three decades and has been reaffirmed by indicators of its effectiveness of combating the epidemic.

The second form of integrated world economic order is being created in India, which is the largest true democracy in the world. The key pillars of the integral system in its Indian form were laid by Mahatma Gandhi and Jawaharlal Nehru on the foundation of Indian culture. The nationalization of the banking system performed by the government of Indira Gandhi allowed to put managing the financial flows in line with the indicative plans for economic development. These tailor-made priorities gave an impetus to the development of key areas of the new technological mode, and today India ranks first in the world in terms of economic growth rate. In order to improve public welfare, the state regulates market processes like they do in China, encouraging investment in production development and the assimilation of new technology. In addition, there are monetary and financial restrictions in place that keep capital within the country, and state planning leads business activity to the production of material goods.

The third form of the new world economic order can be distinguished in the fog of the growing pandemic of mass psychosis. There are claims for the formation of the new world order pushed forward from the inside of the deep state of the USA. The pandemic development is used to establish the institutions that have pretensions to govern humanity. The Gates Foundation controls World Health Organization (WHO) activities in terms of mass immunization. While doing so, they use vaccination to promote the technology of biological programming (on which that have worked for a while now) aimed to reduce the birth rate and to establish total control over the behavior of vaccinated people. This technology combines the achievements of bioengineering and computer science: vaccination is accompanied by chipization, which allows to set any restrictions on human life.

It must be no coincidence that Bill Gates, trying to draw the desired image of the future of humanity nearer, repeatedly announced the approaching pandemic (Hoffower, 2020). In his speech in 2015, he declared in the alarmist-style that the world is "not ready for the next epidemic". At a discussion about epidemics held in 2018 by the Massachusetts Medical Society and the *New England Journal of Medicine*, Gates warned that a pandemic could occur within the coming decade. On October 18, 2019, the center for health security at Johns Hopkins University (which is the source the world is using now to track the coronavirus epidemic), in partnership with the World Economic Forum and the Bill & Melinda Gates Foundation, held the "Event 201" (Johns Hopkins Center for Health Security, 2021) devoted to the problem of high-level response to the pandemic. The meeting was held in the form of a strategic game, which prototyped the spread of a pandemic of a persistent virus transmitted airborne, as well as by handshakes and other tactile contacts. According to the strategic game scenario, a special thing about the virus was a lack of an effective vaccine and selective mortality of the population mainly among people with weakened immunity.

D. Rockefeller is another well-known backer of the idea of world government as a necessary tool to save humanity from the threats of overpopulation and pollution of the Earth. At the previous critical stage of technical and economic development, when the world economy was plunged into a crisis due to the end of the 4th technological mode cycle, he initiated the creation of the Club of Rome, which presented the report "The Limits to Growth" (Meadows et al., 1972).[7] Today, the topic of limits in resource consumption self-imposed by developing countries is once again being refreshed by global media. This time, it is augmented by a threat of self-destruction of humanity from unprecedented viruses bursting out of the remnants of wild nature and thawing perpetually frozen ground.

The Rockefeller Foundation's forecast of a viral pandemic generated ten years ago is a striking coincidence with the current situation. In 2010, the Rockefeller Foundation and the Global Business Network published a report "Scenarios for the Future of Technology and International Development" (Scenarios for the Future ..., 2010). One of the scenarios of the report named in the spirit of special missions of the US secret services from Hollywood blockbusters – "Lock Step" – describes, in fact, a modelling of global destabilization through a virus pandemic. The above-mentioned report states: *"During the pandemic, national leaders around the world flexed their authority and imposed airtight rules and restrictions ... Even after the pandemic faded, this more authoritarian control and oversight of citizens and their activities stuck and even intensified. In order to protect themselves from the spread of increasingly global problems – from pandemics and transnational terrorism to environmental crises and rising poverty – leaders around the world took a firmer grip on power".* Since viruses respect no state borders, it is hard to escape a conclusion that it is necessary to create global institutions for regulating human activity.

In other words, the third form of the new world economic order implies actually the establishment of a world government under the leadership of the American ruling elite in the interests of the financial oligarchy which controls

---

7   "The Limits to Growth" – a report to the Club of Rome published in 1972. Contains the modeling results of the growth of human population and the depletion of natural resources.

the world currency emission, transnational banks and corporations and the global financial market. This continues the trend of liberal globalization added by authoritarian technologies for controlling the population of countries deprived of their national sovereignty. In the view of traditional confessions, this is the scenario of an "electronic concentration camp" that precedes the Judgement Day, as many anti-utopias describe.

Each of the forms of the new world economic order described above involves the use of advanced information technologies, which are a key factor in the new technological mode and represent the material basis of noonomy. They all use big data processing methods and artificial intelligence systems that allow managing not only unmanned production processes, but also people in the systems that regulate the economy and social behavior. The goals of this regulation are set by the ruling elite, and the method using which they were established determines the essential characteristics of each of the forms of the new world economic order.

In China, power resides in the leadership of the Communist Party, who manage economic regulation in order to improve the people's welfare and direct social behavior towards achieving the political goals of building Chinese-type socialism. Market mechanisms are regulated in such a way as to ensure that the most efficient production and technological structures win the competition, and the profit is proportional to their contribution to the improvement of public welfare. Moreover, there are party organizations in medium-sized and large corporations, including non-state ones, that control whether economic motivations correspond to the moral values of the Communist ideology. On the one hand, they encourage increased labor productivity and production efficiency, modesty and performance of managers and owners, and on the other, penalize abuse of market dominance and speculative manipulation, wastefulness and parasitic consumption. There is a social credit system being developed. It is aimed to regulate social behavior of individuals. According to the intended plan, social opportunities of each citizen will depend on his/her rating, and this rating will be constantly updated based on the balance of right and wrong acts. The higher the rating, the more credibility a person has when applying for a job, career development, getting a loan or delegating authority. This is a developed version of personal files management system familiar to Soviet people. Personal files systems that keep track of a person throughout his/her working life has its positive and negative sides, the assessment of which lies beyond the scope of this chapter. Its main bottleneck is the dependence of high-performance elite-forming tool on artificial intelligence.

The second type of new world economic order is determined by the democratic political system, which may significantly differ across countries. It is most developed in Switzerland, where major political decisions are made at popular referendums. In most countries, it is seriously affected by corruption and is exposed to manipulation by business leaders, which can be patriotic or comprador. The introduction of modern information technologies in the system of elections of people's representatives can significantly improve the effectiveness of this political system through the elimination of vote fraud and ensuring equal access of candidates to media. The distribution of the latter in the blogosphere provokes competition between information sources, thus increasing their reliability and impartiality. The proper legal support for the use of modern information technologies in the election process will set the context for the build-up of an automatic mechanism of regulatory responsibility for the results of their pro-social activities. The more educated and active citizens are, the more effectively the democratic political system works. Its main bottleneck is the dependence of high-performance elite-forming tool on clan and corporate structures that are not interested in transparency and integrity of elections.

Finally, the third type of the new world economic order is determined by the interests of the financial oligarchy that claims to world domination. It is usually achieved through liberal globalization, which consists in the dilution of national institutions of economic regulation and subordination of economic reproduction to the interests of international capital. The dominant position in the structure of the latter is occupied by several dozen interwoven American-European family clans that control major financial holdings, military and security services, intelligence agencies, media, political parties and form the so-called "deep state" (Coleman, 2005). This core of the US ruling elite is fighting a hybrid war with all the countries it does not control, using a broad range of financial, information, cognitive and, indeed, biological technologies to destabilize these countries and to unleash chaos in them. The goal of this war is to create a global system of subordinated institutions that regulate not only the reproduction of the world economy, but also the reproduction of the entire humanity using modern information, financial and bioengineering technologies. The primary problem of such a political system is its complete recklessness and immorality, and the adherence of its hereditary ruling elite to Malthusian, racist, and hate-crazed views.

The new world order will be shaped in competition between these three forms of the world economic order. However, the latter form excludes the first two ones, which can coexist peacefully. Just like the victory of Nazi Germany and Japan in the war against the USSR and the USA would have excluded both the Soviet and the American models of the new world economic order of that time. After the common victory, the USSR and the USA created competing political systems, that divided the world into areas of influence, and avoided direct confrontation.

Thus, there are three forecast scenarios for the transition to noonomy. The material basis they share is the new technological mode with the core of a combination of digital, information, bioengineering, cognitive, additive and nanotechnologies. They are used today to create completely automated unmanned production facilities that manage extensive databases of artificial intelligence systems, transgenic microorganisms, plants and animals, to clone living creatures and to regenerate human tissues. This technological basis is key to the establishment of institutions of an integral world economic order that allow conscious managing the socio-economic development of both sovereign states and (possibly) humanity as a whole. This is achieved through a combination of state strategic planning and market competition based on public-private partnership. Depending on the interests in which the activities of autonomous economic entities are controlled, one of the forms of the new world economic order described above will develop. The first two – the communist and democratic forms – can coexist peacefully, competing and cooperating on the basis of international law. The third version – the oligarchic one – is antagonistic to the first two, since it involves the establishment of inherited world domination of a group of American-European family clans, which is incompatible with either democratic or communist values.

Which of the three forecast courses the evolution of humanity will take depends on the outcome of the hybrid war launched by the American ruling elite against sovereign states. The primary targets of American aggression are China, which has become a global leader in the emerging new world economic order, and Russia with its nuclear-missile shield that negates the advantages of the USA in the military-political area. The strategic partnership between Russia and China is an insurmountable obstacle for the American ruling elite to establish the global domination of financial business tycoons. The power of the latter relies on the emission of world money, the potential of which is limited by the political will of sovereign states that can issue and use their national currencies in international cooperation. Should China and Russia manage to create a monetary and financial system independent of the dollar, at least for the Shanghai Cooperation Organization (SCO), the outcome of the world hybrid war will be a foregone conclusion. Deprived of the feeding of its external balance through the unlimited emission of world currency, the American empire will quickly lose its military and political power.

A special thing about noonomy is the leading role of knowledge in managing socio-economic development at national and global levels. As soon as the arrangement for the emission of world money ceases to be a secret for national monetary authorities of sovereign states, the dominant position of American-European oligarchic clans in the global financial market will be no longer the case. The weakness of their position consists in the fiducial (fiduciary) nature of today's money, the purchasing power of which is based on trust earned by state power. Confidence in the dollar is based on the military-political and economic power of the USA, which is rapidly diluting as a hybrid war unfolds. Each act of American aggression may bring short-term political dividends, but it worsens the status of the USA in the long and even medium term. Indeed, the USA are doomed to defeat in the trade war initiated by President Trump, because China has created such a system of economic development management that surpasses the American one in terms of efficiency by an order. Financial sanctions against Russia are undermining confidence in the dollar as a global currency. Another crash of the US financial market destroys the American capital accumulation center. The coronavirus planted into China causes much more damage to the USA themselves than to China.

Perhaps, in an effort to maintain global dominance, the ruling US oligarchy decided to employ cognitive-biological weapons. Exactly as given in the Rockefeller Foundation's pandemic scenario of 2009, panic-stricken countries block people's movement and paralyze business activity. The paralysis of the economy causes a sharp drop in the standard of living of people and the disturbance of public financial systems around the world. Oligarchic clans, that are linked to the US Federal Reserve and hold a monopoly on the emission of world money, offer their financial assistance to obedient national governments, and a heaven-sent vaccine – to the frightened population. Later on, in accordance with the plan of the B. & M. Gates Foundation, blanket vaccination will be used as a tool for bio-programming the population that agrees with the control of global institutions over the birth rate and access to life-supporting resources.

This must have been the intent of the coronavirus diversion against China. This is evidenced by a sequence of "strange" events, starting from the Rockefeller Foundation scenario and ending with the partial privatization of the WHO by the B. & M. Gates Foundation, as well as investigations into the activities of a global network of American secret bioengineering labs. Still, the Chinese system of mobilization of its population and health care system proved to be much more effective than the American one, which is much more expensive. An attempt by the US authorities and media to inflict China for the pandemic failed. Instead, the Chinese leadership has seized the global initiative and provides all countries with the assistance, as compared to the USA with their social disaster. This manifests the advantages of the integrated world

economic order created by the PRC over the system of global dominance of the
American-European financial oligarchy.

4   Noonomy of the Future World Economic Order

Of the three above scenarios for the formation of a new world economic order,
the world government version looks the least likely. This may be the direction
in which the world hybrid war is unfolding today, but the ruling elite of the
USA is doomed to defeat in it due to the higher efficiency of the PRC's mobilization capacities and the lack of all countries' interest in this war. It can be
stopped by establishing a broad anti-war coalition based on the creation of a
monetary and financial system independent from the dollar, concluding a convention against cyberterrorism, and creating a mechanism for monitoring the
implementation of the Convention on the Prohibition of the Development,
Production and Stockpiling of Bacteriological (Biological) and Toxin Weapons,
which entered into force in 1975.

Assuming the most likely outcome of the hybrid world war waged by the
US ruling elite that will be anything but the winner, the new world economic
order will emerge in competition of the communist and democratic varieties, with the results to determine their relative effectiveness in exploiting the
opportunities and managing the threats of the new technological mode. This
competition will be peaceful and governed by international law. All aspects
of this regulation, from monitoring global security to emitting world currencies, will be based on international treaties. Countries which refuse to assume
obligations and discard international monitoring of their compliance will be
isolated in the relevant areas of international cooperation. World economy
will become more complex; the importance of national sovereignty and the
diversity of national systems of economic regulation will be recovered against
the background of the fundamental importance of international organizations
with supernational powers.

The competition between the communist and democratic forms of the integral world economic order will not be antagonistic. For example, the Chinese
initiative "One Belt and One Road" with the ideology of "common destiny of
humanity" involves many countries with different political orders. Democratic
EU countries create free trade zones with communist Vietnam. The competitive landscape will be determined by the comparative effectiveness of national
management systems. They all will face the following challenges of the new
technological mode.

First: Mass release of employees engaged in hard labour, which will be replaced by automatic control systems in both material production and services. These people will either have to learn new creative professions or be allowed to retire early. Second: The split of society into a creative community of people engaged in innovative self-realization and a precariat that settle for the role of service personnel and consumers. Social harmony between these two groups requires the availability of social elevators and social security systems, allowing the poor to receive proper education, and the under-educated – to enjoy a normal standard of living.

Third: Fragmentation of society by social networks differentiated with respect to worldview, moral values and needs. The state will have to integrate these network communities through the harmonization of their interests in achieving common goal of public welfare improvement. Fourth: The concentration of power in the hands of noocracy, whose knowledge creates unlimited opportunities for the use of technologies that are potentially dangerous for society. These people have to agree to restrict their creative freedom in the areas that pose a threat to humanity, including bioengineering, nuclear physics, system programming, fine chemistry and so on.

Fifth: The dilution of social groups based on a physical sense of solidarity due to autism and sociopathy of a growing part of the population isolated in the virtual realm. These people need special conditions for survival and self-realization that require appropriate tools for social adaptation. Their social integration becomes an important task of national security. Sixth: The growing share of spare time due to the release of people from labor-intensive areas of activity. The creative use of spare time requires the development of such areas of creative self-realization that are not related to work for the sake of consumption. The solution of this challenge opens up the door to noonomy.

The list of challenges of the current technological revolution can be continued. The institutions that can recognize them and use them in a constructive way are formed within the framework of the integrated world economic order. The common denominator of its two basic varieties is noonomy, which determines the ability of the management system to create and regulate the automatically reproduced processes of social and economic development. The effectiveness of both the democratic and communist images of the integral world economic order will depend on balancing the negative impact from subjective management factors and the promotion of their positive role. The positive selection of these factors is achieved via an automatic mechanism of accountability of decision-makers to society. China is experimenting with the social credit system that is merged with the traditional Chinese Confucian ethics. Switzerland is developing automatic mechanisms of direct democracy that force the government to bow to continuous popular control and expression of will by way of referendums.

Major competition between the communist and democratic forms of the new world economic order is likely to unfold between China and India, which are today's leaders in terms of economic development and pretend, together with their satellites, to a good half of the world economy. Noonomy-based institutions of the new world economic order are successfully formed in Japan, Korea, and the ASEAN countries. The question remains about the future of other countries, including Russia, whose ruling elite opposes the principles of noonomy. It is impossible to create institutions of the new world economic order, either in the democratic or in the communist version, without creating automatically functioning mechanisms of government accountability to society and positive personnel selection. In the absence of the above, it will not be possible to master the production of the new technological mode that requires high professionalism and social harmony.

Noonomy removes resource constraints in providing for the material needs of humanity. Modern agricultural technologies make it possible to feed twice as many people as the population of the planet today. Energy technologies, particularly sun-power engineering, remove the problems with limited non-renewable raw materials. Information technology removes the constraints of the wit of man in terms of data processing. Today, constraints on socioeconomic development come primarily from subjective factors of management, such as corruption, incompetence, favouritism, greed and thirst for power, which are incompatible with the principles of noonomy and the institutions of the new world economic order.

References

Bell, D. (1973) *The Coming of Post-Industrial Society. A Venture in Social Forecasting.* New York: Basic Books.

Bell, D. (1976) *The Cultural Contradictions of Capitalism.* London: Heinemann Educational Books.

Bodrunov, S.D. (2018) *Noonomy.* Moscow: Kulturnaya Revolutsiya.

Coleman, J. (2005) *The Conspirators' Hierarchy: The Committee of 300.* Mosco: Vytyaz PH.

Danilov, I. (2020) Saviour of Great Britain Comes up with the Idea of an Interim World Government. *RIA Novosti*, 28 March. Available (consulted 23 August, 2021) at: https://ria.ru/20200328/1569257083.html.

Engels, F. (1961) Anti-Düring. In: Marx, K. and Engels, F. *Collected Works.* 2nd ed. Vol. 20. Moscow: Gospolitizdat.

Glazyev, S. (2016a) National economy structures in the global economic development. *Economics and Mathematical Methods* 52(2): 3–29.

Glazyev, S. (2016b) Applied results in the theory of world economic structures. *Economics and Mathematical Methods* 52(3): 3–21.

Glazyev, S. and Kharitonov, V. (eds) (2009) *Nanotechnologies as a Key Factor of the New Technological Mode in the Economy.* Moscow: Tovant.

Glazyev, S. (2016c) *The Last World War. The USA Start and Lose.* Moscow: Knizhny Mir.

Glazyev, S. (2018) *Leap into the Future. Russia in New Technological and World Economic Orders.* Moscow: Knizhny Mir.

Higham, C. (1983) *Trading With The Enemy: An Expose of The Nazi-American Money Plot 1933–1949.* New York: Delacorte Press.

Hoffower, H. (2020). Bill Gates Has Been Warning of a Global Health Threat for Years. Business Insider, 15 December. Available (consulted 23 August, 2021) at: https://www.businessinsider.com/people-who-seemingly-predicted-the-coronavirus-pandemic-2020-3.

Johns Hopkins Center for Health Security (2021). *Event 201.* Available (consulted 23 August, 2021) at: http://www.centerforhealthsecurity.org/event201.

Klyukin, N.Yu. and Gutnikov, V.A. (2018) Assessment of Biological Capacity of Agrosphere in order to Determine the Maximum Number of World Population. *Public Administration. E-Bulletin* 69: 482–497.

Kuznetsov, A.V. (2009) New Economy and Post-Industrial Society: Comparison of Concepts. *Bulletin of Chelyabinsk State University no. 2 (140). Economy,* issue 18: 22–27.

Meadows, D.H., Meadows, D.L., Randers, J. and Behrens III, W.W. (1972) *The limits to growth. A report for the Club of Rome's project on the predicament of mankind.* New York: Universe Books.

Riesman, D. (1958) Work and leisure in post-industrial society. In: Larrabee, E. and Meyersohn, R. (eds.) *Mass Leisure.* Glencoe, IL: The Free Press, 363–388.

Scenarios for the Future of Technology and International Development (2010). The Rockfeller Foundation, Global Business Network.

Shveytser, P. (1995) *Victory. The Role of Secret Strategy of the US Administration in the Collapse of the Soviet Union and the Socialist Bloc.* Minsk.

Zynovyev, A. (2000) *The West.* Moscow: Tsentrpoligraf Publishing CJSC.

CHAPTER 2

Noonomy, Globalization and the Pandemic

James Kenneth Galbraith

1 Introduction

"Noonomy", in the usage of Professor Bodrunov (Bodrunov, 2018), describes the potential development of an industrial system that is fit-for-purpose, in the sense of meeting the essential requirements for a just and civilized society given the possibilities of technology and within the limits imposed by the environment. In this system, productive processes will be largely free of direct labor inputs, and society will be largely organized on principles different from the narrow economic criteria hitherto in use.

In some narrow respects, the world as a whole has been moving toward noonomy for some time, through industrial restructuring and automation, thanks to the rise of digital and solid-state technologies and corporate strategies for cost control. Many workers have already been displaced. But neither justice nor civilization nor the environment are served by this process as it stands; it is instead unequal, in some ways brutal and ecologically destructive. And while a large majority of those displaced have found employment in the services sector, with only a relative few forced to rely for the long term on the meager support of the welfare state, the Covid-19 pandemic has exposed the fragility of that employment, and the inability of the system as presently constituted to survive the radical changes in behavior induced by a severe threat to public health. It therefore points toward the steps that will be required if the potential for a sustainable noonomy is to be realized.

2 The Planning System

Whether national, continental or global, an economy with a knowledge-based industrial sector necessarily conforms to the framework of industrial organization and control laid out in the work of John Kenneth Galbraith in *The New Industrial State* (Galbraith, 1967). There is a Planning System, centered on the industrial corporation, that undertakes market research, product design, the engineering, financing and quality and cost control of the production process. The corporation interfaces with its customers, its employees, the public sector and the financial sector, and works to coordinate and control the behavior of each in order to best advance the interests of the corporation as perceived by its management and directors. Since the Planning System at the level of the enterprise remains the crucial actor in the production process, the determination of its interests becomes a central question.

The interests of a large industrial enterprise are determined in part by the political, legal and ideological environment in which it operates. A differential perception of interests distinguishes long-term going concerns responsive to public purpose from entities whose primary objective is the maximization of shareholder value in the short term and the compensation of corporate leadership.

Notoriously, in the United States and United Kingdom, the adoption of shareholder value as the primary criterion of performance, beginning in the late 1970s under the influence of neoliberal economists, led to the erosion of the long-term viability of major firms, much as nomenklatura privatization brought on looting in the breakup of the USSR. But in other countries, and most notably Germany, Japan, Korea and China, the Planning System has continued to function in the interest of the long-term viability of industrial corporations as going concerns, and these countries have retained and developed their technological capacities in a cumulative process through time. It is worth noting that in each case, the Planning System of the corporations exists in a structure of countervailing power (as with the trade unions and other social partners in Germany) or in partnership with government agencies (as in Japan and Korea), or even, as in the case of China, with state ownership of many of the key enterprises. To some degree, these enterprises are responsive to social and environmental pressures, but their main concern continues to be as Galbraith postulated: in their own stability and growth.

Indeed, even maintaining the stability of the industrial system has required creative steps, imperfectly taken. The construction of an economy built around advanced manufacturing necessarily entails a world in which only a small fraction of the employable workforce can be absorbed in manufacturing activities, while a much larger fraction must seek employment in other domains or means of subsistence without being employed. This fact applies to all manufacturing economies, but it is most prominent for those high-wage countries that are actively shedding manufactures to lower-wage trading partners, and most aggressively implementing labor-saving technological change. In these countries, the share of the labor force employed in high-wage manufactures has plunged. The challenge for the Planning System, even otherwise unconstrained by public purpose, is to ensure that there is both demand and supply for the services that support the incomes of the mass of working people not producing physical goods, in order that there may be adequate demand for the physical products of the Planning System. For social and political reasons, with the important but limited exception of the elderly, supported by Social Security and other public retirement schemes, it is not broadly acceptable merely to guarantee incomes to all who need them. So the Planning System has had to foster an economy in which actual employment is widely available outside the goods-producing sectors.

3   Simulacra, Superfluities and Frills

The key to job creation in the post-industrial proto-noonomy has been to foster demand and supply of goods and services that inessential or superfluous, in the sense that they may be forgone without grave loss to welfare; goods and services meeting this description may be described as "simulacra", insofar as they meet needs that are not real needs, but confected desires.

The distinction between the essential and the inessential, lost in neoclassical economics, has its roots in the classical dichotomy between productive and unproductive labor, and in the concepts of pecuniary emulation and conspicuous waste advanced by Thorstein Veblen (Veblen, 1899), as well as his division between the industrial and the leisure class. Thus, for Adam Smith, who adapted the earlier framework of the Physiocrats, servants, soldiers, clerics and most public functionaries were "unproductive", and so were maintained out of a surplus produced through the diligence of farmers, craftspeople and the merchants who organized 18th century British economic life. While for Veblen, the leisure class preoccupied itself with the flamboyant consumption of luxuries and display of wealth, including the maintenance of expensive suites of retainers and servants, all of whom consumed the products of the industrial classes.

In the postwar era, increasing labor productivity meant that the potential for a Marxian "crisis of realization" had to be dealt with. To keep up the demand for its outputs, the Planning System pursued the design and marketing of simulacra in a multiplicity of forms. Initially this consisted, largely, of an increasing diversity of consumer products, their virtues insistently advanced by advertising, a topic well-explored by Galbraith (Galbraith, 1958). But more recently, the process of creating simulacra has moved on to services. Thus, we see the conversion of simple and previously routine actions – such as exercising, or coffee-drinking, or shopping for food and clothing, or pursuing higher education or elective medical procedures – into expensive forms of discretionary consumption, such as can underpin substantial elements of economic life. And so it is in the services sector, not the goods-producing sector, that simulacra have been recently most prominently developed, and that most job seekers in the advanced economies have until recently found employment.

4   A Tripartite World Economy

The process of globalization has thus brought into being a tripartite world economy, first analyzed in Galbraith (Galbraith, 1989: 14). At the lowest level are those countries that are largely confined to the supply of commodities on the world markets ("Resource-Based Economies"), from cotton and cocoa to copper and cobalt, and of course oil. Such countries have a long-standing and traditional economic structure; they must depend on the outside world for manufactures, for investment goods, and for the basics of medical provisioning; their capacity to pay is limited by the price they can receive for the commodities they produce. Short-falls are covered by debt, and periodic debt crises are endemic for countries in this position. These countries are also radically unequal, with the divide being between landowners and tenants, or more broadly those who control the flow of resources and those who do not. Exceptions exist – Cuba comes to mind, and Norway – but they are rare.

At the top level are the countries ("Leading Technological Powers") that supply advanced technological products, capital goods and financial services to the world. These countries typically enjoy high living standards and high real wages thanks to strong currencies and the capacity to import both commodities and consumer manufactures at prices that the broad mass of their households can afford. Their economies are however marked by distinct business cycles, thanks to the cyclicality in global demand for advanced capital goods, and by very large inequalities, owing to the extraordinary capital valuations attained by advanced technology firms, accruing to very small numbers of people, and to the potential for profit and predation in the financial sector. Since labor-intensive manufacturing is largely removed to other locations, the great mass of jobs in these economies are in services, rooted as argued above in the fostering of novel desires and the conversion of routine activities into expensive formulae for the consumption of time.

In the middle tier, we find those countries ("Intermediate Manufacturing Powers") that provide the manufactures to the consuming households of the world, generally importing both capital goods and commodities. These societies tend to be relatively egalitarian and also relatively stable – their principal vulnerability is to fluctuations in demand for their exports and in the prices of their raw materials. Living standards are comparatively modest, but with a tendency to improve over time as the quality of goods improves and costs of production decline. Such countries are also in the position of importing technologies from their more advanced partners, as well as improving their own capacities. They thus pose an implicit or explicit threat to the material dominance of the incumbents in the top tier.

5   Covid-19, Economic Structure and Economic Models

The Covid-19 crisis has brought these differences into focus. It has differentiated countries with balanced and robust industrial systems from those with unbalanced and fragile systems. It has exposed the elements of superfluity, which are sources of economic fragility. It is revealing the consequences of precarity and inequality in the provision of those goods and services, including public services and amenities, that are essential to a civilized, secure and satisfactory life. It has specifically shown that the most globalized economies, those whose structures are most oriented toward a global division of labor and therefore most dependent on simulacra and superfluities in the support of home-country employment, are the most fragile under the conditions of a global health crisis.

Mainstream economics pays little attention to such questions of structure. It treats all consumer spending as driven by equally valid wants, therefore equally necessary; the distinction between "essential" and "superfluous" does not exist. It ignores, by and large, the burden of debts, and overlooks the role of the global as opposed to the local sources of demand for capital goods. Thus, to many mainstream economists, the pandemic was a shock – like an earthquake or the 9/11 attacks – to an economy whose major features are all internal, and which can be modeled in a fashion essentially identical to that used for any macro-economy whatsoever. From this perspective, Covid-19 was an interruption in an otherwise prosperous and stable expansion, long past the phase of "recovery" from the previous debacle, the financial crisis of 2007–2009. It came as a surprise, which suggests that there was no prior underlying problem. The aftermath can therefore be expected to resemble the economic recoveries of the past.

So, to get an economy "moving again", in the mainstream view, what is mainly necessary is once again "confidence" – for consumers return to spending, to use their "pent-up demand", perhaps with the help of a distribution of dollars from the public fisc. In the United States, the Congressional Budget Office (CBO) (Congressional Budget Office, 2020) is explicit in relying on the consumer, and not business or government, to drive the recovery that it expects to begin soon. With support for incomes producing increased consumption, this eventually prompting an increase in business investment, CBO generally expects a full recovery over time. We may call this the "shock-stimulus" way of thinking. It is consistent with the way American mainstream economists and center-left policy makers have thought about recessions and recoveries since the Kennedy-Johnson tax cuts of the early 1960s. It accepts the idea that consumer desires are unlimited, that household consumption is constrained mainly by income, and that the growth path of the economy as a whole is a predictable function of population and incomes.

6   The Covid-19 Crisis in the United States

Real gross domestic product (GDP) in the United States is expected to fall 12 percentage points, the Congressional Budget Office (Congressional Budget Office, 2020) predicts, in the April-June quarter of 2020, or at an annual rate of 40 percent. Given the role of imputed values in the calculation of GDP, about 15 percent of the total, this would represent a decline of about half in actual cash transactions. Moreover, much of the remainder counts as fixed costs, such as for rent, utilities, and government spending; when one takes these into account the rate of collapse in the second quarter, had it continued for a full year, would have nearly eliminated private economic activity in the country. As things stand, visits to physical businesses appear to have fallen by more than half. The fall was probably arrested in the third quarter by the combination of "stimulus" and "reopening", and a partial rebound is likely when those data are published. But even in the best-case scenarios, US GDP will remain well below the levels of early 2020 a year hence, and unemployment of between ten and twenty million persons a fixture of the landscape.

The shock-stimulus model just described projects a steady recovery from this debacle over four or five years. But this ignores the three features of the US economy that have changed as the United States evolved into a fully globalized Leading Technological Power over the course of the past half-century. They are the globalization of industry itself, the rise of simulacra concentrated in services (and relative decline of goods) in consumption and employment within the country, and the rising burden of personal and corporate debts.

In the 1960s, the United States had a balanced industrial economy. It produced goods for both businesses and households, at all levels of technology, with a fairly small (and tightly regulated) financial sector. It produced largely for itself, importing mainly commodities, although it also produced a large volume of its own commodities. This balance no longer holds.

The United States and the United Kingdom are today leading examples of countries that built globalized economies centered on finance and advanced technology industries, such as aerospace, armaments, information technologies, energy services, advanced pharmaceuticals and the like. They correspondingly import a great share of their ordinary consumption goods, including clothing, consumer electronics, appliances and automobiles and automotive parts, from Asia but also Germany and its near neighbors in Europe, and from Mexico in the case of the United States. Specialization is a feature of globalization, and the prominence of finance and technology also means a concentration of incomes and wealth, yet in societies where real living standards are maintained for many by the strong position of the national currencies, which have permitted large-scale importation of inexpensive consumer goods from developing countries.

Second, with rising incomes and new technologies there has been a change in the composition of household spending. In the 1960s, the American consumer (and her British counterpart, to a lesser degree) was still expanding her stock of household basics. Cars, televisions, kitchen and laundry appliances were the driving forces of demand, as everyone wanted what all the others were buying. A stock of physical possessions of good quality and modern design indicated social status; to lack them was a significant marker of economic failure. Today, the low cost of durables made in countries with much lower wages has diminished the status-content of such purchases. This has freed up incomes for services, from restaurants and bars to resorts and casinos, salons, gyms and trainers, salons, coffee shops, massage therapists and tattoo artists. Higher education and even shopping are likewise to be considered, not solely as investment in "human capital" or (in the case of shopping) as a chore, but as, in part, leisure-time and status-seeking activities. These are the simulacra, the activities on which many millions, from college professors to checkout clerks, have relied for jobs and income. The problem is that, being largely simulacra, these activities are also superfluous, in the precise sense that they may be forgone with no grave harm to the buyer. People may have enjoyed their nights out, their shopping, their manicures, massages and tattoos, but these items are not needs; they are pleasures and luxuries, and they may be foregone.

Third, in the 1960s, American household spending was powered by rising wages, and also by growing equity in homes as inflation drove up house values in relation to fixed-rate mortgages. Neither is true any longer. Wages are largely stagnant since at least 2000, while gains in spending have been powered by debt, both personal and corporate – the latter oriented toward stock buy-backs, pushing up corporate equity valuations and hence the purchasing power of high-net-worth households. House values, a major source of middle-class spending power, were hit by the 2008 crisis; lending against houses since then has no doubt diminished net equity, and increased the vulnerability of middle-class net worth to a decline in home values. Meanwhile a paucity of truly public goods, such as parks, libraries, security, clean air and potable water, especially in low-income communities, drives home and aggravates the inequality in private incomes.

In the Covid-19 crisis, the demand for advanced investment goods has collapsed. With air travel down by over 90 percent, half or more of all aircraft are parked on the ground. There will be little demand for new planes, and the major producers – already in trouble in the case of Boeing – are curtailing new production. For many other advanced goods, the demand collapse is a global phenomenon and national policy can do nothing, short of nationalizing the production lines, to stop it. But there are effects that are purely domestic as well. Drilling of new oil wells in the Permian Basin has stopped as those already drilled are unprofitable at present prices. Commercial offices stand empty, shopping malls are closed, so there is no need for construction of new ones.

On the side of households, faced with a radical increase in uncertainty, saving rises and spending falls. Households will save more even if the government replaces their lost incomes for a time. People know very well that stimulus is short-term. They know that job prospects are bleak. They expect their homes to lose value and their credit ratings to decline. They will cut back on things they do not need, in order to be prepared to provide the things they really do need. With less commuting, cars last longer and fewer new ones will be made and sold. Even in health care, some 18 percent of (normal) US GDP, demand for services is down, since with time off and an absence of routine accidents, the health of the uninfected population has improved and the desire to pay for health services, such as tests and diagnoses, even among those who need them, has declined. Some of the activities that previously drove the economy, such as sporting events, conventions, concerts and other mass gatherings, have been canceled and remain so for health reasons. Restaurants, bars, clubs, salons, retail stores and the like are being permitted to open, usually under restrictions to fifty percent or less of capacity. Airlines are flying, but with their middle seats empty and in many cases the rest of the plane as well.

The people who run restaurants and airlines have two problems. One is that they can't cover costs with their capacity limited for health reasons; these are businesses with low margins that survive in ordinary times by packing people in. But the other problem is more fundamental. It is (once again) that very few people, in America at least, need these services as a condition of decent life. Middle- and upper-class Americans, the major repository of national purchasing power, can if necessary eat, drink, socialize and take their vacations at home. So, under the circumstances demand would be down, even if the coronavirus went away. This explains why many services are not reopening even though they are legally permitted to do so. The tragedy of it is that without them, millions of jobs will not come back either. Analysis of the patronage of businesses in the United States, derived from surveillance of foot traffic, supports this analysis. It reveals that the flow of activities has not recovered substantially at time of writing (in September, 2020), despite a very large replacement of income and the passage of time since the initial pandemic panic took hold.

Finally, though incomes and jobs are lost, household debts have continued to mount: rents, mortgages, utilities, interest on loans for cars, education, and ordinary expenses. Stimulus checks have helped for now: defaults and arrears have been modest, and many landlords have been accommodating. But as people face long periods with lower incomes, they will continue to hoard funds, to be sure to meet their fixed debts. To all this, one can add the plight of state and local governments, which rely on taxes raised on sales and incomes. As these collapse, the response is to cut spending and curtail services, compounding the loss of jobs and incomes. Massive intervention by the Federal Reserve, the interruption of investment projects and the rise of savings together explain the rise in the stock market after the initial panic: both companies and wealthy persons had money to place, no desire to spend it, and were not keen on leaving it at zero interest in the bank. This development, while reassuring to those who own capital assets, has no important implications for the recovery of the economy as a whole.

None of this is the consequence merely of incompetence under President Donald Trump. It is the result of systemic changes in the US economy over 50 years. The US has built an economy based on global demand for advanced goods, on domestic consumer demand for frills, and on ever-growing household and business debts. This is not short-term or reversible in the course of few months or years. This market-driven economy was in many ways prosperous and successful; it was efficient, it delivered what people wanted, it had eliminated unemployment without bringing inflation, and many millions had jobs and incomes. But it was a house of cards, and the wind of the coronavirus has blown it down.

7   The Pandemic in Asia: The Case of Intermediate Manufacturing
       Powers

Meanwhile, on the other side of the world, we find economies that have not
collapsed in the pandemic. Some of these, such as China and Vietnam, are
nominally socialist. Others, such as Korea and Taiwan, are ostensibly capitalist. All experienced relatively low death tolls in the end, with varying degrees
of popular mobilization and lock-down required to achieve this objective. All
were able to muster and make use of a broad solidarity and a will on the part
of large and densely settled populations to do the job. And all survived the
pandemic with manageable levels of economic damage.

Focusing strictly on the economics, what they share is more important than
the ideological and historical issues that divide them. All four have national
economies rooted in manufactures, the product of a concerted industrial
development strategy, having retained most of the core industries providing basic consumer goods. They achieved this with a combination of stable
advanced industrial firms, with long-term perspectives and assured financing, in the model of the American industrial corporations of the mid-1960s,
and also large sectors of small enterprises producing low-technology consumption goods such as garments and paper products. Thus, they were not
suddenly short of medical supplies and protective equipment when global
supply chains were disrupted or were able rapidly to make up shortages that
did occur. Chinese production of face masks rose from 15 million to about 110
million per day over three weeks in February, as 3,000 small and medium-
sized enterprises (SMEs) converted production lines. These economies import
advanced capital goods, and they import commodities, but they are well-posi-
tioned to meet the basic needs of their societies in the face of the challenges
of an epidemic.

Further, the services sectors in Asia evidently do not operate in the same
cost environment as in the West. Obligations with respect to rent and interest
and profit are more elastic, and demand by the population is less so. Small
Asian firms are generally not at the mercy of commercial landlords; in China
and Vietnam, hardly at all. Their banks work to keep them afloat, even during
periods with little or no profit; this is deemed necessary for social stability.
Moreover, what they provide is not thought of as "inessential". Asian families
live in very small spaces and need to go outside; they have smaller kitchens, and
they cannot substitute as readily as in the West against the restaurant trade.
Their debt burden is relatively light, savings are relatively ample, and the drive
to save to meet fixed costs is mitigated by the public provision of health care
and basic education, and by strong family structures that provide a backstop

for retirement and emergencies. These factors help account for economic resilience in the face of the disruption that has knocked the leading Western economies to the ground. And that resilience made it possible for governments in Asia to move quickly, with great social solidarity, to get the virus under control so that things could, quite quickly, return to "normal".

8   Conclusion

The study of noonomy falls under the purview of institutional economics, which considers issues of economic structure to be fundamental. So does a closely related body of thinking, biophysical economics, whose principles are drawn from the laws of thermodynamics and set out in three papers by Chen and Galbraith (Chen and Galbraith, 2011, 2012a, 2012b). Biophysical economics stresses that the more advanced and efficient any system – biological, mechanical, or social – the higher the fixed costs and therefore the narrower the margin of safety. The implications of this principle for the effect of stresses, whether emanating from diminished resource-availability, the constraints imposed by climate change, or the Covid-19 pandemic are straightforward.

A peculiar conclusion emerges, behind which a general principle may be found. It is precisely those countries which are at the top of the hierarchy of globalization that are at greatest risk of collapse. And precisely those *not* at the top of the global hierarchy of trading relations, and that have *not* made the transition to the most advanced systems of financial relations and household access to credit, that have proved most successful in dealing with the coronavirus, both in their capacities to defeat the pandemic and their ability to retain the full function of their economies and the stability of their social order. It is clear now in the case of the United States that this has not been achieved.

A short chapter cannot cover the full spectrum of economic structures that have been obliged to react to the Covid-19 pandemic. I have made no attempt to describe the variations present on the continent of Europe, nor in Russia, nor the situation in the poorer regions of the world, such as Latin America and Africa. But the contrast between the polar cases of the US and UK on one side and the PRC, the Democratic Republic of Vietnam (DRV), the Republic of Korea (ROK) and Taiwan on the other is sufficient to illustrate the roles that structure and finance play in determining the economic consequences of the coronavirus.

Some implications may be summarized briefly as they flow from the structural analyses given above and the goal of a true noonomy. First, as the private provision of global investment goods geared to the needs of the pre-pandemic economy has collapsed, the entire capital-goods-producing sector in the advanced world will need to be redesigned to meet the imperative public purposes ahead, most notably with respect to climate change but also in creating and maintaining a sustainable pattern of agreeable life for our populations, consistent with the requirements of public health, social stability and civilized values. Second, the provision of employment and incomes must be restructured along models that are viable and sustainable in a world of reduced consumer demands for simulacra. Very likely, the new model will have to emphasize cooperative structures of control and the prioritization of individual artistic and craftwork achievement, along with a public job guarantee, initially on a very large scale. Third, the prior structure of debts has been rendered non-viable, so that a restructuring of obligations, of the financial sector and of the distribution of wealth is inevitable.

The framework of noonomy tells us that in moving forward, those who design and plan an economic system must balance the new technologies with the requirements of stability, solidarity, fairness and public purpose. The failure to do so may appear profitable and even prosperous for a time. It may meet the ideological test of conformity to the model of the free market. It may be a paragon of cost reduction and profit maximization, of relentless search for a competitive edge. But market efficiency and market fragility are duals. One purchases them in a package, and the bill comes due in the course of time. Covid-19 has come to us, it appears, in the form of a collection agent.

References

Bodrunov, S.D. (2018) *Noonomy*. Moscow: Kul'turnaia revoliutsiia.

Chen, J. and Galbraith, J. (2011) Institutional Structures and Policies in an Environment of Increasingly Scarce and Expensive Resources: A Fixed Cost Perspective. *Journal of Economic Issues* XLV (2): 301–309.

Chen, J. and Galbraith, J. (2012a) A Common Framework for Evolutionary and Institutional Economics. *Journal of Economic Issues* XLVI (2): 419–428.

Chen, J. and Galbraith, J. (2012b) Austerity and Fraud under Different Structures of Technology and Resource Abundance. *Cambridge Journal of Economics* 36(1): 335–343.

Congressional Budget Office (2020) *CBO's Current Projections of Output, Employment, and Interest Rates and a Preliminary Look at Federal Deficits for 2020 and 2021.* Washington, April 24, 2020. Available (consulted 1 June, 2020) at: https://www.cbo.gov/publication/56335.

Galbraith, John K. (1958) *The Affluent Society*. Cambridge: Houghton Mifflin.

Galbraith, John K. (1967) *The New Industrial State.* Cambridge: Houghton Mifflin.

Galbraith, John. K. (1989) *Balancing Acts: Technology, Finance and the American Future.* New York: Basic Books.

Veblen, T. (1899). *Theory of the Leisure Class,* New York: MacMillan.

CHAPTER 3

Contradictions in Technological and Socio-economic Transformations
The New Role of Knowledge on the Way towards Noonomy

Oleg N. Smolin

The twenty-first century has become a period of crises that shook the world economy and affected all spheres of public relations. The economic and financial crisis of 2008–2009, which engulfed most of the world, was not the biggest problem of the coming century, because in the winter of 2019–2020, new cataclysms in the global economic and financial system began, which were aggravated by the pandemic that arose as a result of universal spread of the new coronavirus infection Covid-19.

In such circumstances, global problems faced by the humanity have moved from the space of theoretical discussions to the space of practical issues requiring immediate solutions at the level of individual countries and the world community as a whole. These changes are associated with the new technological revolution in social production, which is being discussed today not only by theoretical scientists, but also by world businesspersons, dominant political leaders of the most authoritative countries of the world. Another context for these changes was the transformation of geopolitical and economic relations in the world, when the People's Republic of China became the second economic superpower by GDP in dollar terms, and the first one by GDP in terms of purchasing power parity.

Fundamental changes are also taking place in the social stratification of society: instead of the traditional class structure of capitalism, a system is being formed, in which, due to the progress of new technologies, growth in the creative content of labor, development of the virtual space of life, etc., new social groups and strata are emerging. On the one hand, there is precarization of workers (see, for example (Toshchenko, 2015, 2018)), and, on the other hand, the creative class is developing, and these processes take place in unity, producing challenges for understanding types of social structures, including strata, in the new society.

All this makes it necessary to give a theoretically reasonable answer to the question of what social opportunities humanity, including Russia, is facing today. One of the answers to these questions is offered in the work of the

Director of the S. Y. Witte Institute for New Industrial Development, President of the Free Economic Society of Russia, Doctor of Economics, Professor Sergey D. Bodrunov. In recent years, he has published a series of books and articles dedicated to the humanity's progress to a qualitatively new social state, which he labeled "*noonomy*" (see, for example (Bodrunov, 2016a, 2019a, 2019b, 2020a)).

The term "noonomy" used by S. D. Bodrunov, on the one hand, evokes associations with knowledge-based economy and, on the other hand, with the noosphere, the concept of which, as is known, was developed by V. I. Vernadsky. In fact, this is about the genesis of a qualitatively new social system, which the author describes not as a special type of the economy, but as a post-economic state of society.

To gain further understanding the essence of this concept, you can refer to a series of works written by the author over the past decades, including the recently published book *Noonomy: Trajectory of Global Transformation* (see, for example (Bodrunov, 2018, 2020b)) by S. D. Bodrunov. The work comprises a series of eight closely related essays, each, as Bodrunov called it, a step towards understanding the nature of noonomy.

The starting point of the theory of noonomy is understanding modern society as a system in which social production still plays the decisive role, but it is a rapidly changing production characteristic of *the new industrial society of the second generation* (NIS.2), which is going to replace both the new industrial state described by J. K. Galbraith (Galbraith, 1969, 1976) and the illusions of post-industrialism that were popular at the end of the past century.

Under the NIS.2, production retains its significance, despite the fact that man is gradually becoming less involved in reproductive industrial labor (in the old sense of "industry"). However, it is production that becomes qualitatively new, "smart", "unmanned", based on the use of nano-, bio-, information, cognitive and social (NBICS) technologies (see (Schummer, 2010; Efremenko et al., 2012)), the Internet of Things, etc.; this is what determines the overall new state of society further discussed by Professor Bodrunov.

It should be noted that Bodrunov's positive analysis of advancement towards the NIS.2 is associated with criticism of the post-industrial society concept, since in the works of D. Bell (Bell, 1996, 1999) and other researchers of this problem, the theory of post-industrialism actually turned out to be an apology (or was used as such) for the process that led to deindustrialization, to the priority development of intermediary activities, and particularly to the development of the financial sector in the United States and some other countries. This theory has been used to argue for the processes of financialization and the dominance of the financial sector (for detailed information on the problems of financialization, see, for example (Ryazanov, 2016; Fine, 2019; Mavroudeas,

2019; Sifakis-Kapetanakis, 2019)) that have flooded the modern world, not only in the economy, but also in the public sector.

This first essay is concluded with description of knowledge as a decisive factor of production in terms of the genesis of the new industrial society of the second generation. Professor Bodrunov introduces the latter category as a property of a qualitatively new state of the industry. Thereby, a kind of the negation of negation spiral is being built: the new industrial society of the first generation – criticism of post-industrialism– re-establishment of the new industrial society of the second generation (NIS.2), in which knowledge is qualitatively new and holds the most significance, along with the development of knowledge-intensive production.

The role of knowledge in modern production is considered by Bodrunov in unity with the process of new industrialization, which he rightly interprets as the integration of science, education and production. At the same time, for modern economy and contemporary society, as well as for the human progress, there is an objective need for life-long learning for everyone. This attitude is quite consistent with the tasks set by the United Nations and the United Nations Educational, Scientific and Cultural Organization (UNESCO), as well as the position of the author of these lines (see, for example (Smolin, 1999:, 2010 10–23: 18–47, 2014: 19–41, 2019)) and other scientists (Yakovleva, 2020a, 2020b).

On the basis of this analysis, Bodrunov describes the next step in the progress towards noonomy as a qualitatively new state of society. This step stipulates the transition to the world of innovative technologies. In this regard, the author of the book under review gives a detailed description of the current technological revolution, as a result of which the sixth techno-economic paradigm arises, and NBICS convergence of nano-, bio-, information, cognitive and social technologies gradually develops; hybrid and additive technologies are advancing, which largely determine the processes described above. This section of the book is written by Professor Bodrunov in a dialogue with the work of Academician S. Yu. Glazyev (Glazyev, 2012, 2015).

The analysis of the nature of knowledge-intensive production continues the logic of theoretical advancement towards noonomy. It is here where the author describes the process of human emergence "beyond the actual material production" (in this case Bodrunov directly refers to K. Marx' foresight), which, though, does not make industrial production as such disappear, but leads to the development of a new quality of this production, including "manlessness" and "knowledge intensity".

According to Professor Bodrunov (and we fully support his point of view), this production should, as we noted above, *be integrated with science and education.* Not only the third essay in the book under review is dedicated to this, but also a whole series of other articles by the author (see, for example (Bodrunov, 2014, 2015, 2016b)), as well as a number of congresses held under the auspices of Institute for New Industrial Development, directed by S. D. Bodrunov (Maslov and Yakovleva, 2019). According to Bodrunov, these technological changes result in the genesis of the NIS.2, which leads to a significant shift in socio-economic relations.

One of the trends of these changes is the socialization of public life, which Bodrunov considers as the transition from the zoological, competitive paradigm to the society built on the principles of assistance, cooperation and personal development (Bodrunov, 2020b). In this regard, I would like to note the following.

First, the trend towards socialization really exists in the contemporary society, similar to how elements of medieval civilization (feudalism) arose within classical slavery, and industrial civilization (capitalism) – within the medieval one. Proponents of traditional Marxism, who argued that socialism could not arise under capitalism, were wrong, as it is now obvious. Moreover, the new stage in the development of capitalism, called by some researchers "social capitalism", which began around the 1950s, combined the market economy and the social state, i.e., some elements to be traditionally considered socialist.

Second, meanwhile, the trend of classical capitalism towards capital concentration has not disappeared. Recently, almost simultaneously the data were published. According to the data, during the pandemic-related crisis in 2020, global billionaires became richer by USD 3.9 trillion (Thomson Reuters Foundation, 2021); and the International Labor Organization (ILO) reported that which workers lost almost the same amount – USD 3.7 trillion (Kaplan, 2021). This can be confirmed by the fact that during the above-mentioned period, sales in the segments of cheap goods and mid-range goods worldwide fell, while in the segment of super-expensive goods they continued to grow. In other words, the rich could afford to increase their consumption, while the meager consumption of the poor further reduced.

Third, these facts show that boundaries of socialization, even at the present stage of the social state development, are quite narrow, and the trend towards socialization (at least in the medium term) is unlikely to become the leading one.

Another trend of changes in socio-economic relations determined by the technological progress emphasized by Bodrunov is the diffusion of ownership and gradual transition of a person to the sphere where key social interactions evolve not on solving economic (in the narrow sense of the word) problems, but on developing a person's creative potential and shaping of *Homo Culturalis*.

But we will return to this topic later. In this case, it should be accentuated that, when describing the new industrial society of the second generation (NIS.2), Bodrunov demonstrates how the labor content changes, and its creative element develops. In turn, this becomes the ground for gradually abandoning simulative needs and shaping needs of a new type.

This aspect of the work should be stressed especially, since, in our opinion, analysis of the modern consumer society as the social medium creating preconditions for the development of simulative needs to be satisfied with simulacra is an important topic to be rightly developed by Professor Bodrunov, who takes into account J. Baudrillard's studies (Baudrillard, 2007), as well as subsequent works by Professors A. V. Buzgalin and A. I. Kolganov (see, for example (Buzgalin and Kolganov, 2012)), who wrote a lot about simulacra products.

Progress towards noonomy, as Bodrunov reasonably demonstrates, is associated with deep contradictions leading to the crossroads that humanity is currently facing (by the way, not for the first time). As a matter of fact, the progress of technologies can cause not only advancement towards noonomy and the new industrial society of the second generation, but also appearance of new threats associated with pressure on the environment, inequality, and geopolitical conflicts.

The author of the theory of noonomy largely describes this crossroads in terms of contradiction between the progress of technologies and current social relations, with big corporate structures and bureaucratic institutions playing the decisive role. These social relations and institutions coming into collision with potential created by technologies are characterized in many ways in terms of traditional Marxist ideas about the conflict between productive forces and production relations (see, for example (Buzgalin, 2018)), including their interpretation in relation to conditions of the twenty-first century.

Actually, philosophers have long discovered the contradiction between the scientific-technological progress and the social one: in industrial society, the former develops rapidly, exponentially; the latter develops much slower; and this discrepancy between them is constantly increasing. Hence the so-called Fermi paradox, formulated by the famous physicist: in his opinion, we cannot find "like-minded creatures" in outer space because, as a result of the discrepancy, having reached a certain level, technical civilizations should self-destruct.

In this sense, contemporary humanity somehow resembles passengers of the RMS *Titanic*: they drink and dance, watch TV and play computer games when it is high time to change the ship's course. It is well known that half a century ago, using complex mathematical models, experts from the Club of Rome proved an alternative for the humanity. According to them, a global catastrophe threatens us already in the third quarter of the twenty-first century, and if

we want to avoid it, it is necessary for us to learn how to control the technological progress and ensure the development of society towards greater social
equality (see, for example (Meadows et al., 2007)).

It is interesting that a couple of years before the conclusion made by the
Club of Rome experts, the same alternative was described in an artistic form
by the famous Soviet science fiction writer and paleontologist Ivan Yefremov in
his famous novel *The Bull's Hour*. The novel depicts a distant future, when on
Earth, after a painful struggle, communism wins, and earthlings come to help
the people of planet Tormance, where, after a global catastrophe, the population decreases tenfold, dictatorship is established, and, in order to avoid new
overpopulation, "palaces of gentle death" are created for the majority of those
who have reached adulthood, of course, except for the select company.

Sharing Professor Bodrunov's anxiety about growing risks, I would like to
remind you that a new wave of technological revolution and, in particular,
mass introduction of robots, in a few decades, will allow us to withdraw people from most branches of material production and provide everyone with so-
called "basic income". However, without changing the social system, this will
lead rather to the models described by Kurt Vonnegut in his *Utopia 14* or by
Aldous Huxley in his *Brave New World*. So, in this case, the ground for optimism
can be an extremely pessimistic alternative scenario. The book by Bodrunov
once again draws the scientific and political elite's attention to this.

It is worth noting that in the articles dedicated to the pandemic review, and
published simultaneously with the book, Bodrunov stresses that the pandemic
is not the cause, but only the trigger for the systemic crisis that has been brewing for a long time (see, for example (Bodrunov, 2020c)). Accordingly, the essay
concludes with the statement that the escalation of risks is inevitable within
the existing economic system.

As we have already noted above, Bodrunov links the genesis of noonomy to
the development of the new industrial production of the second generation,
where creation and application of knowledge, as well as the resulting dual role
of the latter in the formation/satisfaction of needs, come to the forefront. This
role supposes that knowledge is not only the way to create new goods, but also
the condition for their consumption.

This aspect deserves special attention since it is in the field of education
where the person is involved in active work; we emphasize *in active work*, and
not in consumption in the ordinary sense of the word. Due to this, the person
proves to be capable of desobjectivation, by the way, of not only information,
but also cultural goods in general. The author of this review has been guided
by the similar viewpoint for many years, criticizing the so-called concept of
educational services and proving to teachers that they work not in the service

sector, but in the production one, in the field of reproduction of the person as such, which is the most important (see, for example (Smolin, 2020)).

In this context, the conclusion on turning culture into an economic imperative, drawn by Professor Bodrunov, seems to be completely reasonable. In the framework of the author's concept, the main outcome of the progress of production on the way to noonomy is the *Homo Culturalis* as a product of reproduction, and it is in this process where exaltation of the individual takes place. This thesis continues traditions of Russian philosophical and psychological thought, in particular traditions of such Soviet Marxists as R. I. Kosolapov (Kosolapov, 1984), E. V. Ilyenkov (Ilyenkov, 2010), as well as a number of contemporary researchers (Buzgalin, 2018; Bulavka-Buzgalina, 2018). The works of the author of this review are also dedicated to these issues (see, for example (Smolin, 2017a, 2017b)). According to Professor Bodrunov, this is the basis for the transition from economic rationality to rational formation of needs, which is an important shift in progressive development of the humanity. And we cannot but agree with this.

Bodrunov's conclusion on transition to noonomy as the removal of relations characteristic of the economic system as a whole is one of the most important. This thesis of Professor Bodrunov is innovative, although it is based on Marxist ideas, for even Marx and Engels argued that the future presupposes the leap of the humanity from the "realm of necessity" to the "realm of freedom" (for more information on the leap from the "realm of necessity" to the "realm of freedom", see (Engels, 1961: 294–295; Marx, 1962: 386–387)). Representatives of critical Marxism of the twentieth century (V. M. Mezhuyev, A. V. Buzgalin), as well as supporters of neoliberal ideas (D. Bell, V. L. Inozemtsev), wrote about the future society as a post-economic one, but S.D. Bodrunov gave this thesis original interpretation and argumentation. Under the conditions of the genesis of noonomy, there is rejection of narrowly understood economic rationality, and the non-economic way of regulating economic activities arises. At the same time, the humanity enters into new social relations based on an autonomously functioning technosphere and creates a new type of person. Bodrunov does not draw this future in detail (which is quite rightful), but only portrays it as a certain trend that is objectively formed as a result of the progress of technologies. Meanwhile, he time and again emphasizes that contradictions on the way to the new society are deep, and the victory of this particular trajectory is by no means predetermined.

Of course, any new concept predicting the future based on current trends cannot but contain a wide range of provisions that raise doubts and require special studies. Moreover, in my opinion, forecasting the future by its very nature is mainly scenario-based. In this regard, I would like to note only two problems. First, in our opinion, when examining the current trends of advancement towards the future society, Bodrunov focuses exclusively on the need for the gradual evolutionary movement towards this new state and does not consider the possibility of revolutionary changes.

However, while emotionally fully sharing Professor Bodrunov's position on the preference for evolutionary development over revolutionary upheavals, one cannot help but notice that this possibility is hardly realistic. Philosophers of different centuries and schools have long shown, and contemporary science has confirmed by mathematical models, that such complex systems as society can hardly develop only through accumulation of quantitative or gradual qualitative (evolutionary) changes. On the contrary, thinkers who promoted the idea that there was no alternative to the smooth course of history or the concept of achievement of perfect society were always refuted by reality. Perhaps, the last attempt of this kind is the concept of history's end suggested by Francis Fukuyama, who in 1980–1990s became famous for books and articles developing this subject. Among other factors, he argued that history ended with the triumph of liberal civilization, and in the future all countries will move in that direction, whereby the new world will become well-fed, rich, but rather boring.

In a public discussion with the famous philosopher in June 2007 at the US Embassy, the author of this review allowed himself to note that Fukuyama's works set three records at once:

– record of courage, since, after Hegel, none of major thinkers dared to talk about the end of history;
– record of optimism: according to Fukuyama, the future humanity will languish from doing nothing and abundance of choice of goods, but at the same time life will be so boring that it will be tempting to return to history;
– record speed of failure: even those who at the turn of the 1990s, despite the geopolitical catastrophe of the Soviet Union, continued to believe Fukuyama, stopped doing so after September 01, 2001, when the so-called war of civilizations was discovered.

In recent years, even such social models as the French or American ones, idealized by domestic liberals, are obvious to have experienced serious political upheavals. Going back to Ivan Yefremov, let me note that in his concept of the future, a new, more just society is established after a whole era of severe upheavals, revolutions and wars, including attempts to use nuclear weapons. I would like very much for Yefremov to be under delusion, but excluding this scenario is impossible, too.

Second, the book by Professor Bodrunov, in our opinion, does not completely consider the question of those social strata that can perform as both the main actors and opponents on the way to noonomy. Among such opponents, there might be:

- representatives of the state bureaucracy and the ruling elites, who receive considerable economic, social and political benefits from retention of the existing system;
- strata of society, which, in current conditions, are traditionally related to classical industrial production, labor that is reproductive in its content, and which, in the context of technology transformation, may find themselves in position of outcasts, so to speak, with no place in the new social life.

I would also like to mention that the transition from the current state to the status of precaring workers and freelancers, which is positively assessed by S. D. Bodrunov, is in contradiction with relevant findings expressed in works of a number of sociologists, both foreign and domestic. For instance, Zh. T. Toshchenko considers deep contradictions and negative consequences of precarization.

In our opinion, the survey of other possible scenarios, contradictions and obstacles on the way to noonomy could be an important complement to the ideas contained in the concept suggested by Bodrunov. However, these considerations point not so much to the shortcomings of the ideas under review, but to differences between our scientific schools and scientific paradigms, the polemics between which is necessary and useful.

I believe supporters of right-liberal and right-conservative theories will also find some arguments because they will discover a lot of things that they will not be able to agree with in Bodrunov's concept. Their harsh criticism is highly likely to be caused by Professor Bodrunov's description (which I fully share) of the future as a system where property relations will "diffuse" (Bodrunov's term), and where financial capital will lose its dominant role.

But it draws even more interest to Bodrunov's concept of noonomy, which provokes scientific polemics and reveals horizons of the possible future, i.e., the future which, in our opinion, will justly point to the general trajectory of movement towards the system where contradictions of social alienation will be removed – of course, subject to the humanity managing to prevent the global catastrophe which is looming if we persist in modern trends.

References

Baudrillard, J. (2007) *For a Critique of the Political Economy of the Sign.* Moscow: Akademicheskij project.

Bell, D. (1996) *The Coming of Post-Industrial Society. A Venture in Social Forecasting.* New York, NY: Harper/Collins.

Bell, D. (1999) *The Coming of Post-Industrial Society.* Moscow: Academia.

Bodrunov, S.D. (2014) Revival of production, science and education: problems and solutions. *Problemy sovremennoj ekonomiki* 4: 35–41.

Bodrunov, S.D. (2015) Integration of production, science and education as the basis for reindustrialization of Russia. *Mirovaya ekonomika i mezhdunarodnye otnosheniya* 10: 94–104.

Bodrunov, S.D. (2016a) *The Coming of New Industrial Society: Reloaded: NIS.2.* 2nd ed., revised and add. St. Petersburg: S.Y. Witte Institute for New Industrial Development (INID).

Bodrunov, S.D. (2016b) Russia in the Eurasian space: Production, science and education as progress drivers. *Ekonomicheskaya nauka sovremennoj Rossii* [Economics of Contemporary Russia] 2: 19–27.

Bodrunov S.D. (2018) From ZOO to NOO: Man, Society and Production in the Conditions of a New Technological Revolution. *Voprosy filosofii* 7: 109–118.

Bodrunov, S.D. (2019a) *General Theory of Noonomy.* Moscow: Kulturnaya Revolutsiya.

Bodrunov, S.D. (2019b) Noonomy: ontological theses. *Ekonomicheskoe vozrozhdenie Rossii* [Economic revival of Russia] 4: 6–18.

Bodrunov, S.D. (2020a) *Noonomy: Trajectory of Global Transformation.* Moscow: Kulturnaya Revolutsiya.

Bodrunov, S.D. (2020b) On the Path to Noonomy: Man, Technology, Society. *Mir peremen* [The World of Changes] 2: 24–39.

Bodrunov, S.D. (2020c) Global risks during the pandemic: practice corroborates the theory of noonomy. *Ekonomicheskoe vozrozhdenie Rossii* [Economic revival of Russia] 2: 4–14.

Bulavka-Buzgalina, L.A. (2018) Disalienation: from Philosophical Abstraction to Sociocultural Practices. *Voprosy Filosofii* 6: 202–214.

Buzgalin, A.V. (2018) Late capitalism and its limits: Dialectics of productive forces and production relations (on Karl Marx's 200th birth anniversary). *Voprosy politicheskoj ekonomii* 2: 10–38.

Buzgalin, A.V. and Kolganov, A.I. (2012) "Capital" of the XXI Century: Simulacrum as an Object for Analysis of Critical Marxism. *Voprosy filosofii* 11: 31–42.

Efremenko, D.V., Giryaeva V.N. and Evseeva, Ya.V. (2012) NBIC-Convergence as a Problem of Social and Humanitarian Knowledge. *Epistemologiya i Filosofiya Nauki* [Epistemology and Philosophy of Science], XXXIV(4): 112–129.

Engels, F. (1961) Anti-Düring. In: Marx, K. and Engels, F. *Collected Works.* 2nd ed. Vol. 20. Moscow: Gospolitizdat.

Fine, B. (2019) Financialization from a Marxist Perspective. *Voprosy politicheskoj ekonomii* 1: 34–49.

Galbraith, J.K. (1969) *New Industrial State.* Moscow: Progress.

Galbraith, J.K. (1976) *Economic theories and the society's goals.* Moscow: Progress.

Glazyev, S.Yu. (2012) Contemporary Theory of Long Waves in Development of Economy. *Ekonomicheskaya nauka sovremennoj Rossii* 2: 27–42.

Glazyev, S.Yu. (2015) On the urgent measures to enhance the economic security of Russia and set the Russian economy on course to priority development. *Nauchnye trudy Volnogo ekonomicheskogo obshchestva Rossii*, vol. 196: 86–186.

Ilyenkov, E.V. (2010) *Philosophy and Culture*. Moscow: MPSI.

Kaplan J. (2021) *Workers lost $3.7 trillion in earnings during the pandemic. Women and Gen Z saw the biggest losses*. 25 January. Available (consulted 23 August, 2021) at: https://www.businessinsider.com/workers-lost-37-trillion-in-earnings-during-the -pandemic-2021-1.

Kosolapov, R.I. (ed.) (1984) *What the individual begins with*. Moscow: Politizdat.

Marx, K. (1962) Capital, vol. III. In: Marx, K. and Engels, F. *Collected Works*. 2nd ed. Vol. 26, Part II. Moscow: Gospolitizdat.

Maslov, G.A., Yakovleva N.G. (2019) Production. Science. Education in Russia: technological revolutions and socioeconomic transformations. *Ekonomicheskoe vozrozhdenie Rossii* 1: 58–64.

Mavroudeas, S. (2019) Financialization Hypothesis: A Creative Contribution or A Theoretical Blind Alley? *Voprosy politicheskoj ekonomii* 1: 68–81.

Meadows, D.H., Randers, J., Meadows, D.L. (2007) Limits to growth: The 30-year update. Translated from English. Moscow: IKC "Akademkniga".

Ryazanov, V.T. (2016) Cyclical and systemic causes of the crisis in Russia: the role of socialization of finance in overcoming them. *Voprosy politicheskoj ekonomii* 2: 88–106.

Schummer, J. (2010) From Nano-Convergence to NBIC-Convergence: "The best way to predict the future is to create it". In: Kaiser, M., Kurath, M., Sabine, M., Rehmann-Sutter, C. (eds.) *Governing Future Technologies: Nanotechnology and the Rise of an Assessment Regime*. Sociology of the Sciences Yearbook Series. Vol. 27. Springer Netherlands, 57–71.

Sifakis-Kapetanakis, C. (2019) New Actors in Global Finances and the Financialization of Capitalism. *Voprosy politicheskoj ekonomii* 1: 82–93.

Smolin, O.N. (1999) *Knowledge is Freedom. Russian State Educational Policy and Federal Legislation of the 90s. Systematized collection*. Moscow: OOO "IPTK 'Logos' VOS".

Smolin, O.N. (2010) *Education. Politics. Law. Federal Legislation as a Factor of Educational Policy in Contemporary Russia*. Moscow: Kulturnaya Revolutsiya.

Smolin, O.N. (2014) *Education – for Everyone: Philosophy. Economics. Politics. Law*. 2nd ed., revised and add. Moscow: IKC "Akademkniga".

Smolin, O.N. (2017a) Is the world out of "chaos" or the world without "chaos"? In quest of a new model of Russia's socio-economic development. *Proceedings of the Free Economic Society of Russia*, vol. 203: 125–154.

Smolin, O.N. (2017b) "Kudrinomics Minus"? or Once Again About a New Model of the Social and Economic Development in Russia. Part I. *Russian Journal of Philosophical Sciences* 2: 7–18.

Smolin, O.N. (2019) Economic Growth and Educational Policy: Technologies and Ideology. *Ekonomicheskoe vozrozhdenie Rossii* 1: 29–39.

Smolin, O.N. (2020) Serving or Service? On Some Philosophical-Economic Grounds of Educational Policy. *Narodnoe obrazovanie* 1: 7–30.

Thomson Reuters Foundation (2021). *Billionaires have become richer by 3.9 trillion USD, according to the charity organization Oxfam*. 25 January. Available (consulted 23 August, 2021) at: https://www.deccanherald.com/international/billionaires-39-trill ion-richer-as-poor-suffer-in-widening-covid-19-divide-oxfam-943036.html.

Toshchenko, Zh.T. (2015) Precariat – a new social class. *Sotsiologicheskie issledovaniya* [Sociological Studies] 6: 3–13.

Toshchenko, Zh.T. (2018) *Precariat: from the proto-class to the new class*. Moscow: Nauka.

Yakovleva, N.G. (2020a) Technological and socioeconomic transformations in the beginning of the XXI century: role and place of education. *Ekonomicheskoe vozrozh-denie Rossii* 2: 133–142.

Yakovleva, N.G. (2020b) The Role of Education in Human and Social Progress. *Vestnik Moskovskogo universiteta* [Moscow University Bulletin]. Series 7. Philosophy 5: 81–91.

CHAPTER 4

Intelligence Economy as a Form of Noonomy and Its Economic and Social Impact

Enfu Cheng and Siyang Gao

1 The Concept of Intelligence Economy[1]

Intelligence Economy is an economic form which, based on the concept of digital Economy, takes the intelligently perceived information and digitalized knowledge as key factors of production, and the new generation of intelligent technology as driving force (Xu, 2020: 1). The concept of intelligence economy has been widely discussed by scholars in China, marked by the "Development Plan for a New Generation of Artificial Intelligence" (hereafter referred to as "the plan") released by the State Council in July 2017, which specified the goal of developing high-end and high-quality intelligent economy in China.

1.1 *The Definition of Intelligence Economy*
In terms of the nature of economic activities, the explication of intelligence economy in academia can be summarized as follows: first, intelligence economy is an economic activity driven by artificial intelligence (AI) technology as a strategic force that has led this round of scientific and technological revolution and industrial transformation. In recent years, driven by the new generation of AI technology as represented by graphical perception, deep neural network, machine learning and automatic learning, the scale and scope of the AI industry have been expanding, and its driving and transforming effect over traditional economic activities has are becoming prominent.

Second, intelligence economy is a mode of economy which integrates AI technology and real economy. The 'Three-Year Action Plan for Promoting the Development of the New Generation of AI Industry (2018–2020)', released by the Ministry of Industry and Information Technology in 2017, pointed out that China is to "promote the development of AI industry, raise the level of artificial intelligence in manufacturing, and promote deep integration of

---

1 This chapter was translated by Liu Zixu, Associate Researcher at the Academy of Marxism, Chinese Academy of Social Sciences, Deputy Editorial Director of International Critical Thought.

artificial intelligence and real economy" (Ministry of Industry and Information Technology, 2017). In 2019, the Central Commission for Comprehensively Deepening the Reform passed the 'Guiding Opinions on Promoting the Deep Integration of Artificial Intelligence with Teal Economy', reiterating the need to promote the deep integration of artificial intelligence with real economy. In 2020, the 'Proposal of the Central Committee of the Communist Party of China on Formulating the 14th Five-Year Plan for National Economic and Social Development and the Long-Term Goals for 2035' again listed artificial intelligence as the primary field of scientific and technological research and development of the national strategic technologies. To that end, intelligence-oriented development in the fields of industrial system, infrastructure, public service and social governance are listed as specific development tasks. It could be seen that the development of the intelligence economy depends on the integration of AI technology into real economy to upgrade the level of real economy and improve material productivity.

Third, intelligence economy should be a mode of economy with data driving, man-machine coordination, cross-field integration, and joint-creation and sharing. As a socialist country, China's development of intelligence economy should have distinct characteristics. The plan of 2017 stressed the above four basic factors in fostering a high-end and high-quality intelligence economy, which distinguish the development of China's intelligence economy from that in other countries (The State Council of People's Republic of China, 2017).

Fourth, intelligence economy can be divided into two parts: industrialized intelligence and intelligent industry. The positive interaction between them promotes the development of intelligence economy. Industrialized intelligence is the basic part of intelligence economy, namely, the AI industry, which includes such industrial sectors as 'the Internet, big data, cloud computing, edge computing and core technology of artificial high intelligence' (Liu and Du, 2020). Intelligent industry refers to the adoption of AI technology, which bring about increase in output and efficiency to a given industry, including the traditional industries. It is what is integrated with the intelligence economy. Industrialized intelligence drives the development of intelligent industry, while intelligent industry in turn provides the necessary space and data for the development of industrialized intelligence. This will lead to the deep integration of AI technology and real economy.

To sum up, intelligence economy a new mode of economy that is based on the new generation of AI technology, integrates with real economy through AI technology, takes "data driving, man-machine coordination, cross-field integration, and joint-creation and sharing" as its basic content, and follows the route of positive interaction between industrialized intelligence and intelligent industry for its realization.

1.2   *Basic Characteristics of Intelligence Economy*

Intelligence economy has changed the traditional way of labor, trade, management and consumption. As a brand-new economic mode, it has the following basic characteristics in production factors, industrial organization and operation method.

First, data is the key element in the production of intelligence economy. Labor, land, capital and technology are the basic elements of social production, but in the era of intelligence economy, data has become the "new oil" to drive the development of economy. The driving role of data in the production of intelligence economy is embodied in two aspects: labor's object and means of labor. In terms of labor's object, data, as the "raw material" in the production of intelligence economic, can be processed into various data products or services of various functions. In terms of means of labor, data, as the "fuel" for AI technology, can push forward the iterative development of AI technology.

Second, a new generation of AI technology can be applied on a large scale in various industrial fields. In recent years, a new generation of AI technologies, such as machine learning and deep learning, has achieved large-scale integration with various industries in national economy on the basis of Internet platform and mobile communication network. Such integration not only accelerates the process of commodity manufacture, circulation and consumption, but also leads to the technological upgrading of traditional industries and innovation in intelligence industry.

Third, the organization and operation of intelligence economy are mainly accomplished through digital platform. Digital platform is "a general digital infrastructure for collecting, processing and transmitting information on economic activities such as production, distribution, exchange and consumption" (Xie, Wu, and Wang 2019). It is the space for digital economic activities, formed with the support of AI and network communication technologies. Digital platforms bring together disparate and interdependent groups in intelligence economy to form point-to-point connections. Therefore, it has become the basic economic organization that coordinates and allocates resources in the era of intelligence economy, and the core of value creation and convergence.

Fourth, intelligence technology will be integrated with traditional industries. The new generation of AI technology extends to the real industry through the Internet and the terminal equipment with such technology, thus achieving the intelligent transformation and technological upgrading of the real industry. This is mainly reflected in the expansion of the giant corporations of Internet

Industry into the real economy that have mastered the core AI technologies, especially the unicorn corporations in global information technology industry which, through monopolizing data and platforms, has controlled various fields in real economy. In this process, traditional manufacturing and service industries have also used AI technology to extend from traditional business fields to that of intelligent network, thus achieving upgrading in both their business and product research and development (R&D).

Fifth, intelligence economy has the effect of scale economy and scope economy, with "prominent winner-takes-all characteristic" (Zhang, 2020). With the large-scale deployment of 5G networks and the construction of information infrastructure, the related industries of the future intelligence economy will further break the physical restrictions on the production and circulation of commodities, intelligence technology industry will be integrated into modern agriculture, manufacturing and service industries in large numbers, and the economies of scale will be obvious. At the same time, because of the coexistence of high fixed cost and low marginal cost, under the condition of intelligently equipped production, the scale of intelligence economy is enlarged, the output increased, and the unit cost of products is greatly reduced. The scale effect of intelligence economy leads to the emergence of large enterprises, while its scope effect leads to the emergence of a variety of business or products within given industries that meet different needs, thus forming a winner-takes-all situation.

2   Debates in Western Academia on Intelligence Economy and Its Economic and Social Impact

As intelligence economy is still in the process of rapid development, and "the demonstration of its essence is far from complete" (Sun, 2020). Not surprisingly, some Western scholars take this opportunity to engage in heated debates centering on intelligence economy and economic and social impact, such as whether exploitation exist in the non-material labor of intelligence economy under private ownership, how value is realized, and whether the proletariat has disappeared. It is of great academic value and practical significance to probe into these questions.

2.1   *The Question of Exploitation in the Non-material Labor that Drives Intelligence Economy*

Immaterial labor is a concept proposed by Negri and Hart to refer to intellectual labor, emotional labor, relational labor and linguistic labor (Negri, 2016: 4).

This includes both the intellectual work that directly drives AI technologies, such as the intelligent work of engineers, the coding of programmers, and the maintenance of programs by network technicians, as well as users' emotional, relational and linguistic labor that indirectly drive the development of AI economy through data production. The existence of exploitation in the latter has been the focus of dispute among scholars.

Scholars who argue that there is no exploitation of argue that, for one thing, users have signed authorizing agreement with companies in intelligence industry before performing emotional, relational, and linguistic tasks. Based on such agreement, users provide data on immaterial labor in exchange for the services of the company, and there is a free and equal exchange relationship between users and the company, hence no exploitation exists. Besides, emotional, relational, and linguistic labor mostly occurs in non-productive areas such as socializing and gaming, and the data thus produced is not labor product for exchange, so there is no exploitation.

These arguments have received harsh criticism from Fochs, Negri, and Hart. Fuchs and Negri believe that non-material labor contains an exploitation that is greater in extent and more covert in its form. First, in signing the service agreement, users exchange emotional, relational, and linguistic labor for access to the intelligence platform. Capital owns the control and ownership of the data produced. This means that even if users' labor constitutes the source of the data, under the distribution according to the capitalist ownership of the means of production, capitalists get most of the data-based earnings while the laborers get nothing, hence the existence of exploitation. Second, since the emotional, relational and linguistic labor in non-productive areas, such as social interaction and gaming, generate labor and its use value, that is, "the human individual who produces and reproduces as a commodity" (Fortunati, 1995: 69–70), it should belong to the category of "productive labor" (Fuchs, 2020). In such labor, laborers not only produce themselves, but the data they produce is captured, aggregated, and transformed into big data products, which in turn are used for profit by capitalist intelligence companies. This forms the logic of exploitation in immaterial labor. Third, Negri and Hart point out that the universal development of current information technology and artificial intelligence have made possible "a universal intelligence society" (quoted in Sun, 2013) that Marx proposes in his economic manuscripts of 1857–1858. In such society, capital-driven AI technologies "redefine our bodies and minds" (Zhang, 2017). This means that labor is transformed at the ontological level: "Immaterial labor (such as intellectual labor, emotional labor, relational labor, and linguistic labor) becomes the central element for value creation .... It is life itself that is being exploited here" (Negri, 2016: 4).

2.2 *The Question on the Impact of Intelligence Economy upon the Law of Value*

Intelligence economy in capitalist societies have brought about the industrialized intelligence, capitalized data, and coordinated production. Such changes have led to debate among scholars on the formation and existence of value in intelligence economy.

First, according to the research of the H-UTokyoLab, the repaid development of AI technology has made it possible for replacing human labor with technologies in intelligence economy, which will break the traditional law of value formation. This is especially the case at the state of Artificial General Intelligence (see Cheng and Gao, 2021), which, as an automatic laboring machine, will result in "the wide spread of automation without human participation" (H-UTokyoLab, 2020: 25). In commodity production, "dead labor" will completely replace "living labor", "the organic composition of capital tends to be infinite, and the substantial basis on which commodity value is formed naturally disappears" (Huang, 2020). But this view has been vehemently refuted by leftist scholars. Vincent Mosco points out that the replacement of human labor by intelligent machines in capitalist societies does not occur out of thin air. It is based on "the promise that the replacement of 'living labor' with 'dead labor' always leads to substantial cost saving" (Mosco, 2019: 261). In the meantime, it is a process of de-skilling workers, and "this is possible only when dead labor has acquired sufficient artificial intelligence or decision-making capabilities to perform skilled and semi-skilled labor" (Mosco, 2019: 261). In addition, in terms of the value formation of commodities in society as a whole, the varying level of capital's organic composition in different sectors makes it possible for capital to offset the impact on value formation by the decline in living labor in sectors with high organic composition of capital through continuously creating new industries with low organic composition of capital. For example, "the convergence of cloud computing, big data analytics and the Internet of things means that executives in financial service industry are joining the ranks of the unemployed among telephone operators and factory workers" (Mosco, 2019: 261). This means that the application of AI technology in the production field will not have a fundamental impact on the value formation for commodities in capitalist society. On the contrary, the vigorous efforts to promote intelligence economy in developed capitalist countries, such as Japan's super-smart society strategy and Germany's "Industry 4.0" program, on the one hand, and gig economy and subcontract economy on the other, proves the correctness of the law of value formation of commodities in capitalist society.

Second, in political economy, the existence of commodity value as a social construct presupposes the separation and opposition between private and social labor in material production. Therefore, once private labor becomes a part of social labor without going through market exchange, the basis of value in social relationship will disappear. In line of this, Rifkin argues that in intelligence economy, "the Internet-of-things platform is of dispersed, point to point characteristics", which joint together several millions of producers to "form a globally coordinated sharing system" (Rifkin, 2014: XXI). In this system, the private work of every producer has the opportunity to become a part of social work without going through market exchange, such as Wikipedia and free open-source software, which will have a huge impact on the value of the commodity itself. This view, however, has provoked a rebuttal from other scholars. As Joseph Zubov points out, the Internet of things seems to have abolished the market exchange of private labor and directly become a part of social labor, but in reality this is just a new rhetoric for capitalism's free appropriation of private labor. In fact, the goal of capital in actively building the Internet of things and developing a sharing based model of production through network coordination is to have the cognitive activities that should belong to human beings "integrated into the value system of commodity production and capital accumulation" (quoted in Huang, 2020). Indeed, this has been demonstrated in recent years by the participation of intelligence industry in the development of open-source software systems, providing upgrade services, selling derivative software applications, or commercializing user-generated content (UGC) (Huang, 2020).

2.3 *The Question on the Disappearance of the Proletariat*

Intelligent economy has changed the traditional way of labor and exchange, as well as the class relationship. In response to this change, scholars have engaged in debates on whether the proletariat has disappeared.

Under the conditions of an intelligence economy, Negri argues, the proletariat has disappeared and been replaced by a multitude within the realm of the politics of life. The multitude refers to the network of exploited, mobile individuals in the micro-sphere of daily life under capitalism (Negri 2016: 46). For Negri, the multitude represents the historical turn brought about by the intelligent production in contemporary capitalism. The reasons are as follows. First, intelligence economy reshapes the control structure of capital when the intelligent capital's logic of proliferation permeates the non-material labor and daily life of individuals, which is manifested in the control of lifestyle and micro-power. The public then becomes a target of precise exploitation by capital. "When we speak of the intelligentization, feminization, naturalization, the language/relationship/cooperation, and—last but not least—the publicization of labor, we are not proposing a general concept; on the contrary, we are identifying an absolutely decisive turning point in history" (Negri, 2016: 96). Second, "individual labor is the sole source for the value and productivity of capital today" (Negri, 2016: 47). The multitude breaks the limitation of the expression of proletariat's particular interests and expresses the demand of the social interests closely related to all people. Third, the idea of the multitude suggests that the fight against the economic order of contemporary capitalism no longer depends on class revolution as it was before, but on "the democratic passion and common political existence of the multitude" (Negri, 2016: xx).

Innovative as it is, this view has been widely criticized for abandoning the basic theory of the Marxian political economy. As British digital media critic Andreas Wittel points out, "class struggle is clearly at the heart of Marx's polit-ical economy" (Wittel, 2017: 492), and Marx's idea of the proletariat returns in a "personal" (Wittel, 2017: 493) form in the age of artificial intelligence. Such form, however, reflects a politico-economic structure of universal exploita-tion and repression. That is to say, the proletariat has not dissolved under the current development of intelligence economy in capitalist societies. On the contrary, some key related factors, "especially the ideas of labor, value, and property right, which are all interconnected, are of practical significance to the analysis of our media ecology today" (Wittel, 2017: 492). In the meantime, the occurrence of revolution cannot simply rely on the democratic passion of the masses, which can easily turn into a blind impulse deviated from objective conditions. Revolution always depends on the social movements of the pro-letariat because the proletariat is the product of capitalist social formation, which is the inevitable consequence of laborers' resistance under capital's exploitation of living labor.

3   Intelligence Still Remains within the Sphere of Political Economy

The above debates show that only as we return to Marx's system of political economy can we grasp the dialectical relationship between immaterial labor, intelligence technology and capital, and provide the theoretical basis for the high-quality and efficient development of intelligence economy.

3.1   *Immaterial Labor in Intelligence Economy Has the Material Attribute of Labor, Which Is in Line with the Explication of Productive Labor in Political Economy*

In fact, the focus of the debate among Western scholars on immaterial labor lies in whether the concept of non-productive labor is beyond the scope of labor in political economy? The answer is no, for the following reasons.

First of all, immaterial labor in intelligence economy has material attribute. The emotion, social relationship and linguistic work in non-material labor is not a form of labor independent of material, but is the life force exhibited by humans themselves with certain goals and in certain forms. They are activities that take "the consumption of living labor as the main content" (Cheng and Gu, 2007: 76), and cannot be separated from such consumption. In the meantime, all non-material labor involves the transformation of material to certain extent, and is an activity of creating the object world. In addition, we cannot ignore the intelligent platforms and various related devices for carrying out immaterial labor in an intelligence economy, such as various apps that inspire people's desires and the network of fiber optics, broadband, base transceiver stations and smartphones that underpin them. It is precisely the wantonly appropriation and digital "enclosure" of non-material labor by these "front ends of intelligent technology" that shows the complete occupation of the material life of the living labor, and that makes the non-material labor have the material attribute of labor.

Second, the idea of immaterial labor is consistent with the description of productive labor on political economy. For Marx, productive labor consists of three elements, purposeful activity or labor itself, the object of labor and the means of labor. Non-material labor, such as labor of emotion, language and social relations, is a kind of purposeful cognitive processing activity. The object of such immaterial labor operation is the real world, and the operation process is the transformation of material objects in the real world into the non-material forms of the data, code, information and words. Finally, as mentioned above, the material "front ends of intelligent technology" have become the means of labor used during the process of non-material labor. These three elements demonstrate the consistency between the idea of immaterial labor and Marx's description of productive labor.

In a nutshell, the immaterial labor that provides huge amount of data in intelligence economy has the material properties of labor, and is consistent with Marx's explication on productive labor. The reason why non-productive labor in intelligence economy has become the focus of debate among scholars is because this form of labor demonstrates the tendency of expanded scope and greater degree of exploitation with regard to the living labor under capitalist intelligence economy. Therefore, the development of intelligence economy in socialism with Chinese characteristics requires, on the one hand, that we pay close attention to non-material labor, such as labor of emotion, language and social relations, to promote the positive role of intelligence economy; and, on the other hand, we should remain alert to the appropriation and domination of non-material labor by private capital, especially private monopoly capital, so as to prevent the "formal absorption" of living labor by capital through intelligent machines, and to prevent the vitality and creativity of living labor from becoming a tool of capital growth.

3.2 Intelligence Economy Has Not Changed the Labor Theory of Value and the Theory of Surplus Value in Marxism

The reason for the debate among Western scholars concerning the impact of intelligence economy on the law of value formation lies in the intention of some scholars to challenge Marx's labor theory of value and theory of surplus value. This attempt is based on the basic elements of intelligence economy like data as a driving force, human-computer interaction, cross-border coordination, and joint construction and sharing, and the goal is to change the basic proposition of Marxian economics. The challenge would be futile for the following reasons.

First, let us look at the erroneous argument of some scholars that the increase of the organic composition of capital caused by AI technology dissolve the labor theory of value. We believe that it is true that the combination of intelligent technology and the real economy will increase the organic composition of capital in a given field. However, if we look at the process of capital value's formation, as Marx pointed out, "By striving to reduce labour time to a minimum, while, on the other hand, positing labour time as the sole measure and source of wealth, capital itself is a contradiction-in-process" (Marx 2010: 91). Capital would achieve the appropriation of labor and its own growth by opening new industries and in new ways. As Brynjolfsson and McAfee of the Massachusetts Institute of Technology point out, on the one hand, the combination of artificial intelligence and traditional industries in the United States over the past few years has increased the organic proportion of capital in existing industries, and squeezed out the workers in the old industries who could not keep up with the technology. On the other hand, these workers are then absorbed by very low-skilled, low-paid, part-time positions. This leads to the polarization of labor. In the process of merging artificial intelligence with traditional industries, the newly created labor is either high-tech, high-paying jobs that only a few people can do, or part time jobs that are difficult to be automated or that are more cost to be automated. As of 2017, 36% of the US labor force was engaged in part-time jobs (Brynjolfsson and McAfee, 2014: 203–207, quoted in Wang, 2018). Underlying this phenomenon is not only the crowding out of the living labor by the increased organic composition of capital in the creation of intelligent industries, but also the re-absorption of the living labor by intelligent industries through even lower prices and more stringent requirements.

Second, let us look at the myth that some private labor on intelligent platforms and the Internet of things can become part of social labor without exchange. We believe that, as stated above, the intelligent platforms utilized in these cases are capital-driven, and that the value of the commodities produced by this private labor is made up of three components, as is the case with any other commodities. First, the value of raw materials and the depreciation of facilities and equipment used in producing commodities forms the value of production capital of the commodity. Second, the value created by the necessary labor by the producer of the commodity is the value of the means of consumption needed to sustain the reproduction of the labor force. Third, there is value created by the producer of the commodity beyond the necessary labor. These values should be compensated for or realized in exchange in monetary form, but are not compensated because the commodities are appropriated by the capitalists in intelligence economy through the lie of co-building and sharing, the evidence of which is the growth of these intelligent companies and the rise of their market value.

3.3   *Intelligence Economy and Its Economic and Social Impact Are Conditioned by the Social System in Which It Operates*

The above discussion shows that intelligence economy is an economic form and an economic era described from the perspective of productivity and science and technology, but not an isolated form of noonomy since it is constrained by the socio-economic system in which it operates, including the ownership of the factors of production. This means that intelligence economy has certain attributes of the relations of production. It comes into being and grows up under certain social context, and is restricted by the existing social system. This attribute determines that intelligence economy is to serve the social production and reproduction process in its best way, especially the reproduction of the social relations. For example, under the condition of private ownership of the means of production, intelligence economy will not have genuine co-construction and sharing, but will only serve the production process that is capitalistic in nature, such as the production of surplus value, the reproduction of the private ownership of the means of production, and the maintenance of the subordination of labor to capital. Under the condition of public ownership, it is possible for intelligence economy to rely on the social system to adjust the relations of production, so that the development of intelligence economy will be "centered on the working people" rather than "centered on monopoly oligopoly", thus truly realizing the high-end and high-quality development of intelligence economy.

In addition, the social attribute of intelligence economy determines that the discussion of intelligence economy and its social influence must take into account the requirements of the socialist system, such as public capital holding platform, the coordination of capital-labor relationship, the free and all-round development of people, the direct combination of people and the means of production, and so on. We should avoid the tendency to talk about development without consideration of the system when it comes to the research on intelligence economy. Only by fully considering the social system and policies in the development of intelligence economy can we achieve high-end, high-quality and rapid development, and achieve positive development effect of sharing, common wealth and common prosperity.

Finally, we believe that China and Russia, in accordance with their different national conditions, will formulate scientific and efficient strategies and strategies for the development of intelligence economy, and strengthen their joint cooperation, so as to develop the intelligence economy as a noonomy in a good and fast way. We will work together to benefit each country and its people, and to counter the containment of the neo-Imperialism of the United States.

References

Brynjolfsson, E., and McAfee A. (2014) *The Second Machine Age: Work, Progress, and Prosperity in a Time of Brilliant Technologies*. Translated by Y. Jiang. Beijing: China CITIC Press.

Cheng, E., and Gu Y. (eds) (2017) *Cultural Economics*. Tianjin: Nankai University Press.

Cheng, P. and Gao S. (2021) Philosophical Reflections upon the Ethical Status of General AI Entity. *Studies in Dialectics of Nature* 37(7): 46–51.

Fortunati, L. (1995) *The Arcane of Reproduction: Housework, Prostitution, Labor and Capital*. New York, NY: Autonomedia.

Fuchs, C. (2020) Towards a critical theory of communication as renewal and update of Marxist humanism in the age of digital capitalism. Journal for the Theory of Social Behaviour. 50(3): 335–356. https://doi.org/10.1111/jtsb.12247.

Huang, Z. (2020) Value Crisis, Capital's Responses, and Digital Labor's Resistence in the Age of Artificial Intelligence. *Exploration and Free Views* 5: 124–131.

H-UTokyoLab. (2020) *Society 5.0: Human-Centered Super Intelligent Society*. Beijing: China Machine Press.

Liu, G., and Du S. (2020) The Emergence and Development of Intelligence Economy Related Innovation Zone: The Case of Hangzhou. *Humanities* 3: 40–51.

Marx, K. (2010) *Economic Manuscripts of 1857–1858*. In: Marx, K. and Engels F. *Collected Works*. Vol. 29. London: Lawrence & Wishart Electric Book.

Ministry of Industry and Information Technology (2017) Notification of the Ministry of Industry and Information Technology for the Release of the "Three-Year Action Plan for Promoting the Development of the New Generation of AI Industry (2018–2020)". December 14, 2017. Available (consulted 25 August, 2021) at: https://www.miit.gov .cn/zwgk/zcwj/wjfb/zh/art/2020/art_de90191568e94fb0b358864d30c67ae9.html.

Mosco, V. (2019) Digital Labor and the Next-Generation Internet. In: *The Collections of the Classical Works of the Political Economy of Communication*, ed. by J. Yao, Beijing: The Commercial Press, 252–264.

Negri, A. (2016) *Empire and Beyond*. Beijing: Peking University Press.

Rifkin, J. (2014) *The Zero Marginal Cost Society: The Internet of Things, the Collaborative Commons, and the Eclipse of Capitalism*. Beijing: China CITIC Press.

The State Council of People's Republic of China (2017) Notification of the State Council for the Release of the Plan for a New Generation of Intelligent Development. July 8, 2017. Available (consulted 25 August, 2021) at: http://www.gov.cn/zhengce/content/ 2017-07/20/content_5211996.htm.

Sun, L. (2013) Popular Philosophy of Autonomy and Subjective Political Science of Ethics—Critical Reflections upon Negri's Contemporary Explication of Marx's 'Idea of Machine'. *Journal of Nanjing University* (philosophy, humanities, and social sciences edition) 3: 5–14.

Sun, W. (2020) "Intelligence Society under the Marxist Perspective of Historical Materialism". *Philosophical Analysis* 11 (6): 4–16.

Wang, X. (2018) "The Ideology of Work and the Future of Post-Work". *Marxism and Reality* 6: 138–146.

Wittel, S. (2017) Digital Marx: Toward a Political Economy of Distributed Media. In: *Marx Is Back*, ed. by C. Fuchs and V. Mosco, Shanghai: East China Normal University Press, 452–499x.

Xie, F., Wu, Y., and Wang S. (2019) Political Economy of the Globalization of Platform Economy. *Social Sciences in China* 12: 62–81.

Xu, K. (ed) (2020) *The Great Ecological Change in the Era of Intelligence Economy: Winning the Battle of 5G*. Beijing: Posts and Telecomm Press.

Zhang, X. (2020) How Far is Intelligence Economy from Us: Exploration of the Bottleneck and Innovative Development in the Launching of China's Artificial Intelligence. *Social Sciences in Ning Xia* 6: 108–117.

Zhang, Y. (2017) Immaterial Labor and Creative Surplus Value—Reading Negri and Hardt's *Empire. Foreign Theoretical Trends* 7: 35–48.

PART 2

Development Strategy and Noonomy

∴

CHAPTER 5

Mental Objects as a Productive Force

A Contribution to the Critique of Noonomy

Alan Freeman

1 Introduction[1]

Sergey Bodrunov has introduced into economics the term 'No-onomy',[2] a much-needed reminder that mental activity cannot be regarded as a secondary or ignorable aspect of modern production (Bodrunov, 2018). In this chapter I argue that a further concept is required to make proper sense of this fact: that of a 'Mental Object'. The issue is quite simple: How does mental activity, or 'mentation', enter production? And how do its results enter consumption? The response to both questions depends on the answer to a logically prior one: what, actually, does mental activity produce? My answer is that it produces mental objects.

To start the ball rolling, I suggest six examples of a mental object: a computer programme, a scientific theory, an image, a legal judgement, a poem, and a design. This is a diverse assortment, but they have certain things in common: they exist in a variety of physical forms (written, printed, voiced, depicted, represented electronically or in a brain); they nevertheless maintain a distinct identity; and they can be transferred from one form to another without losing this identity.

Other objects share these properties to a greater or lesser degree, and so merit consideration: patents, engineering standards, dance scores, religious

---

1 This paper is dedicated to Andre Vltchek, who we lost on September 20th, 2020. As I write, I hear in my mind his gentle voice, and transport myself to where I can hear his ironic, humanistic commentary on what I write. Perhaps a future society may imagine such a dialogue into some kind of real existence. I would like to acknowledge many useful conversations with Hasan Bakhshi, Aleksandr Buzgalin, Guglielmo Carchedi, Radhika Desai, Hasan Gürak, Peter Higgs, Claudia Jefferies and not least, the alumni and friends of Christopher Freeman. These are (both sadly and happily in different senses) too numerous to list; particular thanks are due to Geoff Oldham, Carlota Perez and Bengt-Åke Lundvall. All mistakes are of course my own.

2 I have added a hyphen in the word 'No-onomy' to avoid misdirecting English readers to rhyme the first syllable with 'Noon'.

beliefs, fashions, and even languages. However, not all mental activities do so. Emotions, for example, are not always transferrable: sometimes one can communicate a state of mind to another, sometimes not. And whilst stupidity can take communicable forms, such as fallacies, it does not always.

Moreover, neither emotions nor stupidity have a distinguishable, unique identity. We cannot, for example, determine if a given stupid habit always corresponds to another given stupid belief, or *vice versa*. Nor may we readily translate the excitement and fear encountered on a roller-coaster into that experienced in mortal combat. In contrast, there are many different poems, and whatever particular form any given poem takes, we can always determine which poem it is. This also applies when the poem changes form, so we can verify whether a spoken text corresponds to the written version, and vice versa.

These reflections yield an initial definition of a mental object: it is a reproducible entity appearing in a variety of physical forms, with an identity discernible independent of these physical forms. I may have missed something, but I think that captures it. One may wish to add that it can be translated from one physical form to another (communicability) but this property is probably deducible from the primary definition above.

The next question is this: since a given mental object can exist in a variety of particular forms (spoken, thought, recorded, broadcast, etc.) what is the relation it and each of these forms? The answer, critical to the argument of this chapter, is it becomes part of that form's being. The function of a book is to reproduce, communicate, and contain what is printed in it. The text is therefore part of what the book *is*: the printed representation of a mental object, its 'content'. Conversely, the book becomes part of the being of the mental object, which exists only as the ideal form of all its concrete representations.

Mental objects are hence an essential element of what we call 'materiality'. This is frequently reduced to mere tangibility, especially by economists: however, as Desai (Desai, 2013) notes, nations are material, yet one cannot stub one's foot on a nation. Money is equally material, but in its many non-physical forms, such as electronic records, is no less so than gold. Indeed, when circulating in the apparently physical form of notes or indeed, coin, its 'being' as money does not reside in a physical substance but in what that symbolises. Erase the Queen, King, President or masonic image from a note or a coin, and it is no longer money. In philosophy, the concept of 'matter' (Inwood, 1992: 107) is remote from mere natural existence, which is why when Marx and Engels called themselves materialists, they did not identify 'matter' with mere physical substance, as even a cursory reading confirms.

For these reasons, we cannot restrict our conception of the objects which production brings into play, either as inputs or outputs, to the natural qualities they possess independent of their relation to humans. We must give rigorous meaning to the notion of their *mental content*.

Persistent attempts to ignore mental content in economic thinking express the limits of the simplistic view which, with Radhika Desai, (Freeman, 2015) I term 'Machinocratic', by analogy with Physiocracy. By this term, we mean that economic activity gets reduced to the production of things by means of machines. This is strongly related to the fallacy that Andrew Kliman (Kliman, 2007: 13) and I term 'physicalism', which views a commodity as a physical entity independent of the social relations that give it value.

Modern economics has responded to these limitations by introducing mental activity as something supplementary or external to production, for example augmenting the idea of production with extra 'factors' of knowledge, information, or technology, thereby compounding the fallacies of the Neoclassical Aggregate Production Function which Felipe and McCombie (Felipe and McCombie, 2013) ably dissect. Bodrunov therefore does economic science a service by insisting mental activity is integral to production.

Nevertheless, mental activity in his writing hovers tantalisingly outside production, as something 'applied to' it or 'facilitating' it. Professor Bodrunov underlines that the product is an object obtained through the transformation of natural materials through the application of knowledge and adapted to satisfy human wants. This statement would be accepted in most economic discourse – yet there is a problem. Materials do not enter production in a purely natural form, to have 'knowledge' added to them after the fact: they are already permeated with human understanding prior to entering production, and could not do so unless so vitalised.

Specifically, they are treated, in production, in accordance with the human qualities inherent in them as a result of being produced or consumed by humans. A chair, when sat on, has the same physical form as when used for firewood, but a very different use. By virtue of this, it is a different thing. Even a simple act like making flour is *purposive*: the miller, not to mention his or her customers, has in mind a concept of what the flour will be used for. It is not therefore an inert collection of fine glutinous flakes but a means of making bread, white sauce, pasta, pizza, pancakes or even *papier maché* maquettes.

This purposiveness infuses the wheat, which thus also embodies mentality. It is not just grain: it is 'a means of producing a substance that will make bread'. Its 'use-value' as Marx describes it, consists in this. It leads the miller to choose wheat instead of corn, acorns, or mere gravel; to describe the wheat as 'natural' is hence utterly to misunderstand what it really is.

One might try to escape this difficulty by some kind of physiocratic regress, tracing the wheat back to the stalk, the stalk to the field, the field to the elements, and claiming that 'ultimately' everything comes from nature. But nature itself is not immune to humanity: indeed, it at risk of being destroyed by it. Nature is cultivated: the field is ploughed; the seed is sown. Even 'found' objects, be they the flowers of the field or the nuggets in a panhandler's ladle, are already mentalized, in that the finder distinguishes between what should be plucked or pocketed, and what should be discarded. Without in any way transforming their physical being, he or she has assigned additional qualities to them, by exercising *judgement*, a mental act integral to the concept of purpose, and has thus defined their *use*.

Marx's treatment of use is farsighted in this respect:

> The commodity is first an external object, a thing *which satisfies through its qualities human needs of one kind or another.* The nature of these needs is irrelevant, e.g., whether their origin is in the stomach or in the fancy ['Phantasie' in the German – AF]. We are also not concerned here with the manner in which the entity satisfies human need; whether in an immediate way as food – that is, as object of enjoyment – or by a detour as means of production.
>
> MARX, 1976:125, my emphasis

But we cannot, from its purely physical properties, deduce whether an object satisfies a need generated by 'Phantasie' because Phantasising is a mental activity. Nor is 'enjoyment' reducible to mere chemical metabolism. Only by combining the physical and intentional aspects of a need do we attain a complete and hence adequate concept of the object that satisfies it.

A similar, but more subtle distinction must be made for labour engaged in production. All labour is in some sense mental, in that the hand is guided by the brain. But each technology requires of the labourer *specific* skills and mental capacities, not just generic mental capability. A mechanic cannot walk into a surgeon's job, any more than a medical education qualifies doctors to fix cars. The capacities of the labour required for any particular job is what qualifies it as 'concrete': it is engaged to produce things with a specific use, which it cannot undertake without knowing how to. The labourer thus possesses not mental capacity in general, but specific, task-related brain and bodily competences. These skills define the 'type' of his or her labour every bit as much as the industry she works in, or the materials she handles.

Therein lies the weakness of the popular concept of 'mental labour': the work of the schoolteacher, the engineer or the doctor is abstractly cerebral but concretely different; it constitutes labour of teaching, of fixing systems, or healing patients. Knowledge is not, to summarise, 'applied' as an external factor to the process of production, but is embedded, prior to production, in its materials, its instruments, and in the labour that combines them. Bodrunov therefore comes closer to the reality when he asserts that nowadays, the development of the technosphere is driven not by instruments of production and their skilled application, but by the power of knowledge which is incorporated in these instruments and underlies the ability to apply them and boost production efficiency.

He need only have dropped the word 'nowadays'. What is changing, in the modern economy, is not the existence of mental content, nor the 'addition' of something which has always been there, but the manner in which it enters production.

2   The Treviso Arithmetic: An Introduction to Mental Technology

How 'new' is mental content? To assess this, I introduce two pieces of technological history: Europe's adoption of the modern numeral system, and the invention of logarithms. To begin with the first: in the early Middle Ages, as the expanding power and influence of the peninsular mercantile city-states took shape, merchants became increasingly preoccupied with the calculating and reckoning quickly. Until the late 12th Century, they relied either on cumbersome techniques involving Roman Numerals, on the Abacus, or on bead-counting systems. This was transformed when Leonardo of Pisa (1180–1230) began studying what was termed the Hindu-Arabic numeral system, which he learned under the tutelage of an Arab instructor. As Swetz (Swetz and Smith, 1987: 11–12) explains:

> He became convinced that the new numerals and their methods were vastly superior to the Roman numerals commonly employed in Europe. Leonardo, also known as Fibonacci (the son of Bonacci) became the evangelist of the new knowledge and published his impressions in a book, *Liber Abaci* (1203). Much of the text was a general introduction to the Hindu-Arabic numerals and their algorithms; however, a special section reflected Fibonacci's professional background and considered commercial applications of arithmetic.
>
> The book and its message were well received in the *fondacos,* or merchant houses, of Pisa, Genoa and Venice, and soon the Hindu-Arabic symbols were replacing Roman numerals in account books, and the use of the abacus was giving way to computations performed with pen and ink. This new mathematical knowledge was also being introduced

into Europe via translations of Arabic works emanating from Spain, but the receptive climate in Italy soon gave the Italians predominance in this art.

Venice became a great centre of innovation, and (another example of a mental object) created the modern system of double-entry accounting which entered widespread use as the 'Venetian system'. Its mental innovations spread very rapidly. Printed works were still to reach Europe, interestingly not because the printing press was not around (woodblock printing on cloth was widespread by 1300) but because there was no serious paper industry. Merchants therefore first hired special teachers to learn the skills and then founded 'reckoning schools' such as the Europe-famed Treviso school, which produced the first printed Arithmetic in 1478.

As Swetz (Swetz and Smith, 1987: 18) notes, "the seriousness of the task is emphasized by the advice of a German father to his son, studying in Venice, to 'rise early, go to church often, and pay attention to the arithmetic teacher'." The remarkable feature of this innovation – in fact a technology – is that it was entirely mental. It involved no physical entity at all, other than the pen and ink of those too slow-witted to reckon in their heads. Indeed, mental arithmetic *displaced* the 'physical' technology of the abacus (though battles, enlivened by public contests, raged between the defendants of the two methods). Yet it transformed the productivity of the merchants and ushered in the age of monetary capitalism.

This runs counter to any notion that human mental capacities evolve later than physical ones. The problem with this view is seen when we ask, 'what is the function of language?' Language not only accompanies, but predates, humanity's subjugation of nature, because without the social organisation it facilitates, humans could do little more to nature than hunt it, pluck it, fall off or into it, or be eaten by it. Mental objects are hence not a 'new' or 'post-industrial' development but have been part of technology from the dawn of human society. They were always there, but large-scale machine production consigned them to the shadows, from which they are now emerging.

This is further clarified by the history of the logarithm, which replaced the mentally difficult labour of multiplication with the easier (and faster) labour of addition. The Scottish inventor and religious zealot John Napier published the first tables in 1614, arguing they would, by "shortening the labours, double the life of the astronomer". Logarithms expanded, exponentially, the *mental productivity* of Hindu-Arabic arithmetic. They came into their own as England's military-monarchic complex became increasingly hungry for accurate gunnery tables and navigational aids. By 1624 these tables were sufficiently accurate to underpin the dominance of a naval system which, within a century, had laid the foundations of the British Empire.

Again, this is a mental technology. It can be embodied in physical devices such as the engineer's slide rule, a universal calculating device which lasted until the pocket calculator. But these physical forms are mere adjuncts. The core is the replacement of slow multiplication with fast addition. These mental technologies are hence a foundation-stone of industrial capitalism. Not for nothing did the Victorians drum into their children, alongside the virtues of frequent churchgoing and early rising, the 'three Rs': Reading, Writing, and Arithmetic. Modern industry would have been impossible without them.

3   The Use of Mental Objects

It may seem, from the above, as if mental objects can be treated without any regard to their physical form. This idea, also found in physicalist economics, is the converse of the fallacy that physical objects can enter social usage without mental content. Precisely because mental objects are indissolubly embedded in physical objects, they never entirely part company from physicality. Even mental arithmetic exists in a physical substrate: the brains of the arithmetists.

The use of mental objects, therefore, *consists in the way they combine with the physical qualities of produced and consumed objects, to constitute material being.* Insofar as they exist on their own outside of production and consumption, they do so only as an abstraction. Whilst this justifies speaking of their ideal nature, it in no way concedes they can enter human society materially in an ideal form. A poem can exist as a sound, a text, or a song, and we may conceive of it ideally by abstracting from the differences between all these forms. But to be *used* it must be spoken, printed, or sung: it must incarnate in the earthly world. Whether the number 2 'exists' in some Neoplatonist astral plane is of no concern to us: when we define its properties as an abstract object, all we really do is describe how it must behave in any concrete form.

The distinction between particular physical form, and its mental content, gives rise to all kinds of ambiguities we are often only dimly aware of. For example, when we say an author has 'written a book' we do not mean she personally put the ink on it, yet we happily refer to the object on the shelf as 'a book'. The word 'book' has two completely different meanings even in everyday usage.

The ideal separation of mental content from the objects in which it manifests also gives rise to wild confusion when the ideal form is treated as if it were physical object. Mental objects do not 'wear out', because they cannot be quantified independently of their incorporation into a quantifiable substance or activity. One cannot deploy 'twice as much' knowledge in one factory as in another or consume 'three times as much' poetry. One may only employ twice as many knowledgeable scientists, twice as many material products (robots, chemical substances, servers, synchrotrons, universities, aircraft carriers) of their labour, or three times as many poems. At best, one may spend twice as much money to get the knowledge or read the poems. The knowledge itself, like the poetry, is devoid of extent.

That is why it cannot be used up. A poem does not cease to exist after we have read it, a computer programme does not get rusty if it is run too often, and a scientific theory does not lose its validity when applied. True, the programme may become obsolete, the poem may go out of fashion, and the theory may be superseded. But disuse is not to be confused with disappearance: except for those lost to both memory and record, the ghosts of all poems ever composed haunt the shelves of our libraries and museums, waiting only for a reader who will consent to bring them back to life by the act of casting an eye on them.

Nevertheless, mental objects gain access to the mundane spheres of production and consumption only in physical garb. Like the gods of Olympus, they consort with humans only in a bodily guise, a coarse physical bearer of their aethereal existence.[3] This is the root cause of the attractive idea that they are freely and costlessly available. But precisely because they can only be used in a definite physical form, their use is not costless. It takes work to recite a poem or make a pill. It takes work to reproduce mental objects: education, child-rearing, museum maintenance, and all aspects of preserving the mental content of civilized life by constantly transferring it to the brains and competences of new people, consume truly immense amounts of social labour.

Actually, they appear costless not only because they are mental, but their physical forms of existence are frequently 'non-excludable'; the fact that one person is listening to a song does not prevent others hearing it. This is in a certain sense a technological accident. In Moses' day it probably took as much work to copy a commandment as to issue it. This may account for the veneration accorded to prophets, who probably came cheaper than stonemasons. Notwithstanding, the general tendency of technology is to widen the gap between the costs of origination and dissemination. Electronic communication

---

3   In the early years of Hungary's liberation from the Communist yoke, an enterprising Budapest café owner is said to have established a bar which served empty cups of coffee. His argument was that people entered cafés not to consume actual coffee, but the experience of drinking it. Therefore, his newly unbridled commercial instincts told him, he could separate the experience from the coffee, relieving the customer of its narcotic side-effects, and himself of the cost of providing them. No trace of this apocryphal philanthropist remains.

is, in this respect, a qualitative leap, worthy of being designated a technological revolution in and of itself: a musical recording can be distributed literally by the million, without restricting the ability of the original owner to listen to it.[4]

In standard economic terminology, mental objects are *public goods*; as Wikipedia currently puts it:

> In economics, a public good is a good that is both non-excludable and non-rivalrous, in that individuals cannot be excluded from use or could benefit from without paying for it, and where use by one individual does not reduce availability to others or the good can be used simultaneously by more than one person.

The illusion that the mental being of a piece of music is costless dissipates, the minute one asks how musicians stay alive. It takes labour to produce a mental object, to use it, and to reproduce it, which is to say, to keep it in existence. This labour is concealed like the base of an iceberg, because it resides in human brains. The reproduction of human mentation is, like the reproduction of physical capacities, performed outside the commodity relation, by the labourers and their families, especially women.

This immense quantity of labour lies beneath the surface of commercial society, unseen and unacknowledged. Yet music without musicians is an absurdity, as indeed is music without instruments, venues, music teachers, rehearsals, practice, and everything that makes the music possible. Every time a mother sings to her children, she breathes renewed life into the song.

Mental objects, in summary, exist not in some no-osphere which we can optionally forget or add in as an afterthought, as an external factor of production, but are inseparable from the labour and materials in whose company they enter it. This calls on us to revise and extend our idea of what production really is: to be precise, to transcend the limitations on thought imposed by notions of production which we have inherited from a mechanical age that we are fast leaving behind.

---

4 This is one of two fallacies underlying Baumol's ((Baumol and Bowen, 1966), see also (Baumol et al., 1990)) celebrated theorem which claims that an orchestra may not increase its productivity because of its service nature – the musicians can't, for example, play faster. But an orchestra with an electronic audience of fifty thousand is obviously more productive than if it plays to a seated audience of a hundred; it has supplied more 'use'. The second fallacy is the idea that the only dimension of use is quantity. In fact, the orchestra can become more useful by playing better.

4   Is There a Successor to Industrial Production?

What lessons may we draw from the above? I intend to question an assertion by Professor Bodrunov which I will, with no offence intended, describe as a half-truth. According to him, humanity has not put forth any new production methods apart from preindustrial and industrial production. I will argue that to the contrary, these new production methods or 'productive forces' are with us today. What holds them back is the way their fruits are appropriated – that which Marx terms the 'relations' of production.

In fact, at least two fast-growing spheres of production exist today whose methods are entirely different from industrial production, though as the Treviso example shows, they have unexpected similarities with pre-industrial methods. These are software, and the creative industries, of which software is a part. Scientific research, especially in its more modern creative forms, is a close third, but the first two are in an important sense 'archetypal' and provide a template, with the aid of which we can understand how mental objects function more generally in society, including in scientific research.

In short, if we wish to stand at the birthplace of noonomy, this is where to look. Just as the factory was the archetypal site of the industrial stage of capitalist production, so software houses and design studios are, today, the site of its embryonic new stage. A considerable body of literature describing these industries is sufficient to establish that their 'system of production' is very different from anything previously encountered. This is precisely because of the decisive role played by mental objects in what they do, how they do it, and what the result is.

I begin with the function of software. What exactly is it? I will define it, quite simply, as a mental object that can exist in a machine. This is too bald to offer much enlightenment, so I begin with a simple list of its defining features, identifying those that, in my opinion, justify classifying it as mental. I'm sure others can improve on the definition, but I hope to provide some kind of scaffolding for a more complete concept.

The scaffolding rests on two quite simple propositions, both fully justified in modern mathematical logic and in computational linguistics. The first is that software by its essence is a mechanical mental system. The second is that there is, in general, no definite mechanical way to satisfy purposes. The result is a division of the world of mental objects into *mechanical* or *algorithmic* objects, characteristic of software, and *purposive* or *predicative* objects, characteristic of human thought. This separation may not exist for ever, but is characteristic, and determining of, the current stage that our productive systems have attained.

The mathematical foundations of these claims are usually found in the arcane theorems of modern mathematical logic. I will try to convey the findings in a more accessible form because, I hope to persuade my readers, they are fundamental to our understanding of the new forms of production now taking shape. I begin by studying, at greater length, the idea that production is purposive.

Bodrunov notes that natural sciences more or less adequately describe objective natural processes, while technical equipment uses this information to manage such processes more or less adequately by converting them into purposeful, i.e., technological, processes. [emphasis added – AF]. The notion that production is purposeful is essential to any adequate conception of what it is. Without it, one is doomed to recognise any act of transformation as an act of production. However, neither the slow growth of trees, nor their flowering, nor their fruiting, is an act of production any more than the fusion of elements in the sun to produce the heat, or the evaporation and precipitation of the water that combines with that heat to render fructiferousness even possible. These are all transformations – but they are not acts of production. Producing means making something with a use, with the intention of satisfying a need. That in turn is what we mean by a purpose.

Marx expresses this in a well-known passage about the difference between humans and bees:

> A spider conducts operations that resemble those of a weaver, and a bee puts to shame many an architect in the construction of her cells. But what distinguishes the worst architect from the best of bees is this, that the architect raises his structure in imagination before he erects it in reality.

We must add the proviso that the 'imagination' consists not just of a plan to conduct the building, but a vision of what it will be. Production is purposive precisely because it seeks to bring about a state of being, and cannot be reduced to a sequence of instructions that will achieve that state.

The same stricture, however, applies with equal force to the work of a machine. Paolo Giussani once made to me the astute observation that an entirely automatic factory, which makes ice cream with no human intervention, is no longer a factory but an ice-cream machine. A vacant mill with its sails turning idly in the wind, an abandoned Duracell energizer bunny, and a space satellite which has left the solar system and lost radio contact, but continues measuring the universe, are not 'producing': they are merely functioning.

Production, like the objects that enter it, is from the outset and by definition the combination of a physical and mental process directed by desire, imagination, and mental intention. This implies judgement as to whether the result satisfies the purpose: we rank cooks not by their skill in reading recipes, but by what they set in front of us to eat.

It is for this reason, incidentally, that when people worry that machines will replace labour, they miss the point. What should concern them is machines that can form intentions. So far, no such machine exists and nothing on the drawing-boards remotely resembles one.[5]

With this in mind, let us now dig into the world of software. What more can be said of it? Much. I have defined it as a mechanical mental system. The notion of mechanising mentation is actually quite old: the legend of the Golem dates back to early mediaeval times, but the earliest actual mechanical calculator is attributed to Leibnitz, who devised a machine he called a 'stepped reckoner' in 1673 and completed it in 1694. It relied on an ingenious gear with teeth of variable length which was still in use in calculating machines as late as the 1970 Curta handheld, which today retails for $2,500 on E-bay. The engineering techniques of the day did not quite stretch to making it actually work, a problem not unfamiliar to Microsoft users; nevertheless, the design was sound, and it was the progenitor of mechanical calculation including Babbage's more famous Differential Engine, and in many senses, the electronic computer. Leibnitz's justification sheds interesting light on early modern concepts both of productivity and the role of labour:

> it is beneath the dignity of excellent men to waste their time in calculation when any peasant could do the work just as accurately with the aid of a machine.

It is often said, rightly, that the step from mechanical calculation to an automatic computing engine came into being when Lady Ada Lovelace, working on the prospects for Babbage's Difference Engine, realised that a machine might make its own choices about what to do next. Leibnitz's machine, like its successors including the Curta, require the user to enter the data and decide what to do at every step, until the answer comes out. The computer was born with the idea that a machine could 'branch' – could decide the next step for itself.

---

5 They abound, of course, in science fiction, such as Philip K. Dick's prescient *Do Androids Dream of Electronic Sheep,* which made the big screen as *Blade Runner,* or Ian Banks' 'Culture' universe in which droids are fully sentient beings with legal and social rights and aspirations.

Though this is how the story is usually told, this aspect of automation is not my focus. I am not concerned with the machine, since any machine will do, but on its instructions – on the mental object that constitutes a programme. What is new about this is not just the automatic character of its application, but the fact that it exists free of the machine that applies it. A programme, at least a well-written one, will run on *any* computer. The key feature of software is hence that it exists independent of any particular physical form. It can be transported from one computer to another; with the arrival of 'high-level languages' (FORTRAN, Algol, C, C++, Java, Ruby, Python ....) it can also exist on machines with very different physical structures. This is what lends it its 'ideal' character. But just like any mental object, it plays an active role only when combined with ('run on', 'instantiated in' or 'downloaded to') a particular physical structure; it then *alters* that structure – it is *transformative*. Also just like any mental object, it is *communicable*: it can be taken from one physical environment to another. It possesses *identity*: when we download a programme, we can check that it is the exact same 'thing' that we ordered by inspecting its checksum.

All these are characteristics we enumerated at the start of this piece, shared in common with mental objects we are all familiar with: books, poems, songs, theories. If we admit that the idea of a mental object is useful, it makes no sense to rule out software. Moreover, what we have described above covers most of what we mean when we use the word 'thinking' or 'thought'. What is a thought, but a communicable ideal object with the transformative capacity to alter a physical form when incorporated in it?

Software has further characteristics that it holds in common with some, but not all, other mental objects. First, it is a language or, to be precise since there are many computer languages, it is a linguistic system. Second, it is a 'grammatical' system. By this I mean that computer languages have a structure; certain sentences or statements 'make sense' to the compiler, and others do not and are reported as 'errors'. Moreover, the structure imparts a meaning. If I write the statement

$$x = 2$$

then in more or less any computer language, I am stating that there is a variable x, and I wish the computer to make it equal to 2. To head off a diversionary discussion on Semiotics and Deep Structure, I do not claim that the objects in a programme receive their entire meaning from its syntax; only that the structure conveys part of that meaning. Syntax is therefore part of the essence of software.

A further feature of software isolates its specific character: it is 'algorithmic'; it consists of a sequence of actions to be carried out in time.[6] The order of execution matters. This is not so for an image, which the viewer may traverse in any preferred order or indeed, simply render it internally as a *gestalt*.

It is also not the case for a belief, or a judgement. To state that 'this apple is tasty' is to make a statement about the apple, without requiring the apple to be tasted. We can verify (or refute) the statement by tasting the apple, but we don't have to do that in order to make the claim. The claim is a mental entity that exists independently of any action we may take, and hence of any specific time-ordering of activities.

Indeed, new students of computer languages often misread '$x=2$' as a statement about x. But it isn't: it is an instruction to the computer to 'put the number 2 into x', that is, to make the predicate 'is equal to 2' true of the variable x. It is, in short, a means to bring about a change of state.[7] This leads us into the fundamental distinction between algorithmic mental objects which specify a temporal sequence of actions that bring about a change of state, and predicative mental objects which make a judgement on what the state actually is. Table 5.1 (in which the objects on the left and the right only partially correspond) may serve as an aid to reflection.

The above distinction is rooted in modern logical theory, originating in George Boole's *Laws of Thought*, which essentially attempted to set down the laws of logical proof in a systematic way. Many of these laws were already codified in particular by Aristotelian 'syllogisms' – statements of what may be deduced from what, as when, from the statement 'All thieves are dishonest' and the statement 'Barnabas is a thief' one may deduce a third statement, that Barnabas is dishonest.

What Boole seems to have realized is that two different types of mental activity are involved in syllogistic reasoning. Deducing that Barnabas is dishonest is an action, which combines the two premises and produces a third; in fact, it produces a new predicative mental object from two existing predicative mental objects. When one makes the *judgement* that Barnabas is dishonest,

---

6 For the geeks among my readers, neither multitasking nor asynchronous programming alter this fact. A trigger that activates a callback in response to an event is still synchronous in that it responds after, not before, the event. Though several processes may be going on at once, each one of them performs its actions in a definite order.

7 Some languages, for example Microsoft's DAX, use distinct symbols such as ':=' for 'assignment' and some such as Python use special symbols such as '==' to indicate that a comparison is to be made. I played some part in these mental innovations.

TABLE 5.1   Distinctions between algorithmic and predicative mental objects

Algorithmic mental objects	Predicative mental objects
Computer programme	Consumer rating
Deductive proof	Mathematical theorem
Court procedure	Legal judgement
Musical score	Aesthetic pleasure
Laboratory procedure	Experimental result
Instructions to a labourer producing a car	Car performance
Cooking recipe	Tastiness

one enacts a distinct mental activity. It is comforting when the deduction leads to the judgement or, as mathematicians put it, that the judgement is consistent with the deduction, but the two activities are distinct and, as we shall see, do not coincide in general.

At first sight, and when confined to simple propositions, we are conditioned to believe that the connection is obvious, and we assume that making the deduction, and making the judgement, are just two ways of doing the same thing. Indeed, within the limited logical system termed the 'first order predicate calculus', sometimes called the propositional calculus, an important theorem known as the completeness theorem guarantees that an algorithm exists to prove every conceivable predicative statement that can be made about the objects of the system.

But – and this is a big *but* – this is not so for the more general mental system known as the second-order predicate calculus, which is much closer to everyday life. In this logical system *predicates count as objects*, and we can make statements about them, such as "Winnipeg and Moscow have something in common". This asserts, formally, that there exists a predicate that applies to both Winnipeg and Moscow, for example "they are cold in winter". This is a statement about predicates, as well as a statement about cities. We need to be able to make such statements to express most of the ideas that we use in everyday life.

Unfortunately – or perhaps fortunately – the second-order calculus is incomplete. Quite minimal second-order systems contain statements that cannot be proved: to be precise, statements which can neither be proven nor disproven by logical deductive reasoning. This is the outcome of Gödel's celebrated 'incompleteness theorem' which established that this problem exists in any system that contains arithmetic.

Gödel's example is somewhat arcane, and it is tempting to dismiss it on the grounds that the objects he constructed are so difficult to understand that we need not fear meeting them in the course of daily life. More telling, however, is a theorem known as Church's 'undecidability' theorem, formally identical to Turing's 'halting' theorem, and sometimes termed the Church-Turing theorem. Church responded to a question posed by Hilbert, which can be described in lay terms as asking for an algorithm to decide whether a given statement is provable.[8] The Church-Turing (CT) theorem proves that no such algorithm exists.

We can make, therefore, quite reasonable statements without knowing if they can be proved. To put it another way, we will always run up against problems we do not yet know how to solve. There may be a solution, but we cannot build a machine to find it in advance of encountering the problem. If the solution exists, it will have to be *discovered*. A quite simple example of this difficulty is that it is not possible to write a general-purpose translator. Given any two languages, we are likely to be able to translate one into the other. However, there is no way to instruct a computer to produce a translator before we meet the languages. Similarly, there is no algorithm such that, given any two computer programmes, can determine if the effect of one is the same as the effect of the other.

To cut to the chase, there is no mechanical way to answer all questions that can be asked. There will always be problems such that we don't know the answer without discovering it, and we can never be sure of discovering it. Answering new questions is, therefore, a distinct productive activity from mechanical calculation: creation. So far, it is only done by humans.

5   Creativity, Culture and the Limits of Mechanism

Having established that predicative mentation is necessarily distinct from mechanical mentation, we can finally assess the new productive technologies. Two main modern spheres of mental activity have attracted attention: scientific

---

8   That is, an algorithm to decide whether another algorithm exists. A subtle but crucial point. The issue is not whether, given a new problem, we can produce an algorithm to solve it. The question is whether we can write a 'God' algorithm, that will produce the algorithm on our behalf, for all problems that may be stated predicatively, in a calculus in which predicates are objects. Church and Turing prove we cannot.

and technical production including R & D, and the 'creative industries' – which include software. The overlap between these two spheres is surprisingly small (Bakhshi et al., 2016), and both are independently large. Between them, they accounted in 2011 for 3.44 million jobs, 12% of the UK labour force. I will set aside scientific production for reasons already given, and software since we have already dealt with it, and focus on the so-called content industries: Music, Photography, Performance including the visual arts, Crafts, Architecture, Advertising, Publication, Film, and Television and Radio.

These are often subsumed under 'cultural production', which I will argue is a mistake that bedevils the proper understanding of what they really do. This is a pugnacious statement, so I will justify it, but undertake to respond constructively to responses. First of all, there is a basic difficulty in defining production solely in terms of what it produces. How are we to distinguish the sword-makers of ancient Damascus, whose works to this day are renowned for their remarkable qualities, from the workers in Bessemer's first foundry, let alone the five-mile-long behemoths of today, solely on the basis that they all 'make steel'?

Second, the literature is startlingly unforthcoming about what this product actually is. Culture flamboyantly defies definition. As Terry Eagleton (Eagleton, 2016: 1) citing Williams (Williams, 1983: 76) notes, it is "the second or third most complex word in the English language" whilst Williams himself (Williams, 1983: 87) says 'the difficulty about the idea of culture is that we are continually forced to extend it, until it becomes almost identical with the whole of common life'. Throsby (Throsby, 2001: 3) cites Borofsky (Borofsky, 1998: 64) who describes attempts to define culture as 'akin to trying to encage the wind' whilst earlier writers like Mumford (1938) who lean heavily on the word 'culture' simply take its meaning for granted, happily employing it without any real concern for what it is.

Third, the very fact that nobody can agree what culture is, should at least provoke some hesitancy before trying to say what produces it. This does not stem a flow of confident works on 'cultural production' nor the satellite accounts of the statistical agencies of the USA and Canada detailing how much of it comes out.

The most fundamental difficulty, however, is this: the term's most frequent users are arbiters of taste; those who, precisely because the term is indeterminate, can create a role for themselves as definers of what it is. This allows them to act as referees for what constitutes 'genuine' or 'excellent' culture, to be supported and of course, funded, as opposed to 'bad' culture which always seems to coincide with popularity. In short, the very lack of definition in the term is the basis for a small industry devoted to explaining who should be paid to do it, taking a small consideration on the way, thank you Sir for your appreciation of good taste. This may, or may not, be a useful way to construct a social order: it is, however, no basis for a rational account of what cultural actors in fact do.

Elias (Elias, 1939) offers a valuable way out of this blind alley, via a historical account of the origin of the term. It originates in 18th Century German romanticism, when the rising German middle classes needed to counter the power of the nobility by confronting its notion of 'civilization' as a product of breeding manifested in good manners. *Kultur* signified something produced by an artist, who did not have to be well-bred, but in deference to the mythology of 'superiority' that permeated aristocratic society, could be decorated as an *achievement*, indeed the product of genius, distinguishing the talented artist both from the nobility, and from the common crowd.

This is the origin of the profoundly élitist concept transmitted into English society by early capitalism's custodians of public virtue, like Thomas Carlyle (Carlyle, 1829), who held that society needed a distinct and privileged caste of persons he termed the 'clerisy' who would be responsible for designating what would be good for the masses, and what would not.

The clerisy is still with us today, through the major part 'culture' plays in maintaining class distinctions. Culture, however we choose to define it, is indestructibly universal. Everyone is involved in producing and reproducing it, and we all bear equal responsibility for it. That should be the end of it: who is to say that Darnella Frazier's recording of George Floyd's last moments has contributed less or more to American culture than the speeches of Robert E. Lee?

Yet in no sphere of human activity is so much attention paid to distinguishing 'good' from 'bad'. Most modern creative activity, from jazz, rock, jive, salsa, movies and indeed photography, to today's graffiti, rap, punk fashion, video games, has had to fight for acceptance past well-meaning – and well-to-do – guardians of culture. The mass commercialization of popular culture adds an ironic extra dimension to pre-existing disparities of wealth, since those who can afford to socialise culture among themselves sneer politely at its purchase with mere money by the masses.

That which the pundits call culture, reduced to its abstract essentials, thus consists of the production and reproduction, as Bourdieu's (Bourdieu, 1984) classic study demonstrates, of social distinctions. These are of two types. What we may term 'horizontal' distinctions are between types of creative activity people can engage in, such as sport, music, travelling, performance, film, game-playing, study, and so on. This is further differentiated into types of sport, types of music, and so on, down to the level of the fan clubs and followers of individual performers, teams, and so on. This diversification is entirely positive and consists in essence, in extensions to the capabilities of humans. They are what 'being human' is really about.

But in class society, distinctions are also 'vertical'; they divide culture into 'high', 'low', 'medium' and so on, and preserve social hierarchy, which, it goes without saying, includes racialised hierarchy. Distinctions become signifiers of wealth and of status, whose function is to signal and maintain class member-ship. This is necessary because classes need to reproduce themselves which, as with any exclusive collectivity, means they must reproduce their membership. They do not do this simply by the reproduction of wealth, though wealth is the vertebral column of the system, because wealth is inherited, so it must be determined who is fit to inherit it. This is managed by family and association, in the maintenance of which the management of taste plays a critical role. Such issues as who children marry, what schools they go to, who they hang out with, not to mention what language they speak, what church they worship in, the colour of their skin and the shape of their hair and extremities, assist in maintaining a complex hierarchy of status and property. The culture indus-try controls *access:* it functions, in effect, as the Western equivalent of a caste system, a network of exclusive employment agencies in cahoots with a giant marriage bureau.

These two types of distinction intersect, but conflict with one another. Anyone can play the violin, but only the privileged are deemed worth of so doing. The vertical distinctions require restricted access and exclusion, to demarcate those worthy of a place on each rung of the social ladder. This exclusivity is directly contradicted by the multiplication of human capaci-ties of the ordinary person corresponding to the multiplication of horizontal distinctions.

How, then, have the 'creative industries' become a mass industry? Because distinction is purchased with discretionary income and has come within the reach of large numbers of people. The fact that the discretionary income is concentrated at the top does not alter this fact: every new capitalist product – cotton clothing, railway travel, the car, television – enters consumption first as a luxury confined to a few and then, as costs fall and economies of scale set in, as an item in the budget of ever more people. In 1996 a crossing-point was reached, the UK Household survey shows, when the 'average' family first spent more on 'leisure' than on physical consumption. The gap has grown ever since. Of course, once this aggregate is decomposed into income groups, it is found that the bulk of the demand for non-basic consumption comes from the rich end of society. No matter: the crucial point is that it is now a mass source of demand. To give some idea of the scale of this development, let us note that the combined capitalization of the 'seven dwarfs' of the media industry

(Time-Warner, Bertelsmann, Disney, etc.) was by 2016 greater than that of any oil major.

The concept of 'culture' provides some insight into this process but focusses from the get-go on the wrong end of things: it asks what the product is. Instead, it should be asking how it is produced. This brings us to the why discretionary income has risen. In part, this expresses rising incomes, but this simplification does not capture *why* incomes have risen: because costs have fallen. The productivity of labour in those industries devoted to the production of tangible goods is now so high that the proportion of the labour of industrial societies devoted to the production of such goods has fallen to 15–20% of the workforce. The focus of ever more industries is therefore the production not of quantity but of variety.

In this mutation, a new element of the mental content of produced goods emerges: that of distinction as such. The purchaser of a t-shirt, a pair of trainers, a music track, a movie, or a ticket to a hockey game, wants a particular design on the t-shirt, a fashionable pair of trainers, etc. and pays not just to clothe or entertain herself but to do so in a particular way which distinguishes her from others. The manufacturer satisfies the demand for *difference*, which becomes an additional component of the use of the product. When a customer pays five times as much for a handmade cup as for a mass-produced one, she or he is paying to be the proud and distinguished owner of a different cup, not to drink more, or even better, tea from it.

The demand for difference is by nature predicative. Of course, purchasers always make the primitive judgement on whether what they buy satisfies a 'basic' need – the cup must contain tea, the car must drive, the shoe must fit, and so on. But with the pursuit of distinction a further element arrives and with it, *design* becomes a universal feature of production. Gone are the days when Henry Ford could tell his customers 'you can have any colour you want, as long as it's black'. Every model must now be different, in colour, style, accessories, performance, or gadgets. The social status of the buyer is inversely related to the number of people with an identical vehicle, as testified by numerous advertising strategies and slogans – My Other Car is a Porsche, The Car in Front is a Toyota, and so on. Alongside greed, envy takes its place as a motor of economic expansion.

But now we come to the cause of the new structures of creative production: *mechanical* calculation is not up to the job of working out how to satisfy a goal specified only by the judgement that will be made at the end of it. A figure interposes herself between calculation and consumer: the creator. Creative human labour – the labour of devising how to satisfy predicative needs – comes into play.

This occurs at every step of the creative chain. A film producer (and film is in many senses archetypal in this respect) engages a huge team of people from camera-people to makeup artists, each of whom responds to a predicative requirement. Their function is to solve problems, to interpret needs generated by the complex collective task of creating the giant product that is the modern film.

Creative labour, in short, undertakes all those tasks which cannot be mechanised. Again, some sense of the scale is required. According to the calculations we made at the Greater London Authority (GLA), using the methodology developed there and in Australia's Queensland Institute of Technology, and then refined to an unambiguous and statistically well-grounded methodology (Bakhshi et al., 2013) in conjunction with the UK's National Endowment for Science, Technology and the Arts (NESTA), one in every six Londoners was by 2008 a creative labourer. Studies dealing with the USA and Canada (Nathan et al., 2016; Freeman and Miles, 2021) suggests that creative labourers make up at least 12 % of the labour force, and similar results apply in other countries. Creative employment is also growing, in fact rapidly: by 2016 in the UK at the rate of 8%, well above any other industrial sector. This is thus an exceedingly dynamic area of production. What its nature, and what is driving it?

The answer comes from a defining characteristic of creative labour: its use is heavily concentrated in specific industries. These are the creative industries. Our research established that these employ between ten and 20 times more creative workers, in proportion to their workforce, than in other industries. Creative labour, in short, has become a *productive force*. It is the defining feature of an entire branch of industry.

6 Creative Labour as a Productive Force

To grasp the issue at stake, we must ask the simple question: why can't this work be done by machines? This boils down to asking what exact aspect of mechanical calculation prevents it yielding the solution to predicative requests on demand. It is not merely the fact that it is repetitive, though this gives us the clue. The key limitation is that the repeated operations are drawn from a finite set of objects. This can be very small indeed – Turing famously showed any programme can be reduced to binary operations. Modern computer languages are less sparse, but their instructions are confined to a fixed set defined in advance. When Kernighan and Ritchie wrote the manual of the C language, they specified every single thing it could do. The list can be read in a couple of hours.

Mechanisation, reduced to its essence, consists of the indefinite repetition of a finite number of identical actions, or sequences thereof. In this, it is no more or less than the reproduction in thought of the physical principle of mass industrial production. The enormous advances in productivity that followed the Spinning Jenny, the Water Frame, the Arkwright loom, the Steam Engine and all the paraphernalia of Victorian Steam Punk arise simply because these machines can repeat the same action over and over again: moreover they can be replicated, so the action is carried out by an army of machines, and the machines can be speeded up so the results come out a hundred, a thousand, a hundred thousand times faster than when performed by humans.

Nevertheless, we forget at our peril that the precursor of mechanical production is mechanical labour, as Braverman reminds us. When Bodrunov notes that the Primitive had no concept of machines, he expresses a common idea that calls for correction. From the earliest days of labour, it consisted of repetitive, that is to say, mechanical actions. Repetition is intrinsic to the life not just of humans but the animal world: it consists of seasons, the succession of night and day, the passage of the planets, rhythmic actions like walking, pounding, eating, and so on. Even primitive gods were charged with maintaining the rhythms of nature – the Sun god to switch the lights on in the morning, gods to separate the seasons and manage the weather, and in the Graeco-Roman pantheon, a god for every planet. These were the divine machinery of the universe.

Indeed, structures like Stonehenge had a computational function: the very word 'computation' derives from the dog Latin term *Computus* (McCarron, 2019) and refers to calculating the date of Easter, a recurring event of great primitive significance because of its relation to the solstice, and the confusing non-coincidence of lunar and solar years.

Moreover, the earliest tools were constructed in a mechanical manner, as when for example chipping flint. Rotatory mechanisms appeared early in history, probably with the rise of the war chariot. Forty thousand years of mechanical activity therefore prepared the Victorians to introduce machines: all they had to do was construct machinery first to imitate, and then replace, the rhythmic activities of human production.

Mechanical activity has thus always been a universal feature of life; what the industrial age achieved, however, was to transfer the agent of this activity from the heavens to the factory. It would probably be as true to refer to the stage of capitalism from which we are emerging as 'mechanical capitalism' as the mor current 'industrial capitalism'. Computation is simply the child of a mechanical age. It should not surprise us that a mode of production dominated by mechanical labour and production should yield, as its characteristic mental object, mechanical thought.

Here, however we encounter the limits of the mechanical age, and grasp the centrality of creative labour to the new productive systems. Mechanical actions consist of repetition: but one may only repeat something if it is identical at each repetition. Predicative objects, however, are characterised by their diversity. The consequence is that some kind of absolute limit is being reached in what can be achieved by mechanisation, which brings us to the threshold, or rather, poses the necessity, of noonomy. The result is a *transformation of labour.*

Freeman (Freeman, 2015) demonstrated, as noted above, that over the past seventy years, the character of the labour force in the industrialised economies has transformed radically. All the tangible goods produced in the US come from industries employing fourteen percent of the workforce. But therefore, *eighty-six percent* of the US labour force is not engaged in physical production, but in what is (erroneously) termed 'service' production. Similar proportions are found in all fully industrialised economies. Moreover, the phenomenon is also transforming the process of industrialisation itself: in China despite a rapid decline in the agricultural workforce, manufacturing employment is falling as 'service' employment rises, not because Chinese industry is in decline but because its productivity growth outstrips its output growth, which is to say fewer and fewer labourers are required to produce more and more output. In this situation, Rostow's 'stages' of development no longer apply; the mental future of humanity is knocking at the door.

This challenges dearly held prejudices of conventional economics, of which the most pertinent is the claim, which the economics novitiate encounters as a kind of catechism on which the rest of the doctrine rests, that capital and labour as *substitutes*. Students are introduced to the neoclassical aggregate production function

$$Y = f(K,L)$$

in which Y is output, K is the 'quantity' of capital (whatever that may mean) and L is the quantity of labour. They are taught that any combination of L and K yield a definite output, that the curve defining Y is 'convex' (bulges outwards) and that therefore, given the price of labour and the price of capital, there will be an optimum choice of L and K for which either output is maximised for a given budget, or cost is minimised for a given output. Both economics and popular journalism deduce that, as the price of K falls, capital will displace labour. This same idea prevails in common thinking, in the perception (often based on harsh reality because of the destructive manner in which this occurs under capitalism) that industrialisation inevitably destroys jobs.

But in creative labour this relation does not hold.[9] Machinery can increase the productivity of labour, but cannot easily replace it. Our London research (Freeman, 2002) established that the creative industries were part of a 'benign productivity revolution' – they increased output without cutting the labour force, which, indeed, was increasing rapidly.

In short capital no longer behaves, in this new form of production, as a substitute for labour but as a complement to it. The output of creative products can only be increased by simultaneously hiring more creative labour and providing more capital – especially ICT but also infrastructure such as venues – to support it. This cannot be achieved by driving out labour for which there is no substitute.

In a certain sense, this is an obvious outcome of the mechanical stage of economic growth: if machines drive out labour, but the labour force itself persists, this cannot continue indefinitely. What does the rest of the labour force do? Those things that machines cannot. However, there is a *social* constraint on the realisation of this potential, pointing to one of the contradictions explored in our final section. The tasks left to humans extend to wide sectors in which humans are simply preferred over machines, such as care and hospitality. These are typically unrewarding in present society, both as to the quality of the work and the level of pay. And in many countries, especially the global South, labour finds no stable employment at all but concentrates in *Favelas* on the margins.

In summary the displacement of mechanical labour does not on its own create a mass demand for the products of creative labour, but merely creates the conditions to meet such demand. Precisely because the purchase of creative products depends on income levels, the immense disparities that typify modern economies restricts the monetary demand for them to the upper income levels of society.

Beside this, a new supply-side constraint appears. Creative labour, like all labour is not produced capitalistically but 'reproduces itself' through family and personal labour. However, unlike mechanical, undifferentiated labour its creativity must also be reproduced, and requires substantially greater resources. It requires education, access to resources (musical instruments, art materials, sports facilities, computers) and not least, time to develop. But the wage system does not finance this, and even less does the precarious nature

---

9 Designating the counterpart of labour 'capital' is misleading since it is actually impossible to calculate a 'quantity' of capital and for other reasons, which Felipe and McCombie ably demonstrate. However, my purpose is to exhibit the flaw in the neoclassical substitutability argument, which I therefore present in its own terms.

of the 'gig economy' that characterises this sphere of production outside of those industries, like software, which have either learned to stabilise the production process or in which the rapid rate of expansion ensures that workers can always 'move on' to the next gig.

In these two facts – the restricted demand for creative products arising from income disparities, and the restricted supply of creative labour arising from the inability of existing property relations to provide for its production and reproduction, we encounter basic limits on both the growth, and the potential, of this new productive system. These limits, we now argue, arise from capitalist property relations themselves.

7   Capitalism and the Future of Mental Production

Traditionally, in analyses influenced by Marx's approach (as is this essay), a new productive force should be expected to enter into contradiction with the existing relations of production, which contradiction should be expected to drive forward the evolution of society. But even in a neoclassical analysis, it would be insufficient to celebrate the achievements and potential of a new productive force; we would have to ask what new problems it presents, and what are the limits to its full development.

Two issues have already been alluded to. These are:

1)   The stunted character of the demand for creative goods in an unequal society, and the limited opportunities for employing labour displaced by mechanisation

2)   The conflict between the public character of mental goods and the private character of appropriation

To this we should add a third, which we might term 'beyond quantity':

3)   The purely quantitative character of mechanical mentation

The first difficulties can be summed up in the failure of our current society to make creativity a *universal* feature of human life, that is to say, to make the full and free development of the innate human capacity to create and to enjoy the fruits of creation, a real and material right of all citizens.

We have already discussed the first issue to some extent. Unlike the second, we may conceive of simple redistributive mechanisms to resolve it: a substantial reduction in inequality, a greatly augmented provision for education, measures like Guaranteed Minimum Income which leave labour sufficiently free from the threat of non-survival to take time out to develop itself, and to take up the time between gigs, and so on.

Much more serious is the vexed institution of Intellectual Property (IP) which governs the manner in which creative producers, and their employers, receive incomes. The critical point to grasp is what allows creative enterprises to generate a *stable* source of income, and how that income is distributed. IP has been criticised from the right and from the left, and the criticisms are unexpectedly similar. Both criticisms, I suggest, fail to adequately address the essential point, which is that creators do require income in order to pay for the labour of creation, and moreover, performers and disseminators need an income to pay for the labour of performing and disseminating.

The left criticism (Buzgalin, 2017; Buzgalin and Kolganov, 2013) centres on the restrictions that IP places on free access to mental products. As we have mentioned, in their abstract form of independence from any specific physical form, mental objects are public goods: non-excludable and non-isolatable. Moreover, the cost of merely reproducing them in this abstract form, independent of putting them to use, is low compared to the cost of creating them. To *print* a musical score, or a book, costs next to nothing in comparison to the work of the composer or the scientific inventor.

These goods are then held to constitute a new kind of 'commons' – infinitely available for all to use without constraint. The institution of IP is then seen as a new kind of enclosure, a modern instance of the crime which figures in Ricardo's pointed barb at the landlords, that they 'love to reap where they do not sow'. The income from IP is then a particular kind of rent, arising from ownership alone, devoid of connection to production.

From the right comes the neglected critique of the modern Austrians, for which IP constitutes an obstacle to free competition, a restraint on trade. It creates an artificial monopoly, preventing new entrepreneurs from entering the market immediately a new technique is available, and thus stifling the competition that would lead to it being used in the most efficient way possible. Indeed, the critique of the libertarian right is remarkable enough to cite at some length. Heubert (Heubert, 2010) explains things thus on the von Mises Institute website:

> For a long time, libertarians were conflicted about "intellectual property" (IP). On the one hand, libertarians support property rights, so IP sounds like something they should favor. On the other hand, IP empowers some people to use government to limit other people's speech and actions ...
>
> The people who enacted IP laws in the first place ... were not recognizing some preexisting natural property right, but just granting a temporary privilege. This is clear in the wording of Article 1, section 8, clause

8 of the US Constitution, which gives Congress "the power to promote the Progress of Science and the useful Arts, by securing for limited Times to Authors and Inventors the exclusive Right to their respective Writings and Discoveries." The language shows that Congress would be granting a positive right to serve a specific purpose, not recognizing some preexisting natural right.

We can contrast this, for example, with the First and Second Amendments, which state that certain rights "shall not be infringed," implying that those rights already exist. Congress didn't need to grant those rights because they derived from individuals' rights to their lives and property and therefore preceded the formation of the government ...

The current generation's libertarian scholars in the natural-rights tradition have largely rejected the legitimacy of IP. The most influential figure in this intellectual revolution has been lawyer and legal scholar Stephan Kinsella, whose article, "Against Intellectual Property", appeared in the *Journal of Libertarian Studies* in 2001 and was published separately as a monograph in 2008. According to Kinsella, the problem with IP is that it isn't grounded in property rights – as all libertarian rights must be – and in fact requires government to violate property rights for its enforcement.

The difficulty with both analyses is the same: they omit entirely the role of labour, not only in the creation of mental objects, but in their *use*, especially use in production. One cannot in any case leave the creators without recompense, or they will be unable to live from labour of creation, and therefore will cease creating.

Although superficially the libertarian right at least addresses the issue of income in speaking of the original purpose of patent and copyright protection, it still (as is to be expected from a tradition in which property is conceived of as property over labour as well as things) the critical point is that the bulk of creative labour does not consist in origination but in reproduction – in particular, but not exclusively, performance and dissemination, which make up the vast bulk of what goes on in the creative industries, not to mention the science-based industries.

The vast bulk of creative labour is concerned with putting it to use, in the company of the material objects, charged with mental content, on which they work. The purely physical aspect of their labour is recompensed by the wage, as is the labour of the Victorian hod-carrier. But the mental element of creative producer's labour is formed outside the production process, in her education, her self-development, and the conditions that allow her to apply the mental technology not merely efficiently, that is to says in the old *mechanical* sense of minimising the time of labour required to accomplish a task, but in the *predicative* sense of the designer, of ensuring that the creative object meets a distinct social need. This extends, incidentally, to the incorporation of socially determined ethical objectives in design, not least that it should not encourage toxic activities, should contribute to the curation of the environment, and so on. Needs are generated not just by individuals but by societies; a typical shortcoming of the Austrian world view is its rejection of this fact.

Heubert does not recognise that mere efficiency is no longer the sole criterion that applies to the full development of either the social, or the economic potential of any new technology. But equally, the left critics of IP fail to recognise that this development requires labour, and this labour must be sustained and indeed, expanded, out of the product of their activities.

The reproduction of any abstract mental object includes reproduction of all the physical forms in which it exists, not least the brain and body of the labourer that applies it. The practical effect of IP is, hence, to create a stream of income out of which, if re-applied productively, the reproduction and use of mental objects can be sustained. The problem does not lie in its existence but in the fact that it does not achieve the purpose for which it was institutionalised. Like any form of rent, it lives a life apart from the labour that creates it. There is no mechanism that ensures it is applied either productively, nor in such a way as to nourish and sustain the labour of the creators, nor the creative users of the mental objects they produce, far less general social conditions for their full development – schools, time for creative development, functioning family or other social relations sustaining the maturation to creative completion of young lives, and so on.

It therefore takes toxic forms. The elevation of envy into a general determinant of demand gives rise to the prioritisation of unnecessary and frivolous needs (Panayotakis, 2021). The maintenance of restrictive monopolies of high technology integral to the domination of the global North (Freeman, 2019) lead to perverse reactions such as the USA's attempts to frustrate, instead of extending, the flow of its technical knowledge to other countries, as testified by its rapidly escalating trade war with China. The defence of forms of IP that focus only on its capacity to extract rent leads to provisions, such as the extension of the period of all IP to 70 years in 1996, which make sense only as a means to deprive them of any intention of providing income to individuals, and turn them into the private preserve of corporations.

At the same time, employment practices in the creative sector, especially the 'gig' economy, make it extremely hard for creative workers to enjoy even the minimal stability of the waged labourer. The notion that creative production can be the terrain of a complete free-for-all with no means to provide a stable income for the creative labourers, is a non-starter. The task is hence to devise alternative, legal mechanisms which provide that stability, and are devised to meet social and ecological needs by ensuring that creative activity is indeed rewarded to an extent that reflects its real contribution to society.

The central issue of 'where does the income of the creative labourer come from' brings us to the brink of the problem that is really central to the future of creative production, and which reaches far wider than the Aleksandr Buzgalin's 'creatosphere' or indeed, any imaginary boundary we may want to erect between physical and mental production: this is the limits set on both production and human development by private property *as such*, not merely the private ownership of intellectual products. In conventional economics it is simply assumed that the owner of a productive process will pay the actual producers, via the wage relation.

The core ideological prejudice of this idea is that the private owner, as representative of the capital invested in the enterprise, is the true source of the wealth it creates, and magnanimously distributes it to the wage-earners. But in the sphere of creative production this does not happen, because the vast bulk of the labour in this sphere does not consist of origination but creative reproduction. This however breaks the link between the labourers in the industry and the 'owner' of the intellectual product, idealistically supposed to be the originator but these days, most usually the faceless corporate entity that has appropriated all the rights pertaining to this 'original' product. The owner of a patent or copyright has no interest in sustaining the lives of the vast army of labourers that are engaged in the mental processing of its content to produce consumable commodities, and does not pay them wages. This vast army is therefore as bereft of a true and stable source of income as the landless peasant of mediaeval times, whose highest aim was to acquire a master.

What is actually required is a system of distribution that allocates, to this army, the means of existence allocated on the principle of *right*: artists, performers and creators alike are entitled to an income not because they own anything, but because they produce; and because what they produce is valuable to society. Such a principle transcends the boundaries of purely private ownership and requires the recognition, and instantiation, of a principle of social ownership of creativity and social responsibility for nurturing it.

But this in turn is not merely the problem of 'mental' labour as distinct from physical labour or of 'mental property' as opposed to physical property: it is the universal problem of all labour and all property since, as we have shown, mental activity and mental content are an indissociable component of all human production. The lowliest common labourer works with both hand *and* brain; and that is what makes her human. The apparently new problem posed by the new divorce of the mental labourer from the mental means of production merely poses this difficulty centrally, throwing it athwart an prospect for a further development of humanity's productive forces.

The solution therefore is to progress, with the greatest possible speed, to the genuinely social ownership of all property, and to the universal acknowledgment that all labour which creates wealth based on the use of that property is entitled to a dignified portion of the proceeds, equal in magnitude to that appropriated by the labour of all others, on the basis of justice instead of privilege, and need instead of greed.

References

Bakhshi, H., Freeman, A. and Higgs, P. (2013) *A Dynamic Mapping of the UK's Creative Industries.* London: NESTA. http://www.nesta.org.uk/publications/dynamic-mapping-uks-creative-industries.

Bakhshi, H., Davies, J. and Freeman, A. (2016) *The geography of the UK's creative and high–tech economies.* London: NESTA.

Baumol, W.J. and Bowen, W.G. (1966) *Performing Arts, The Economic Dilemma: A Study of Problems Common to Theater, Opera, Music, and Dance.* Cambridge Mass.: MIT Press.

Baumol, H., Baumol, W.J. and Rubinstein, A. (1990) On the Economics of the Performing Arts in the USSR and the USA: A Preliminary Comparison of the Data. *Working Papers* 90–36, C.V. Starr Center for Applied Economics, New York University.

Bodrunov, S.D. (2018) *Noonomy.* Moscow: Kul'turnaia revoliutsiia.

Borofsky, R. (1998) Cultural Possibilities. In: UNESCO. *World Culture Report.*

Bourdieu, P. (1984) *Distinction: A Social Critique of the Judgement of Taste.* Harvard University Press.

Buzgalin, A. (2017) Creative Economy: Private Intellectual Property or Ownership by Everybody of Everything? *Sotsiologicheskie issledovaniya* 7: 43–53.

Buzgalin, A. and Kolganov, A. (2013) The Anatomy of Twenty-First Century Exploitation: From Traditional Extraction of Surplus Value to Exploitation of Creative Activity. *Science and Society* 77(4): 486–511.

Carlyle, T. (1829) 'Signs of the Times' ['The Mechanical Age']. *Edinburgh Review.* Vol. XLIX.

Desai, R. (2013) *Geopolitical Economy: After US Hegemony, Globalization and Empire.* London: Pluto Press.

Eagleton, T. (2016) *Culture.* New Haven and London: Yale.

Elias, N. (1939[2000]). *Über den Prozess der Zivilisation.* Haus zum Falken. English translation Elias, N. 2000. *The Civilizing Process.* Oxford: Blackwell.

Felipe, J. and McCombie, J. (2013) *The Aggregate Production Function and the Measurement of Technical Change: Not Even Wrong.* Cheltenham: Edward Elgar.

Freeman, A. (2002) *Creativity: London's Core Business.* London: GLA.

Freeman, A. (2015) High End Labour: the foundation of 21st Century Industrial Strategy. *Valdai Discussion Club public website*, 15 August. Available (consulted 23 August, 2021) at: https://valdaiclub.com/a/valdai-papers/valdai_paper_26_high_end_labour _the_foundation_of_21st_century_industrial_strategy/.

Freeman, A. (2019) Divergence, Bigger Time: The unexplained persistence, growth, and scale of postwar international inequality. *Geopolitical Economy Research Group Data Project Working Paper* 2 (March 2019). Available (consulted 23 August, 2021) at: https://www.academia.edu/39074969/Divergence_Bigger_Time_The_unexplained _persistence_growth_and_scale_of_postwar_international_inequality.

Freeman, A. and Miles, G. (2021). *Culture in a time of Covid: An Early Warning Reporting System for Canada's cultural and creative economy.* Unpublished Manuscript.

Heubert, J.H. (2010) *Libertarianism Today.* Praeger, 2010, Chapter 10. Reproduced in *'Mises Daily Articles'* as Heubert, J.H. (2011) 'The Fight against Intellectual Property'. Available (consulted 23 August, 2021) at: https://mises.org/library/fight-against -intellectual-property.

Inwood, M. (1992) *A Hegel Dictionary.* Oxford: Blackwell.

Kliman, A.J. (2007) *Reclaiming Marx's Capital: A Refutation of the Myth of Inconsistency.* Lanham, MD: Lexington.

Marx, K. (1976). *Capital: A Critique of Political Economy. Volume I* (Capital Volume I). London: Penguin.

McCarron, M. (2019). *Bede and Time: Computus, Theology and History in the Early Medieval World.* Routledge.

Mumford, L. (1938) *The Culture of Cities.* London: Martin Secker and Warburg.

Nathan, M., Kemeny, T., Pratt, A. and Spencer, G. (2016) *Creative Economy Employment in the US, Canada and the UK.* London: NESTA. Available (consulted 23 August, 2021) at: https://www.nesta.org.uk/report/creative-economy-employment-in-the-us -canada-and-the-uk/.

Panayotakis, C. (2021) *The Capitalist Mode of Destruction: Austerity, Ecological Crisis and the Hollowing out of Democracy.* 1st edition. Manchester University Press.

Swetz, F. and Smith, D. (1987) *Capitalism and Arithmetic: The New Math of the 15th Century, Including the Full Text of the Treviso Arithmetic of 1478*, Translated by David Smith. Open Court Publishing.

Throsby, D. (2001) *Economics and Culture*. Cambridge: CUP.

Williams, R. (1983) *Keywords: a Vocabulary of Culture and Society*. London: Fontana.

CHAPTER 6

Predictive Potential of Noonomy to Justify the Development Strategy

Andrey I. Kolganov

Building a strategy for the socio-economic development of society, which concerns both the promotion of long-term development goals and the choice of the means to achieve them, is fruitless without relying on theoretical research that has predictive potential. However, there is a clear lack of scientific concepts that would give us guidance for making far-reaching strategic decisions now.

The once popular concept of a post-industrial society, although some of its forecasts made in the 1960s and 1970s of the last century proved correct, has never been able to draw a well-founded holistic picture of the prospects for socio-economic development. Its key premise turned out to be false: the world economy has not become post-industrial,[1] despite a significant reduction in the share of the industrial sector in developed countries. Overall, though, there is no reduction in the share of industrial production in the world economy, nor is there a reduction in employment in the industrial sector. In reality, the advancement of the "post-industrialization" concept is a disguise for the ongoing transfer of industrial production from developed to developing countries during capitalist globalization that aimed to exploit cheaper labor (Smith, 2012). Thus, despite the fact that the ideas of post-industrialism have sprung into considerable popularity and the term "post-industrial society" is widely used (often without understanding its real meaning), post-industrialism cannot possibly claim that it opens our eyes to the future of humanity.

The more interesting is the scientific hypothesis of the movement of modern society towards noonomy (non-economic mode of business activity), developed in the latest publications of Professor S. D. Bodrunov (Bodrunov, 2018b). It can be assessed as a rather promising theoretical and methodological starting point for the study aimed at exploring the expected trends in the evolution of business systems. What makes it possible to regard the concept of noonomy as a scientific methodological platform for further study? It is the

---

1 Foremost American economists and sociologists also agreed with this point (Inozemtsev, 1998).

fact that noonomy relies on a synthesis of a series of real objectively developed trends in technological and socio-economic development.

The technological trends that underlie the concept of noonomy are the enhancement of knowledge intensity of modern production, the increase in the knowledge capacity of the products produced, further withdrawal of man from material production and the rise of scientific knowledge and information in technological development, which results in deeper integration of science and education production. Besides, in the framework of the concept of noonomy, it is very important to study trends such as the increase in the course of technological development resource load on the environment and the expansion of direct intervention in human nature, because these trends set the limits for the current economic order of society.

The growing importance of knowledge as a factor of economic development has been repeatedly confirmed by renowned economists since Karl Marx advanced a thesis that production is turning into a "materially creative and subject-oriented science" (Marx, 1969: 221). For example, Alfred Marshall argued that "knowledge is our most powerful engine of production" (Marshall, 1920: 115). Joseph Schumpeter insisted also, that it is the new combination of knowledge that forms the basis of innovation and entrepreneurship in general (Schumpeter, 1911: 57), and knowledge itself is the main engine of economic growth (Schumpeter, 1939). Later, the importance of acquiring and disseminating knowledge was emphasized in the 1960s–1970s of the twentieth century from various viewpoints in the works of Fritz Machlup (Machlup, 1962), John C. Galbraith (Galbraith, 2008: 37) and Daniel Bell (Bell, 1973). Since then, focused attention to the role of knowledge and to the knowledge "economy" has become an integral part of modern economics.

The new thing that S. D. Bodrunov adds to the study of this trend is the reconstruction of such consequences of growth of knowledge intensity of production, that are reflected in the structure of the business system itself. Besides, Bodrunov's views differ from the once popular one-dimensional interpretations of this trend in the concepts of "post-industrial society" theorists, who regard knowledge and information as not only the most important resource of production, but also the most important result of human activity. The concept of noonomy, while being based on the fact that the importance of knowledge and information is growing, arrives at a different conclusion: about the transformation of modern production into knowledge intensive material production, and its product – into a knowledge-intensive product (Bodrunov, 2018a: 8, 14). This emphasizes the importance of material industrial production and the fact, that knowledge and information have no economic value without their technological application.

The question of the transition to a new phase of industrial production and industrial society is not the only one raised by the concept of noonomy. It also considers the process of withdrawal of man from the process of direct production in terms of analyzing its impact on the socio-economic structure of society. So far, such questions have been mainly an arena where futurists and publicists could practice their skills, but neither economists nor sociologists conducted any in-depth study of the consequences of this trend through the discourse of their area of science.

The manifest growth of human technological power makes it possible to create a basis for better satisfaction of needs, though it results in higher risks that threaten human existence through the loss of man's own nature. These trends, that are described in the works of S. D. Bodrunov, are fully confirmed in the ongoing processes of development of the fifth and sixth technological modes that we witness now. It stands to reason that all these new technologies have higher knowledge intensity than the technologies of the previous stage. In addition, these technologies are characterized by the synergy of various branches of scientific knowledge in accordance with the current processes of technology convergence and hybrid technology formation (Roco, Bainbridge, 2004: 1). It is this increase in production capacity and the effect of synergy and technology convergence that reduces both the material and energy consumption of products and services. As exemplified by, say, additive technologies developed based on the use of 3D printing technologies, these knowledge-intensive technologies can significantly reduce material consumption and create a high degree of non-wastefulness of production (Dresvyannikov, Strakhov, 2018: 17; Suleymanova et al., 2018: 73). A similar increase in knowledge intensity typifies such current closely intertwined trends as the creation of so-called smart factories (Burke et al., 2017), the employment of the Industrial Internet of things (PwC, 2016; Buntz, 2019), the use of artificial intelligence technologies, the application of methods for managing technological processes based on automatic processing of big data from built-in sensors. In addition, all these trends ensure the withdrawal of man from direct production with the increasing role of human creative and goal-setting functions.

That said above about additive technologies is true for cutting-edge biotechnology, nanotechnology, quantum technologies, and so on. Indeed, all modern technologies are based on the growth of knowledge capacity of production and ensure the corresponding reduction of material resource intensity and the withdrawal of man from direct production processes.

Technologies of the sixth technological mode, primarily information and cognitive technologies (artificial intelligence, the Internet of Things, big data processing ...) gave a new impetus to the development of robotics. Universal industrial robots were widely used as early as at the turn of the 1970s–1980s, with the annual increase in their number reaching tens of thousands. In the 1990s, however, this growth slowed down sharply. It was only in the mid-2000s that technologies of the sixth mode were first applied in practice and a new stage of rapid growth of industrial robotics began. If we compare the number of industrial robots with the number of industrial workers, we will see that robots accounted for 2% in the USA in 2017 (Robot ..., 2018), in 2018 in Germany and Japan – 3.3%, in South Korea – 7.7% and in Singapore – 8.3% of the number of people employed in industry. China is growing the number of industrial robots at breakneck speed. In 2018, there were 154,000 industrial robots installed in China – more than in the USA and Europe combined (Welcome ..., 2019: 8, 13).

However, the socio-economic trends of the modern age that are developing on the basis of this technological progress are rather contradictory. On the one hand, we see growing technological opportunities to meet human needs, but on the other – we also see the proliferation of false, phantom, imposed needs in the context where a part of humanity cannot even meet their vital needs properly, and social polarization is growing. On the one hand, there is a development of methods of conscious socio-economic regulation, but on the other – the force of market processes is still able to undermine and impair these efforts, plunging the economic system of humanity into another crisis.

New opportunities created by modern information technologies for big data processing are employed not to give economic development a well-ordered character, but to manipulate consumers for to impose simulated needs in the pursuit of growing sales of anything that can bring profit (Maltsev, 2019: 67–68). Not only critics of modern capitalism point to these facts, but even Nobel prize winners in economics, who can in no way be considered opponents of the free market and entrepreneurship (Akerlof, Shiller, 2015). The huge marketing and advertising costs highlight that the consumer is now made to pay not only the production costs of the product, but also the efforts that are spent on trying to impose this product on him/her!

The processes of globalization of world economy are developing, which reflects an objective need for internationalization of production, the growth of global interconnectedness and interdependence. But, on the other hand, we see that globalization is exploited as a tool in the fight of some influential states and extremely large-scale capitalist groups for world hegemony (Stiglitz, 2002). The financialization of world economy, on the one hand, provides rapid-fire flow of capital in its most liquid form, thereby expanding the ability to manage the processes of structural and technological restructuring of production. However, on the other hand, it has caused the financial sector to swell, which retracts material resources from production and can undermine the real sector of the economy (Levina, 2006).

These contradictory processes are captured in the thesis that we have now entered a context of new normality. This thesis actually represents a disguised embarrassed statement of the ongoing dismantlement of the world economy. Market volatility is growing, traditional levers of state regulation are weakening, the level of investment in production is decreasing, the rate of economic development is dropping, and the growth of the population's welfare is actually frozen. Thus, the development of technologies and the evolution of the modern economic institutional order bring along an increase in both, new development opportunities and threats.

One of such most serious threats is the increasing burden on the environment. The whole humanity has exceeded the threshold of the global ecosystem's ability to self-repair for several years now, and today we follow the path of ever-increasing deterioration of our own living conditions. At the same time, despite all attempts to limit the activity of this kind, the threat of interference in human nature is growing – both direct, through various projects of body restructuring, up to the interference in the genetic apparatus, and indirect – through informational, psychological and other effects on the consciousness and lifestyle of man.

This makes us be serious about the conclusion that the crisis of modern civilization is approaching, that it is coming to its bifurcation point, which requires us to urgently find ways to resolve the escalating contradictions of development. It is on these facts that Bodrunov relies when concluding on the need and the objective tend of transition to the next generation of a new industrial society, which would ensure our potential to get out of these contradictions. This very new industrial society of the second generation is modelled in the concept of noonomy just as a conclusion from the analysis and the opportunities that are developing now, as well as the contradictions that are created by the modern stage of development of human civilization. The transition to a new second-generation industrial society does open up the opportunities to significantly mitigate these contradictions, but their decisive overcoming requires a qualitative transformation of the entire structure of modern society and, of course, the ways of its economic activity, due to the fact that both, we see new opportunities created by technological development and these opportunities within the framework of the modern economic system, inevitably provoke destructive trends.

Actually, going beyond the limits of the capitalist social system is not enough: it is necessary to go beyond the limits of economic society in general. Admittedly, the forecast of the onset of a post-capitalist and post-economic society has long been made in the Marxist tradition, but it must be said that Professor Bodrunov's concept of the future of society differs from this Marxist forecast in a variety of ways. First, the concept of noonomy provides a detailed description of the technological basis that makes it possible to move to a post-economic society, to go beyond economic necessity and economic rationality. I must admit, however, that some modern Marxist developments on the assessment of technological changes converge with this position. Second, Bodrunov uses the analysis of this technological basis to draw a conclusion, which was not explicitly formulated in classical Marxism. He concludes that the exit of man from direct participation in material production is accompanied by the regression of human relations about the participation in this production, that is production relations. There will be no production relations between people in noonomy at the social stage of noodevelopment.

Third, Bodrunov models the way in which economic activity will be regulated after man has been withdrawn from direct production. There has been no such concept developed in Marxism so far. And from his point of view, it will be a system of guiding and goal-setting human actions in relation to a rather autonomous manless technosphere, functioning on the basis of self-organization of the activities of technetic creatures.

Finally, fourth, the concept of noonomy argues the thesis of a new criteria-based business activity in the context of noonomy. This criteria basis will determine the goals of production, the formation and satisfaction of human needs, and it will grow out of changes in the nature of human activity, which will be increasingly concentrated in the creative space, in the process of learning and in the process of technological application of new knowledge. This creative nature of the primary human activity will also cause a change in the structure of human needs, which will be focused not on the extraction and absorption of the largest possible amount of means of living, but on ensuring the development of man himself, on the exaltation of human culture in all its manifestations.

Accordingly, it is these cultural imperatives that will become the fundamental internal criterion determining the goals of production, the formation and satisfaction of needs. At the same time, the saturation of needs will be evaluated in a way different from how we do it now, not in terms of volume indicators, that is how much of everything we were able to consume (no matter, with or without benefit). The saturation of needs will be assessed by the satisfaction of specific rationally determined human needs aimed at man's own development. If we can meet these specific needs, it means that we are a success. The question is not how much we have consumed, but whether we have met our needs.

Such a forecast of the future development of humanity cannot definitely be founded only on the publication of a single monograph and a series of articles. It is increasingly evident that the scientific hypothesis of the movement of society from economy to noonomy requires a much deeper study of this trend and the underlying objective processes. Thus, noonomy is becoming not just a discovered phenomenon of civilizational development: closer study of this phenomenon gestates noonomy as a special discipline focused on in-depth study of the entire complex of problems set within this concept. Interest in noonomy as a discipline is growing, and one of the featured characteristics of the birth of a new branch of science is the fact that noonomy as a scientific hypothesis is now accepted for studying as an academic discipline (a course on noonomy is now planned in several universities in 2020). Noonomy is being built up in parallel with economy as a real phenomenon around us. It is being formed both as a reality that comes up in our current existence, and as a discipline that studies how this reality unfolds.

The prognostic view of the concept of noonomy on the prospects for the development of human society provides us with methodological and theoretical prerequisites for setting a very wide range of research targets. Such targets include, for example, the study of intermediate stages of progression to a new second-generation industrial society and to noonomy, and, accordingly, the study of the patterns of formation, evolution and change of such stages. Besides, it is now more and more relevant to assess the immediate prospects of socio-economic development in terms of their compliance or non-compliance with major strategic route towards a new stage of society's living, to a new stage of human civilization. This also affects a certain understanding of the route of technological progress, and the changes required in socio-economic institutions, economic policy, and the social structure on the whole.

In this light, the reindustrialization of Russia appears not only as a necessity of nowadays, but also as an imperative arising from the insights into the future. In this sense, we need reindustrialization not only to accelerate economic development, not only to strengthen its competitiveness in the world economy and to raise people's welfare, but also to set the necessary prerequisites for progressing to the next stage of social development. If we do not want to content with position of always laggards, we need to adjust our development in this context in such a way as to reach the most advanced frontiers determined by the very strategic prospects for social evolution.

This also requires a specific policy of technological modernization, which should be aimed at tackling the very challenges that are in line with the most important development trends and form the basis for the progressive changes not only in the present, but in the future too. This requires an appropriate strategic planning and the corresponding active industrial policy which would ensure a focus on solving the challenges of technological breakthrough aimed at implementing promising long-term trends: the increase in the share of knowledge in production and its product, the reduction of the share of material resources in the total costs, and the withdrawal of people from the direct production process.

The solution of these problems will definitely require a backup by the advanced development of the creative potential of man. And the latter implies a significant increase in the share of investment in education, research and development, and healthcare too – but not only in the medical industry as such, but in the development of all elements of healthy lifestyle, including human environment. If we assess the challenge from a strategic position, the required increase is estimated not by a percentage, but manifold compared to the achieved level.

One rather common comparison is: memorably, when the Soviet Union first entered the space, the USA, trying to understand how the Soviet Union had deserved the privilege to overcome the world's leading power in space exploration, concluded that one of key factors was the education system in the USSR. Currently, we allocate less than 4% of our gross domestic product to education, while the Soviet Union spent 10–12% of its national income in the post-war years to create the conditions for space exploration (the did not calculate GDP at that time), and even in 1988, the period of Soviet decline, these allocations amounted to 6.4% of GNP (National Economy.., 1991).

If we fairly evaluate the current technological gap between Russia and not only the most developed, but also many of the developing countries, we will come to an unambiguous conclusion: the scale and complexity of the challenges to be tackled are of an extraordinary nature. Just compare the little Singapore, which installed 4,300 robots in 2018, and huge Russia with only 1,007 robots. In Russia, there are only five robots per 10,000 of those employed in industry, while in Singapore – 831. At the same time, only 4% of the robots installed in our country are Russian made. The country, that used to be at the forefront of robotics production during the Soviet era, has completely lost its serial production of industrial robots. Such a low level of robotization of production in the country cannot be explained by the cheapness of labor, just because China, where labor is cheaper than in the RF, has as many as 140 robots per 10,000 of people employed in industry, and it is increasing this number at an unprecedented pace (Skrynnikova, 2019; Welcome ..., 2019: 8, 13).

Therefore, as the extent of our disadvantage is so extraordinary, the measures to address this and similar problems must be just as extraordinary. The fine-tuning of the existing socio-economic institutions must seem much more seamless, but it is fraught with the risk of aggravation of our disadvantage, procrastination with the solution of problems, which will make them much more expensive to overcome and associated with increased social risks.

No country that has successfully overcome its underdevelopment has managed without measures that are fraught with extreme costs. But such is the inevitable price that must be paid for a long-term waver of the policy of technological modernization. The mobilization of resources for a technological breakthrough and a surge in the creative potential of people will definitely disrupt the existing balance of economic interests (which is actually the main reason for procrastination with the relevant decisions). But if we respect the interests of actors who benefit from the current situation, we will never be able to seriously progress in our development.

In the end, it is impossible to solve the problem of rapid development of our country by constantly underinvesting in both, the advancement and application of new technologies and the development of human creativity. It is not without reason that the theory of noonomy highlights the tasks of human development as the main shift in the structure of satisfaction of our needs. Since the technological possibilities to meet people's vital needs are expanding with the progress of technology, the problem bumps up against the fact that the system of social relations inhibits a significant part of the population from taking advantage of these opportunities.

Of course, the development of nooproduction is a prerequisite for the shift from better satisfaction of basic needs to the development of a human need in self-development as a basic one. If man's activity is not limited to earning money for survival, but is based on the actualization of his creative potential, then the nature of human needs will change accordingly. At the same time, this should be facilitated by a shift in social relations that will not be subject to the standards of economic rationality based on boundless increase in consumption. The new standards of rationality will no longer be economic in their nature. If a person's activity is aimed at the development of his/her personality, that is at growing his/her cultural maturity, then the standards for his/her needs will be primarily cultural in nature.

Therefore, we shall abandon the outdated view of the development of science, education and healthcare as a waste of state budget funds, and start regarding them as the most promising investments into our development. It goes without saying that a man of education and culture cannot be developed in the technological semi-desert that represents the Russian economy of today. If we don't keep the highest rate of creation of new high-tech industries and the corresponding jobs, the cost of mastering knowledge and high skills will be fruitless. Therefore, solving the problems of a technological breakthrough and increasing the creative potential of our nation shall definitely go hand in hand.

We shall also remember that the transition from economy to noonomy has not occurred yet, and we are in a tough competitive economic environment. Russia's position in the world economy will depend on the prospects for our technological development. So, will we manage to abandon the role of a raw material colony of the world economy and become one of technological leaders? The countries that can make the best use of the development potential of modern knowledge-intensive technologies will become economic leaders relying on their scientific and technological monopoly; others are destined to be content with their dependent position. The chosen solution to this issue will determine our position in the geoeconomics and geopolitics of the modern world for many decades to come.

References

Akerlof, G.A., Shiller, R.J. (2015). *Phishing for Phools: The economics of manipulation and deception*. Princeton, NJ: Princeton University Press.

Bell, D. (1973) *The Coming Post-industrial Society: A Venture in Social Forecasting*. New York: Basic Books.

Bodrunov, S.D. (2018a) Neo-Industrial Production: Step Towards Non-Economic Development. *Ekonomicheskoe vozrozhdenie Rossii* 1: 5–15.

Bodrunov, S.D. (2018b) *Noonomy*. Moscow: Kul'turnaja revoljucija.

Buntz, B. (2019) Predictions: IoT Market to Expand, but Challenges Remain. *IoT World Today* (11 December). Available (consulted 23 August, 2021) at: https://www.iotwor ldtoday.com/2019/12/11/2020-predictions-iot-market-to-expand-but-challenges -remain/.

Burke, R., Mussomeli,A., Laaper, S., Hartigan, M. and Sniderman, B. (2017) The smart factory. Responsive, Adaptive, Connected Manufacturing. *Deloitte Insights* (31 August). Available (consulted 23 August, 2021) at: https://www2.deloitte.com/us/ en/insights/focus/industry-4-0/smart-factory-connected-manufacturing.html.

Dresvyannikov, V.A. and Strakhov, E.P. (2018) Classification of Additive Technologies and Analysis of their Economic Use. *Models, Systems and Networks in Economics, Technology, Nature and Society* 2: 16–28.

Galbraith, J. (2008) *New Industrial Society*. "Anthology of Economic Thought" Series. Moscow: Eksmo.

Inozemtsev, V.L. (1998) Rethinking What's Coming. The Largest American Scholars about Modern Development. *World Economy and International Relations* 11.

Levina, I. (2006) On the Relationship between the Financial Sector and the Real Economy. *Voprosy Ekonomiki* 9: 83–102. (In Russian) https://doi.org/10.32609/0042-8736-2006-9-83-102.

Machlup, F. (1962) *The Production and Distribution of Knowledge in the United States.* Princeton, N.J.: Princeton University Press.

Maltsev, V.A. (2019) *Karl Marx and Big Data.* Moscow: Rodina.

Marshall A. (1920) *Principles of Economics.* Eighth edition. London: Macmillan and Co., Ltd.

Marx, K. (1969) Economic Manuscripts 1857–1859. In: Marx, K. and Engels, F. *Collected Works.* Vol. 46, Part II. Moscow: Politizdat.

National Economy of the USSR in 1990 (Statistical Yearbook) (1991) Moscow: Finansy i statistika.

PwC (2016). *The Industrial Internet of Things. Why it Demands not only New Technology – but also a New Operational Blueprint for Your Business.* Available (consulted 23 August, 2021) at: https://www.pwc.com/gx/en/technology/pdf/industrial-internet-of-things.pdf.

Robot density rises globally (2018). *International Federation of Robotics. IFR Press Release* (consulted 23 August, 2021) at: https://ifr.org/news/robot-density-rises-globally.

Roco, M., Bainbridge, W. (2004) *Overview Converging Technologies for Improving Human Performance.* In Roco, M., Bainbridge, W. (eds). Converging Technologies for Improving Human Performance: Nanotechnology, Biotechnology, Information Technology and Cognitive Science. Arlington.

Schumpeter, J. (1911) *The Theory of Economic Development.* Oxford: Oxford University Press.

Schumpeter, J. (1939) *Business Cycles.* Second Volume. New York: McGraw-Hill.

Skrynnikova A. (2019) Automotive Industry is the Largest Buyer of Robots in Russia. *Vedomosti,* 9 September. Available (consulted 23 August, 2021) at: https://www.vedomosti.ru/technology/articles/2019/09/19/811579-bolshe-vsego-robot/.

Smith, J. (2012). The GDP Illusion. Value Added versus Value Capture. *Monthly Review* 64(3): 86–102.

Stiglitz, J.E. (2002). *Globalization and Its Discontents.* New York – London: W.W.Norton&Company.

Suleymanova, L.A., Pogorelova, I.A. and Marushko, M.V. (2018) The Essence of Additive Technologies in Construction. *University Science* 2: 70–74.

Welcome to the IFR Press Conference (2019). International Federation of Robotics, September 18, Shanghai. (consulted 23 August, 2021) at: https://ifr.org/downloads/press2018/IFR%20World%20Robotics%20Presentation%20-%2018%20Sept%202019.pdf.

CHAPTER 7

Science and Technologies

Property and Public Progress through the Prism of the Cuban Experience

Jesús Pastor García Brigos

1   Problem Statement

What is the role of the process of scientific cognition and the development of technologies in the modern society? What place did they occupy when the current global problems emerged, and how can they affect the resolution of these problems?

Marx and Engels in the *Communist Manifesto* argue that the bourgeoisie, during its rule of scarce one hundred years, has created more massive and more colossal productive forces than have all preceding generations together. Subjection of Nature's forces to man, machinery, application of chemistry to industry and agriculture, steam-navigation, railways, electric telegraphs, clearing of whole continents for cultivation, canalisation of rivers, whole populations conjured out of the ground – what earlier century had even a presentiment that such productive forces slumbered in the lap of social labour? (Marx and Engels, 1955).

And this would not have been possible without rapid development of science and technologies in the modern day and age, the development that became the foundation for the ideas of the founders of the modern vision of socialism as a process: modern *systems of* capital and new socialist ideas are the products of the modern development of science and technologies. And the post-twentieth century socialist experience, like capitalism in its imperialist phase, has so far developed in a *contradictory relationship with the development of scientific knowledge and technologies*. But this does not mean that in the context of the modern development of the *'knowledge society'* and the general problems of the humankind it makes no sense to distinguish between socialism and capitalism.

Ultimately, as in the case of some approaches to the 'new industrial society', these statements constitute variations of the *'convergence theory'*. Nowadays there are questions that require an even more careful analysis by supporters of socialism and capitalism, since all of them understand that the first thing that needs to be ensured is *the very existence of the humankind*. Is it possible to resolve the so-called *general human problems* within a *capital system* based solely on the inexhaustible opportunities that have opened up in recent years with the development of science and technologies?

As Fidel Castro noted, "It is possible, however, that the destructive power of modern weapons, which could disrupt peace worldwide and make human life impossible on the surface of the Earth, is the most serious threat hovering over it at the moment. Our species will disappear, as did dinosaurs. Who knows whether there is going to be a time for new forms of intelligent life, or the sun will melt all the planets of the solar system and their satellites, as many scientists whose theories are known to us, uninitiated laymen, predict. In this case, practice-oriented people must expand their knowledge and adapt to reality. If our species continues to live much longer than expected, future generations will know much more than we do, but first they will have to resolve a serious issue: find a way to feed billions of people who will inevitably face shortages of drinking water and necessary natural resources" (Las frases ..., 2016).

For these questions that are critical for the existence of the humankind, there is only one correct answer. The only correct answer to the challenges of the 'destructive progress' of recent years is associated with our *political activities*. Fidel Castro always perceived that, so at the Seventh Congress of the Communist Party of Cuba he emphasized that "some of you and, perhaps, many of you are wondering when we are going to start talking about politics in this speech. Trust me, and I say this with chagrin, that politics underlies everything I said in these humble words" (Las frases ..., 2016). Nevertheless, Fidel and I do not abandon Marx's fundamental ideas about the role of productive forces and production relations in the development process. Quite the opposite.

Marx and Engels revealed the most important elements for cognizing the limits of the development of *capital*, and at the same time recognized the great importance of capitalism for the development of productive forces. This is not a paradox. In fact, this reemphasizes the need to approach the analysis of the social process dialectically. They did not give 'easy recipes'. They laid out the necessary elements to not 'just' explain the world. We respectfully add that we often even explain the world incorrectly. The humankind needs, consciously and purposefully, to 'change' this ever-increasing in its complexity world, for it is *the only world that we all have*.

In this context, let us turn to a contemporary world-renowned theoretician who has been developing these ideas – S.D. Bodrunov, who wrote, "In global terms, those who recognise the arrival of the New Normal are right. But they focus on its present outlook without exploring the essence of its origin, its genealogy, which renders the establishment of real cause-and-effect relations and evaluation of potential effects impossible. Only by finding the roots of this phenomenon we will be able to assess: objectivity/biases of the arrival of the New Normal; inevitability/non-inevitability of its occurrence; necessity/possibility of overcoming it; or its consequences and the options available for developing the economy. (...) The New Normal is the reality today. The reality that is new for all of us. And, in fact, it is the "norm" (the reason why I used quotation marks here will become clear later on). It is certainly new, i.e., unusual, to us. And it is under-explored and under-developed by economists, so to speak. It has fallen on the society of scientists, managers, asset owners, regular people, etc. who were wholly unprepared for it. And its features, in general terms, have been described correctly. Moreover, it is both objectively happening and inevitable – and is therefore dubbed "normal." It originates from objective things – the start of the transition to a new stage of our civilisational development, the initial phase of a new industrial society of the next (second) generation. After all, we have *reached the limit of the existing development model's efficiency*. And this constitutes a deeper basis for the changes that we anticipate now, vacillating on the razor's edge, burying our heads in the sand and calling this positioning on the verge of an abyss the new (un)normal. Changes are coming that have never been witnessed before, but soon will be. Profound reforms are necessary" (Bodrunov, 2018a: 56).

These processes, i.e., a change in the development model, take place in all countries. And Cuba is no exception, but a specific and unique case. The essence of the Cuban Revolution is inextricably linked to Fidel's ideas and practices. Cuba is a fine example of how the existence of a specific social organism depends on the attention paid to the development of science and technologies and on understanding the content of productive forces and their development. Currently, it is clear. In fact, anyone can see that this claim is substantiated if they look at the results of Cubans' biotechnology advances in the fight against the new coronavirus.

It is the full and comprehensive human development that has always been and remains the focus of the Cuban Revolution. We build on our understanding that *'public life is essentially practical'*, and it constitutes an activity that transforms the world around us and ourselves: *the totality of all production relations*.

It is necessary to remember the ideas of Marx and Engels, but not just repeat them as religious dogmas. We must develop them critically, on the basis of experience drawn from attempts at a communist transformation of the Great October Revolution, revolutions in Asia, the Cuban Revolution and revolutionary transformations in Africa, Venezuela, Bolivia and other countries of Latin America.

It is necessary to resolve all problems that threaten the human existence. And they can be resolved, first of all, by consciously and purposefully pursuing a comprehensive and complete expanded reproduction of each person's abilities in accordance with his/her humane essence – with the *"aggregate of all social relations,"* i.e. by consciously and purposefully seeking to achieve *a comprehensive and completely free, expanded reproduction of each person's abilities as a result and a necessary condition for the development of a comprehensive and completely free, expanded reproduction of the abilities of the humankind as a whole, as an entity inseparable from nature, in the closest unity with the surrounding natural environment.*

This requires a new nature of public relations and humans' different attitude to nature: *a new method of public process function.* Where can we 'find' this method? It is not immediately available, so *it must be built.* We may be skilled 'architects', but we are no bees (as Engels said), so we need to have a preliminary idea of what we want to build. In this case, the task is particularly difficult. The humanity has been functioning and developing in a different way for thousands of years. And to this day 'architects' who tried to draw blueprints and build new 'public buildings' have not achieved all the expected results.

Perhaps, we need to revise the 'blueprints', not just the 'structures', but also *the content of the construction process itself.* We need to reassess our concepts critically and determine how they have worked so far, whether they have allowed us to successfully move forward in the direction of a new vision of the future society.[1] An invaluable contribution to the theoretical development of this problem was made by Bodrunov, both in the aforementioned book and his other work (see (Bodrunov, 2017)), and by general research conducted under the aegis of s.w. Witte Institute for New Industrial Development (INID) (Bodrunov, 2018b, 2019, 2020).

The very concept of 'practice as a criterion of truth' is often used to substantiate the narrowest pragmatic approaches which tend to forget that "anybody who tackles partial problems without having previously settled general problems, will inevitably and at every step "come up against" those general problems without himself realising it. To come up against them blindly in every

---

1 Here we use the central concept of *predictive* analysis. This method is rarely used and is often used incorrectly: a certain categorical apparatus serves as the foundation for diagnosing one system, one process, and it is used to develop an image of the desired future for it, *a vision of the future.* After that, a group of experts (not only scientists) applies different methods, including mathematical methods, to suggest probable paths leading to *this vision of the future. On this basis, a general policy and actions are developed to achieve set goals, which will be constantly and systematically refined along with the application of appropriate methods.*

individual case means to doom one's politics to the worst vacillation and lack of principle" (Lenin, 1962). It is necessary to act so that the solution of current problems not hinder, but, on the contrary, promote, the implementation of the development strategy in practice. This will become possible only as a result of the interconnectedness of political activity (as a process beyond the simple 'use of power') with the possibilities arising from the process of cognizing the integral world, and not just material production.

The Cuban process of change, which began after January 1, 1959, teaches us that if we want to continue on the path of progress, we must systematically conduct critical analysis of the concepts that serve as the basis for our actions. It is worth starting with the very notion of the 'socialist revolution'. But we also should regularly and consistently consider concepts that are common to *all social processes* (such as political activity, state, democracy, property, planning, market, etc.) from the dialectical perspective.

It is also important to pay attention to the following problems:

- The issue of the state's *decline* as a process within the framework of communist transformations: how is this process related to the complex essence, of the phenomenon, to the transformation of the economy, politics, all social relations and institutions, ideological relations; to the transformation of the entire functioning of society, and in particular to planning and the market?
- Do we really consider property as a system *responsible for integral functioning of the society,* as Marx emphasized in his criticism of Proudhon, "*In each historical epoch, property has developed differently and under a set of entirely different social relations. Thus to define bourgeois property is nothing else than to give an exposition of all the social relations of bourgeois production. To try to give a definition of property as of an independent relation, a category apart, an abstract and eternal idea, can be nothing but an illusion of metaphysics or jurisprudence*" (Marx, 1955: 173)?
- How should we construe state property in general and public socialist property in particular? What are the distinctive features of public property under the socialist transformation perceived as the beginning of the conscious genesis and development of the 'kingdom of freedom'? How should we construe *public efficiency* of public property? What should be the role of the government and public property as a truly leading format in the property system?
- How does planning operate as part of the social process functioning? Is it a universal factor in human progress?
- How did the market emerge, develop and operate? Is it a universal factor in human progress?

- How did planning and the market interact in the process of human development mankind, and how did they combine as factors of progress? Should this interaction change during the communist revolution, in the process of a *complete metabolic transformation of the society* in its unity with nature?
- Within the framework of existing socialism building experience, what was the answer to the question on what serve as the basis for combining market and planning during the socialist (communist) transformation?
- What is the role of the so-called general human values (for example, 'democracy') in the process of "going beyond capital"?

We are not talking about final and universal answers to these questions or about a fully developed and complete theory that could provide all the necessary answers for practical application on what needs to be changed and how it can be done. We believe it is necessary to develop an integral and systemic view of the processes occurring within each system and in its environment resulting from the interaction between a constant and continuous analysis of reality with its contradictions and the analysis of suggestions for reforming this system.

Human progress stipulates the closest interaction of all individuals targeting the resolution of the most pressing problems facing the planet, whereas people are always acting both as subjects and as objects of requisite changes. We, not only Cubans, must clearly develop a *vision* of 'progress' as a strategic goal and resolutely reject what hampers or does not facilitate its achievement. It is necessary to identify tactical steps that will contribute to the achievement of strategic goals, without improvisation or voluntarism. Improvisation and voluntarism ultimately just lead to mistakes and failures.

2   Challenges for the Cuban Society: Answers for Cuba and the Entire World

In the end of the second decade of the twenty-first century – perhaps that goes against 'common sense' – the most acute challenge for Cuba is not economic, but ideological. There is a struggle of ideas in Cuba. It began on October 10, 1868 and continues in more difficult conditions than ever before: the defeat will make it necessary to start the struggle for independence anew ... or disappear as an independent nation, which would signify betraying all those who gave their lives for the progress that was made and not just those killed in action.

Cubans must accept that our society requires many changes. For our part, we humbly suggest careful analysis of ongoing events' specific conditions as a way of resolving issues and guaranteeing progress. In this regard, it is necessary that we take into the following into account:

- perceive the *"meaning of the historical moment"* and use it as the foundation for carrying out all *"urgently necessary changes"* in pursuit of *"complete equality and freedom"*; pointedly develop a *"humane attitude towards oneself and others"* while seeking *"liberation based on own resources"*, despite all the challenges posed by the *"dominant forces within and outside social and national boundaries."*
- tirelessly *"protect the values that we believe in at the cost of any sacrifice"*; this struggle should be waged *"modestly, selflessly, with altruism, solidarity and heroism"*(...).
- lead *"a bold, far-sighted and realistic struggle"* strengthening *"unity, independence, fight for our ideals of justice for Cuba and for the rest of the world"* with *"a staunch rejection of lies and loyalty to ethical principles"* and with *"a deep conviction that there is no force in the world capable of overcoming the power of truth and ideals."*

We should heed these ideas that Fidel suggested to Cubans not mechanically, like dogma. Instead, we should analyze them and put them into practice *in accordance with specific conditions* and taking our experience into account. These ideas have helped us address acute issues that are a threat to progress in our transformation process. We are talking about components that comprise the concept of 'revolution' understood as *"the basis of our patriotism, our socialism and our internationalism."* But these components hold deep methodological content for all those who are genuinely interested in the progress of the humanity.

Humanity needs a real *public revolution* if it wants to withstand the threats caused by prior developments. And it is impossible to lead the revolution forward, in the words of Che Guevara, with an old *"rusty tool"*; it is impossible to use the *tools of capital* to continue the revolutionary process, but it is also impossible to do it with the tools that were used by socialist countries, which eventually suffered a defeat in the past century, regardless of all the positive results and undeniable successes.

We cannot explain here in detail what needs to be done because this is not a task for one person or for one group of eminent scientists or professional politicians. This is the responsibility of everyone who is interested in continued existence of the humanity. It is important to understand that it is necessary to go "beyond the limits of capital", and in this sense we offer some ideas that are the result of our research on Cuban and partly international processes.

It is necessary to overcome the narrow understanding of 'politics', according to which it is but an activity concerning the issues of power. Politics as an activity has always existed and will always exist in accordance with human nature. We propose to approach its content as a set of processes[2] arising from activities of individuals, allowing for the perception of personal, private and social needs (of a social group, a class, etc.) and targeting organization and direction of resources (material and non-material) of all public process participants (individuals, groups, organizations, parties, ... social formats that bring people together) *with the purpose of meeting perceived needs through joint efforts, based on the capabilities of this system and in accordance with the goals (vision) of this collectively developed project.*

With such content of political activity, it becomes possible to take a different approach to the relationship between subjective and objective aspects of this form of activity, to develop a different understanding of its *material and physical* basis: to understand politics as a universal activity inherent in human activity.

We propose to *actually* understand *property as a system and not just an empty slogan.* We must act consistently in order to define *a specific system of property,* i.e., "*to give a description of all public relations*" of production within a given social system, specific social organism, at a certain point in history. At the same time, let us pay attention to the fact that "*to try to give a definition of property as of an independent relation, a category apart, an abstract and eternal idea, can be nothing but an illusion of metaphysics or jurisprudence*" (Marx, 1955).

It is necessary to approach property as a historically set system of relations, its active elements stemming from labor relations, the relationship between humans and nature and people's ideological concepts. This system underlies the entire process of the society's functionality. It changes historically and depending on the specifics of a given process: production of living conditions and the individual himself; production, development and expanded reproduction of conditions and life itself by members of the society. Our focus is on *public relations that are inseparable from relations with nature in a historically specific changing labor process.*

Historically, specifically defined *processes of public management* constitute essential components of this system: *politics* is perceived as an integrating activity, not only and not simply as a '*concentrated expression*' of economic activity. These two points are dialectically related. This dialectic is based on contradictions between *alienation* and *emancipation, the individual* and *the society,* in their specific manifestations associated with the processes of *social*

---

2 These matters are discussed in more detail in the author's forthcoming book and his other works, i.e., in the book *The System of People's Power and Economic Model Update: Necessary and Possible Changes* (García Brigos, forthcoming).

division and *hierarchical social division of labor.* When these contradictions are resolved, the *state* emerges, functions and develops, with content and specific expressions (structures, processes, etc.), with the corresponding historical *types of the property system,* and there are also planning and market as historically specifically defined systems.

Let us identify *three historical types of property systems.* They can exist at the same time in different places:

– initial, primitive, 'original' system, which can still be found in Africa, Latin America and other regions of the world;
– as such system disintegrated under various conditions, a system of '*private hostile property*' appeared, which developed in different ways in different conditions, up to the emergence of a capital system;
– as Marx showed, and as our life experience indicates, the capital system as an expression of the private hostile property system generates conflicts that cannot be resolved by the system itself and must be removed (*aufhebung*) by a new property system.

Contradictions of the private hostile property system force the humanity to perform *a revolutionary transition* 'beyond' (*aufhebung*) capital or disappear. Going beyond the limits of capital means going beyond the limits of the old 'social metabolism', going 'beyond' the entire system of private hostile property, as opposed to just removing or transforming its elements. Human progress depends on succeeding in this process. And this is closely related to the development of scientific knowledge ... and much more.

3   Cuba 2018: What May Come Next?

> Theory and practice of socialism should be developed and recorded.
>
> FIDEL ALEJANDRO CASTRO RUZ
> *One Hundred Hours with Fidel,* Chapter 19

Cuba is seeing a struggle of ideas, and the course of this struggle will decide the future of the Cuban nation, for experiencing other attempts at socialist reformation leads to fatal consequences. Cuba is now at a peculiar stage in the development of the process of socialist transformation: it is undergoing *a radical restructuring of the entire system of public relations.* We observe the transformation in all elements of the *functioning* of the process of production and reproduction of public life.

The reform is referred to as the 'process of renewing the economic model', the foundations of which are set out in The Conceptualization of the

Socio-economic Model of Cuban Socialist Development. In this regard, there are important documents, such as Directions of Economic and Social Policy of the Party and the Revolution until 2021 and Fundamentals of the National Plan for Economic and Social Development until 2030: Vision for the Nation, Axes and Strategic Sectors.

The process of socialist transformation in Cuba has so far been driven by a complex of forces. This system results from the resolution of contradictions inherent in *socialist transformations* as the initial processes of the society's *communist transformation under* Cuba's *special circumstances*. These circumstances were largely determined by Cuba's relations with various US governments, which have consistently sought to achieve their goals with respect to Cuba since the eighteenth century.

Cuba began its socialist path from the state of *a country that did not develop*: it is *a dynamic state* – not just an 'undeveloped country' – the content of which is *not limited to economic backwardness and is determined not only by the peculiarity of structural internal features*; *external relations* play a decisive role in it. In overcoming this situation, it is very important to consistently apply the Marxist understanding of productive forces' development. In the case of Cuba, this situation was also determined by the fact that until January 1, 1959 the country was actually a neo-colony of the United States.

In the current process of reforms, we see *objectively* a radical transformation of the foundations and *the Cuban system of property*, which constitutes *the core of the system of production and reproduction of life* adopted by the Cuban society. The reform begins in the context that results from the interaction of *targeted changes based on conscious, well-thought-out economic actions which began in 1990s and sought to overcome the crisis of the 'special period'*. Such changes interact with others, and *some of them* deliberately have a detrimental effect on the socialist development. An *unstable context* is now emerging in Cuba: in mathematical and physical terms, it is a special 'inflection point' in the course of Cuban socialist development.

There is one very important feature of the current moment that must be borne in mind when we analyze ongoing processes and especially when we conceptually develop these processes and justify the direction of reforms and decisions made. Cuba has already gone relatively far down the path of socialist transformations, with its successes, shortcomings and mistakes, under special external geopolitical conditions that cannot be ignored, and which significantly influenced internal processes.

Cuba has been developing *its own public system* and preserving special public relations in production and reproduction. These relations provided the basis for the country's response to the severe economic crisis of the 1990s and ensured that Cuba did not collapse and did not dismantle this system, in spite of experiencing strong shocks in all its constituent elements. This situation is dramatically different from the one that Cub a found itself in after the victory of the 1959 revolution.

Now it is necessary to significantly 'correct the course' and improve (in accordance with our experience and taking into account the experience of other countries) all elements of the *development* process, the structure and features of the system's *functioning*, while maintaining the essence of the strategic goal: *the process of communist emancipation*. It would be a gross mistake to think that now it is possible to 'start from scratch' and completely abandon the achieved level of *public relations*, as if everything that has been done is 'worthless'.

Now we need to move to a new level. It is necessary to deliberately and purposefully *break away* from the old *way of production's functioning and reproduction of the system of public relations, while maintaining the continuity* of the development of emerging socialist relations. It is necessary to consolidate everything positive that has been achieved over more than 60 years and completely eliminate all the causes of errors and shortcomings in order to achieve harmony and stability in actions that determine the pace and content of changes, *while ensuring that progress is self-sustaining*.

Today, more than ever, it is important to act carefully in the process of resolving all the contradictions of the public life and to look ahead. In order to achieve this, it is necessary to study as accurately and closely as possible *all potential trends in the processes of societal development and finds ways to resolve old and new contradictions*. It is necessary to abandon spontaneity, improvisation and voluntarism in decision-making. We must have a clear idea of the desired future not as a predetermined scheme, but as a constantly refined picture.

The slogan of reforms has been put forward during the socialist transformation in Cuba under different names more than once but has not been termed 'the reform'. Constant calls for 'a correction' and for a return to attempts at resolving old problems that have gone unresolved during prior attempts make us pay attention to the fact that "an organism that is constantly undergoing corrections may, as such, cease to exist" (see Alonso Arrastía, et al., 2001: 101). This is a real threat to our process of socialist transformation.

In the current process of 'correction', it is necessary to pay attention to two essential components of public development as a whole, which are even more significant in the context of communist transformations and *are interpreted differently in political science and in practice*:

- optimization of the *functioning and development of the system of productive forces perceived as achievements in the widest range of spheres of the public life*.
- improvement of political activity. We require *intensification of people's socialist participation* in the public process and – closely related to such intensification – improved *interaction between politics and the economy in the process of socialist building*.

In the current reform process, there is *an emphasis on the economy*, on searching for ways to achieve the necessary development results, *on better results of the functioning* of our system of production forces and on the result of the production of material goods and services. And this approach is assessed using narrow criteria of profitability and economic efficiency.

Processes in the economy are often perceived merely as processes of *obtaining new resources* as opposed to *socio-economic processes* that produce and reproduce relations between individuals in economic structures and in the society as a whole. There have been deficiencies in analyzing the consequences of *how the defining processes of functioning and development of material production pan out as elements of the property system; and core of the process of production and reproduction of people themselves and learning about human nature*.

In this sense, there are tendencies towards the formation of potentially conflict situations in the correlation between *short-term goals pertaining to the development of productive forces*, achievement of quick economic results and *strategic goals of ensuring socialist public development inextricably linked with the tasks of ensuring Cuba's existence as an independent nation*.

These contradictions are exacerbated by the fact that, in contrast to previous reform processes, the current 'renewal process' exhibits shortcomings in actions targeting systemic improvement of political activity. We require new theoretical approaches to economic and political activity, and on this basis there is a demand for new practice in the Cuban transformation process. Many may fund it paradoxical that the Cuban process perceives itself as consistently following the ideas of Marxism. Some will say that 'the truth in its entirety has already been said by Marx and Engels', while others will argue that what was said by Marx and Engels is already outdated'. But both statements are incorrect. Marx demanded the development of political economy through the analysis of labor, and together with Engels they proposed ideas that need to be analyzed and developed holistically, and not by selecting fragments of the text, often without even taking into account the nature of the text. They laid the foundation for movement towards a new economy associated with a new content of politics as part of a new method of production and development of social relations. The ideas of 'noonomy' that study changes in material production, the results of scientific knowledge and technologies in their relationship with social relations can undoubtedly make a significant contribution to movement along a new path, the path of actual 'human emancipation'.

We imply a systemic improvement of political activity, which is required by the very process of revolutionary transformations. This will become a transition to the *necessary and possible* level in our context. We need economic growth backed by engaging in politics those individuals who are *interested in the socialist development of society*, in the process of *socialist management of economic transformations* and in countering all threats and difficulties. *We need a new content of politics during the socialist transformation of the society with the 'disappearance of the state', 'disappearance of classes', with the transformation of the 'market – planning' combination, etc.*

In Cuba, the essence of this process is to improve (in accordance with the National Vision, which was analyzed and accepted by the majority of Cubans following the Seventh Congress of the Communist Party of Cuba) the functioning of the *unity* of the Communist Party of Cuba and the form of state organization – the People's Power System. They must act in unity with our system of public organizations, especially trade unions. But at the moment, the shortcomings and mistakes exposed during previous reform processes persist and reproduce, and sometimes exacerbate.

The critical 'spirit' – the approach which stipulates systematic critical analysis and implementation of everything necessary in order to ensure continuous pursuit of improvement – must be an integral part of our process of socialist transformations, and in this sense, it must be a constant and integral part of this process. This approach was expressed when Fidel Castro defined the content of the 'Revolution' concept, which we consider to be a precise definition of what should characterize a *socialist revolution*.[3]

---

3   In his speech on May 1, 2000, Fidel Castro said, "Revolution means to have a sense of history; it is changing everything that must be changed; it is full equality and freedom; it is being treated and treating others like human beings; it is achieving emancipation by ourselves and through our own efforts; it is challenging powerful dominant forces from within and without the social and national milieu; it is defending the values in which we believe at the cost of any sacrifice; it is modesty, selflessness, altruism, solidarity and heroism; it is fighting with courage, intelligence and realism; it is never lying or violating ethical principles; it is a profound conviction that there is no power in the world that can crush the power of truth and ideas. Revolution means unity; it is independence, it is fighting for our dreams of justice for Cuba and for the world, which is the foundation of our patriotism, our socialism and our internationalism." (Speech by Dr. Fidel Castro Ruz, 2000).

But along with consistent revolutionary critics, there are those who conform to changes seeking personal gain and unconditional supporters of what is "proposed" by the authorities. Neither are helping to advance the reform process. Their actions contradict the principles and approaches that were outlined by the leaders of the revolution at the previous phases of the reform processes. Accepting everything that comes from the authorities without its critical analysis means to deny the true spirit of socialist transformations, to actually act against what Fidel and Raúl Castro have repeatedly required from all of us. Ultimately, this approach does not help to correct mistakes, but, on the contrary, makes them worse.

Moreover, we are currently seeing conservative tendencies engaged in contradictory interaction with 'extreme perestroika' tendencies. All of them *agree* on the approach justifying the need to try to achieve *"socialism that is possible under our circumstances,"* and they may be concealing regressive tendencies and direct attempts at opposing socialism building in Cuba. All this, of course, poses a clear threat to the current reforms, which are directly related to objective change of top leadership. The threat is growing before the announced and inevitable changes in the higher structures of the party and state following the death of Fidel.

It is necessary to ensure that our reform process proceed without splits or a "traumatic generational change". In this respect, we should heed the sad experience of the Soviet Union. A necessarily conscious process and practice, socialism demonstrates how difficult it is to change the consciousness of individuals in the course of socialist transformation. The Cuban experience, with its achievements and results, is no exception in this sense, and, therefore, the Cuban leadership has always emphasized the role of ideological work.

We now note significant shortcomings in ideological work, from conceptualization of the renewal process to the way it is presented in political speeches. The threats are now multiplying many times over because we have to resist attempts at revising our course of development, attempts which do not constitute openly expressed ideas or openly counter-revolutionary political actions. For the most part, they are presented in a veiled format as 'new', 'fresh ideas', 'necessary' for building socialism that is 'possible under our circumstances'. These ideas are presented as examples of a 'new way' for building socialism, but in fact they are introducing the values of liberalism and social democracy.

Even after the approval of the Seventh Congress documents (Conceptualización, etc.), we still lack *publicly recognized ideological conceptual guidelines* that would help formulate approaches that are necessary for the development of specific actions towards the 'desired future' to which we should aspire.

Mistakes are especially noticeable when we discuss the importance of various forms of ownership, the course of reforming the enterprise management system and the role of the market. We lack sufficiently profound analysis of the market as a *special public system* of relations. We do not have a deep understanding of the need for a new content of *state* activities, *the role of elected representatives* during the socialist transformation and their specifics at the present stage. In particular, there is no analysis of the role of the state in the new content of the public planning process.

Planning has always been interpreted as a defining feature under the socialist development and has been perceived in opposition to the *market*. Planning is the core of socialism functioning and development. But planning also exists under capitalism, and it does not reproduce 'socialism' in capitalist countries. As a market, *specifically the capital market*, it continued to characterize the entire experience of socialist transformations. So, what is the real essence of such a contradiction? Do we understand the role of market and planning in human development? What should be the combination of these phenomena in the process of socialist building? Why is the functioning of planning in the course of socialist transformation interpreted as a narrow economic process?

The reason for the reproduction of such errors is the lack of guidelines (conceptual samples) and ideas about the desired socialist reproduction of the society. This is also influenced by the emergence of some 'other landmarks' that play a prominent role in the work of our media. In this sense, it is striking how actively our press covers the activities of enterprises of new forms of ownership, (non-state and mixed, with the participation of foreign capital) highlighting their 'economic successes'. The media constantly hail the 'efficiency' and 'effectiveness' of 'new forms of economic management', and, at the same time, we do not see sufficiently profound analysis of the consequences of spreading such forms in the society and the specifics of their functioning as *special systems of socio-economic relations*.

Now there are already examples of such enterprises functioning de facto according to the rules of the crudest capitalism, with relations of cruel exploitation and the absence of social rights of illegal workers. Even if workers are officially employed, they must endure various forms of 'hidden' exploitation and failure to comply with legal requirements due to weak and ineffective public control, an insufficiently clear role of the party, trade unions and public authorities, and vague definition of the relationship between the state and different forms of ownership.

Another problem is the one-sided presentation of information by our media. For example, when reporting news from some countries that are still considered socialist, the media avoid any criticism. This contributes to the fact that this experience is presented as an impeccable example, a possible 'model' of development for our country.

The aforementioned problems and shortcomings intertwine and have a significant impact on the development of purely instrumental approaches to analyzing contradictions of our reform process. These negative features hamper clear formulation and classification of emerging contradictions and, thus, impede the development of a necessary systemic approach when making political decisions and taking targeted action during our 'renewal process'.

In particular, the identified shortcomings hamper the consolidation of the *planning process*, i.e., planning as not just a narrowly economic process, but a complex integral process that begins with individuals at the workplace, in the family, at home ... in all instances of the process of reproduction of the public life *as a holistic process.*

We see the creation of conditions for an ever-wider application of narrow, pragmatic approaches that allow for the resolution of specific problems within our system of productive forces. But they risk creating new subjects and social practices that do not reproduce the socialist nature of the society, but will try to participate in the political life and become involved in political activity. This can become a factor in the decomposition of the very 'model' that created the conditions for their emergence and existence and will ultimately begin to reproduce the tendencies that undermine socialism.

Such approaches are clearly manifested when party documents do not accurately interpret the topic of property, commodity-money relations, market as a system, planning as a social process, their place and role in the process of production and reproduction from the moment of creating material foundations of life to ideals and spiritual components of the society's socialist transformation.

The documents proclaim that the system of socialist planning is the *main means for managing the national economy,* and it is necessary to take into account changes in the *methodological, organizational and managerial aspects* of planning. This involves *taking into account the functioning of the market, influencing it depending on its characteristics,* mastering various forms of sectoral and territorial planning and developing new methods of control, which opens up new potential opportunities for the development of public relations.

Nevertheless, planning continues to be interpreted *in a narrow sense,* as an essentially economic and technical process. Without denying that it touches upon all spheres of the social life, it is argued that the planning process covers, first and foremost, *production of material goods and technical ways of organizing it.* At the same time, the role of individuals in all manifestations of their public life is not sufficiently considered, and there is no interpretation of the planning process as a truly public process from the moment of its very genesis and deployment.

The understanding of commodity-money relations and the role of the market in our society remains at the level of discussions of the past, which have already proved their inconsistency and incompatibility with the task of creating premises for successful socialist transformations. These approaches suggest that we use a '*controlled*' market or separate elements of the market in our economy, assuming that '*under the socialist conditions*' they will not have the same consequences as under capitalism. Such approaches, which do not even explain how planning will be '*combined with the market*' and do not account for '*its peculiarities*', forget about the essence of the market as a dynamic system of relations. This is fraught with risks and real threats in Cuba's specific circumstances. In addition, it is necessary to take into account the historical experience of socialist transformations, which led in a number of countries to the restoration of capitalism in the twentieth century. These issues are very important when introducing new forms of ownership and when changing state ownership formats.

Little attention is paid to emerging changes in socio-economic relations: the *economic* process ('management') is inseparable from the system of property relations and constitutes its essential element. We are lacking the necessary analysis of social consequences, which are already objectively manifested in the growth of differentiation in people's standard of living despite the fact that the result of individuals' selfish and 'new philistine' behavior – as opposed to the result of one's own labor, efforts and benefit to the society – are becoming significant factors in increasing personal wealth.

Such changes, along with other consequences, require a different role of the state compared against its role before the emergence of new forms of ownership. This state should not just act as a 'regulator state' or an external 'coordinator', as some suggest. This state should be a *system* through which *everyone participates in public governance under the efficient leadership of all those interested in socialist transformations.*

Implementation of economic reforms has a significant effect on the entire system of public relations, from material production to ideology. As the experience of the USSR and Central and Eastern European countries indicates, such changes significantly affect the core of the system of production and reproduction of public life, and mistakes in this area can strategically have negative consequences.

The process of implementing the main provisions of party documents serves as the foundation of the current 'renewal process', which objectively changes the public system as a whole. But this process is not systemic, nor is it complex. The 'renewal process' is a fundamental change in *all public and pro-duction relations within the Cuban socialism. It stipulates radical transformation* of the system of public relations from purely objective to ideological relations. *Objectively operating system of property in Cuba is being reformed.*

We need to achieve the hegemony of the system of *state enterprises* (in general, *public property* in all its manifestations) which will be 'renewed' after the reform and would play the pivotal role in articulating various forms of ownership. This is a *necessary result and a prerequisite* for an effective process of public planning *as a collective building effort starting from individuals as manufacturers and consumers.*

In order to achieve synergy of launched transformations' effects, all *political decisions and targeted actions* should be systematically *thought out and implemented*, based on the leading role of the following *key public actors*: (1) workforce (2) territorial units; (3) the state as a social institution capable of expressing the actions of individuals in the production and reproduction of a new nature of public life.

Taking into account the external context of the Cuban transformation process, special attention should be paid to 'normalization' of relations with the US government, which officially began on December 17, 2014. The very use of the term 'normalization' has ideological implications, as demonstrated by events in Cuba and Trump's actions. We have no room for error, just as we have no right to be naive. It is also necessary to account for the situation around Cuba, e.g., potential changes in Venezuela and Latin America in general.

Last, but not least, even while agreeing that the party documents provide an important basis for working on changes, we have to admit that there are very serious shortcomings in their conceptual basis and their conceptualization. By overcoming these shortcomings, we could help ensure broader and more efficient implementation of transformational goals by developing and enriching their interaction with more precisely and accurately defined contradictions of reality which we want to influence. This would create a *consistently systematic approach* to the development of political decisions and the implementation of targeted actions. Such mistakes allow for the strengthening of tendencies towards improvisation and voluntarism and determine the lack of coherence in the process of renewal, which hampers effective reformation of the *system of public relations.*

We do not suggest final or universal answers to the questions considered herein, nor a fully developed and complete theory that would supply answers required for practical implementation, i.e., what needs to be changed and how it can be done. We believe it is necessary to develop an integral and systemic view of the processes occurring within the system and in its environment resulting from the interaction between a constant and continuous analysis of reality and its contradictions, on the one hand, and the analysis of proposals for reforming the system, on the other hand. This suggests close interaction of all individuals interested in strengthening the process of socialist development and our public institutions as subjects and objects of the necessary changes. We must resolutely reject what does not support or even contradicts the strategic goal of transformations and define those tactical steps that will promote the achievement of strategic goals without improvisation or voluntarism.

Improvisation and voluntarism ultimately only lead to mistakes and failures, which, as demonstrated by the experience of other attempts at socialist reformation, has fatal consequences. *It is not enough to realize that a lot needs to be changed; it is not enough to be dissatisfied with the current state of affairs and seek to introduce a different arrangement. We need a clear idea of what needs to be changed, for what purpose, in what direction and how. It is particularly important to define all this in the course of a discussion involving all subjects interested in the socialist process.*

Cuba today needs economic changes required to maintain and effectively stimulate socialist development. But they must be accompanied and, if possible, preceded by political changes. This is a complex dialectical interaction. If you do not pay attention to this problem, it can lead engender trends which go against the socialist trajectory of development. We must admit that such tendencies are already present in the Cuban society and find their reflection in selfish behavior with the reproduction of *individualized* individuals who egotistically think exclusively about themselves.

The fight of Cubans' ideas continues in more difficult conditions than ever before. And in this fight, the decisive role is attributed to sciences, in particular social sciences, which provide the framework for the development of the economy per se in close interaction with political science and other sciences.

References

Alonso Arrastía, F., Alhama Belamaric, R. y Cuevas Cañizares, R. (2001). *Perfeccionamiento empresarial. Realidades y retos.* Playa, Cuba: Editorial de Ciencias Sociales.

Bodrunov, S.D. (ed.) (2017) *Galbraith Restored.* Moscow: Kul'turnaia revoliutsiia.

Bodrunov, S.D. (2018a) *Noonomy.* Moscow: Kul'turnaia revoliutsiia.

Bodrunov, S.D. (2018b) Noonomy. The future: fourth technological revolution requires profound economic and social changes. *Ekonomicheskoe vozrozhdenie Rossii* 2: 5–13.

Bodrunov, S.D. (2019) Noonomy: The conceptual basis of the new development paradigm. *Journal of New Economy*. 20(1): 5–12, DOI: 10.29141/2073-1019-2019-20-1-1.

Bodrunov, S.D. (2020) *Noonomía*. Mexico: Plaza y Valdés S. A. Editores.

Las frases de Fidel Castro (2016). Available (consulted 25 August, 2021) at https://www.vozdeamerica.com/estadosunidos/fidel-castro-frases-celebres-hasta-la-victoria-siempre.

Lenin, V.I. (1962) The Attitude Towards Bourgeois Parties. In: Lenin, V.I. *Collected Works*. Vol. 12. Moscow: Foreign Languages Publishing House, 489–509.

Marx, K. (1955). Chapter Two: The Metaphysics of Political Economy. Section 4: Property or Ground Rent. In: Marx, K. *The Poverty of Philosophy*. Moscow: Progress Publishers, 173–187.

Marx, K., and Engels, F. (1955) *The Communist Manifesto*. Ed. by S.H. Beer. New York, NY: Appleton-Century-Crofts, Inc.

Speech by Dr. Fidel Castro Ruz, President of the Republic of Cuba, at the mass rally called by the Cuban youths, students and workers on the occasion of the International Labor Day at the Revolution Square. May Day, 2000 (2000). Available (consulted 25 August, 2021) at: http://www.fidelcastro.cu/en/discursos/speech-mass-rally-called-cuban-youths-students-and-workers-revolution-square-occasion.

PART 3

Noonomy: Reflections of Political Economy

∵

CHAPTER 8

Noonomy and Geopolitical Economy
Natural Allies

Radhika Desai

Modern thinking about the good society has inevitably involved the conception of plenty created by the development of the social productive capacities of human societies that has been advancing so spectacularly for centuries now. This is true whether we think of Marx and Engels's vision of 'Scientific' as opposed to 'Utopian' socialism (Engels 1970[1880]) or of Keynes's (1963[1930]) vision of the 'Economic possibilities for our Grandchildren'. Production and its technology were critical. Though in our own times ecological challenges – of climate change, biodiversity loss and pollution – have caused many to speak of 'degrowth' (Victor, 2008 is a persuasive argument), and while these perspectives are certainly right to say point to the environmental consequences of growth and of the endless and mindless desire to consume, we must make at least three caveats. First, over the neoliberal decades, growth has been slower even as ecological damage has accelerated. Clearly, low growth *per se* is not synonymous with environmental protection. Depending on how growth is measures, a very green economy that cuts down on resource and land use and even eliminates fossil fuel consumption could register as growth. Second, the challenges themselves imply better technology that works in harmony with the natural environment even without growth. So socially determined priorities for production and a cultural sphere free of the commercial impulses that stimulate meaningless and socially destructive consumption will be critically necessary. Finally, action on the environment therefore assumes, even if this is not always specified in so many words, a democratically planned economy of precisely the sort that Marx or Keynes had in mind.

The West faces, however, some very critical obstacles to achieving these objectives. Mainstream discourses, refined over four decades of neoliberalism, merely celebrate capitalism, giving it credit for delivering the pinnacles of growth and technological development without overall or centralised planning. Of course, one expects little else from it. However, over the same neoliberal decades, the Western left has evolved its own form of neoliberalism, a consensus against planning and against party politics to bring it about. Instead, it adheres to what I have called Proudhonist economics of small, decentralised production and a party-less network politics or small, local and single-issue groups, connected, if at all, only on loose networks (Desai, 2011). Thanks to the incursion of the Trojan horse of neoclassical economics into the very citadels of Marxism within a decade or two of the latter's emergence (on this and its ruinous long-term effects on Western Marxism, see Desai, 2010, 2016, 2017, 2020a, 2020b), most of the Western left, including its Marxist core, indeed, often led by its Marxist core, considers capitalism a practically Promethean system. It is considered superior to any other, certainly any planned system, in terms of its ability to develop social productive capacities, or, to put it in Marxist terms, to develop the forces of production.

The fall of the Berlin Wall and the disintegration of the USSR, though it happened for reasons quite independent of Western pressure or Western economic success (Kotz, 1997), prompted an entirely unwarranted Western triumphalism, complete with announcements that history had reached its terminus in capitalism and liberal democracy. This too strengthened the tendency of the Western left to distance itself from any notion of centralized planning or parties.

What is astonishing is that this view was strengthened over the neoliberal decades, precisely when it should have taken a beating. After all, neoliberal policies were unable to revive capitalism after its growth slowed down in the 1970s (Brenner, 1998, 2009) despite increasing the freedoms of capital to revive its 'animal spirits', removing the 'dead hand' of the state and beating back union power. Worse, more state-interventionist and planned economies, led by China with its Communist party-state and including the other BRIC economies, grew faster in the same decades (Desai, 2013b). Already by the end of the 2000s, leading opinion-makers were preparing Western countries for their impending eclipse as the world's dominant nations (O'Neill, 2001). This process only accelerated after 2008 when decades of financializations – the series of international and national financial bubbles whose bursting punctuated the progress of neoliberalism with remarkable regularity – which had been delivering at least weak growth through their 'wealth effects' (while also holding up the dollar's value by creating artificial financial demand for it, see Desai, 2013a) peaked. Thereafter, though international financial flows recovered after their precipitous drop, they remained over 65 percent short of their 2007 peak and growth in the West, already slow throughout the neoliberal decades, slowed to a barely crawling pace. Thanks to the policy combination of austerity for the many and bailouts and central banks support for the tiny financial elites, electorates in leading neoliberal countries – not just in small countries of less moment such as Hungary – elected insalubrious populist leaders who could only make matters worse.

Having nursed the Promethean conception of capitalism so long, it is no wonder that the Western left finds itself dumbfounded (Desai, 2020c) by the pandemic and its exposure of the weaknesses of Western neoliberal financialised economies and their policies. The failing public health systems, gutted by decades of neoliberal underfunding, corporatization, privatization and contracting out, could not be expected to deal with the onslaught of the virus. Ironically, considering they were supposed to protect the people, they now had to be protected by the people staying in their homes, unable to work, study or play (Desai, 2020e). Under the lockdowns that ensued, neoliberal economies were devastated. Over the decades, they had outsourced the most essential production to lower wage locations and now found themselves unable to procure essentials, including medical essentials. Meanwhile, reliant on sucking in monopoly and financial rents from the world over, their own economies were geared to the asset-income fuelled consumption of the rich and the debt fuelled consumption of the rest. This had led to an economy geared to producing inessential 'frills' – travel, tourism, restaurants, personal services – that were precisely the worst affected by the lockdowns.

After remaining in denial for weeks, wasting precious time, neoliberal governments responded only after the seriousness of the situation could no longer be denied. When they did finally respond, they did so in true neoliberal fashion, to save the financial sector alone. Their greatest public effort consisted in an almost diarrheal issuance of Central bank liquidity. It came first in response to the expected and then to the real fall in asset markets in March – *inter alia* those for stocks, bonds and derivatives. In doing so, for instance, the Federal Reserve managed to use up in a few weeks all the 'ammunition' it had managed to save over the previous many years by incrementally raising interest rates, carefully limiting the pain it inflicted the coddled financial sector.

The liquidity injection was so great that, over the next two months, it wiped out nearly all the losses incurred in March. Needless today, this liquidity-fueled market recovery had no basis in the actually rapidly deteriorating economy. Even the financial press did not expect it to last (Desai, 2020g; *Financial Times,* 2020). However, at least the reckoning had been postponed and the assets of the financial sector and the elite preserved and even increased.

Beyond this, however, neoliberal governments could not do much. Economies tanked under lockdowns as much as due to the chaotic public responses that could barely control COVID-19. Discontent swelled. Amid all this the performance of China in particular, with its planned economy in control of the pandemic and resuming growth, could not form a sharper contrast. Its technological prowess, already clear in the years before the pandemic, was no longer tolerable. Three months into the pandemic, with the West once again threatened by a potentially superior socialist productive power, a New Cold War was declared against China.

Clearly, the path on which neoliberal capitalism was set is overdue for a major course correction. There is already much talk about 'building back better' and a whole slew of policy ideas for how to do so, whether sound or not: Modern Monetary Theory, Universal Basic Income, redesigning cities, transforming employment. The list is long. However, we will also need larger ideas that explain how and why capitalism got into this mess and how to get out of it. Among the more critically important are Noonomy and Geopolitical Economy and, as this paper argues, the two are natural allies. They are jointly able to point progressive forces to the real dynamics involved in the expansion of the world' productive capacities.

Noonomy explores the conditions of development of productive capacities, historically and in twenty-first century conditions, particularly how the world may transition towards what it calls the New Industrial Society 2.0. It recognises that these conditions are social and purely 'economic rationality' of private ownership can only have a predatory relation with them. Geopolitical economy shows, by contrast, how, historically, the social and state contribution has been and has hand to be the key in expanding productive capacities of countries around the world. While many fail, there is no other path to success than getting it right. Geopolitical Economy can explain how and why the leading neoliberal nations got things so wrong and how and why China got it right. Thus, a considerable part of the explanation of why the neoliberal, financialised capitalist world finds itself in the mess it does, and of mapping the route out of it lies in the intersection of Noonomy and Geopolitical Economy. Let us take them in turn.

1   Noonomy

In proposing the science of Noonomy (Bodrunov, 2018b), Sergey Bodrunov develops Marx's insights into human history as that of the development of the forces of production and therefore of human knowledge and technology. He joins that with currents of European thought that have long emphasized the critical role of knowledge in human history and in the development of human productive capacities through ideas of the noosphere. He defines Noonomy as a system of economic management in which relations among people not connected with material production will be of paramount importance. It will form a basis, a foundation of the future society which, however, may become a reality with the rational development of human civilization (Bodrunov, 2018a).

Noonomy involves 'the transition to knowledge-intensive material production'. While there is much talk today of 'the knowledge economy', 'cognitive capitalism', the 'fifth Kondratieff' and a new industrial revolution of information and communications technologies, Bodrunov is aware that contemporary changes and transitions are a matter of degree, not quality.

Knowledge has always been at the centre of production, as Marx knew well. He opened his chapter distinguishing the Labour Process, a trans historical reality, and the valorisation process, a process specific to capitalism, with the famous assertion that labour in the first sense is simply the 'metabolism' (283) between humans and nature. While the original humans might have engaged in this metabolism instinctively, the essence of humankind is that it soon develops labour into an exclusively human trait that also transforms humankind. In this exclusively human form, labour always involves knowledge. As Marx put it in his famous distinction between bees and architects,

> ... what distinguishes the worst architect from the best of bees is that the architect builds the cell in his mind before he constructs it in wax. At the end of every labour process, a result emerges which had already been conceived by the worker at the beginning, hence already existed ideally.
>
> MARX, (1867[1977]): 284

Interestingly, Marx goes on to remark that

> The writers of history have so far ·paid very little attention to the development of material production, which is the basis of all social life, and therefore of all real history. But prehistoric times at any rate have been classified on the basis of the investigations of natural science, rather than so-called historical research. Prehistory has been divided, according to the materials used to make tools and weapons, into the Stone Age, the Bronze Age and the Iron Age.
>
> MARX, (1867[1977]): 284

Though Marx does not say this explicitly, he appears to imply that the more consciously human beings devise their labour processes, the more their history encompasses the age of noonomy.

This process, which has always involved changes in the labour process and, by the industrial age, in industrial production, has brought us today to a new stage. We are witnessing 'a drastic reduction in the role of material factors of production, [and] an increase in the role of knowledge, acceleration of scientific and technological progress, and many other things' (Bodrunov, 2018a).

Moreover, the development of human knowledge, its processing and transmission, are themselves becoming branches of human economic activity, this is partly signified by the development of the information and communications technology sector. According to Bodrunov, Information/communication (nowadays widely known as digital) and cognitive technologies which, unlike all others, demonstrate their high capacity to penetrate technological processes of any kind, will allow them to become an integrated technological platform capable of combining diverse technologies into hybrid technological processes. In fact, information and cognitive technologies will serve as a channel for embedding knowledge in technological processes – via big data processing and artificial intelligence (Bodrunov, 2018a).

However, just as the shift from hunting and gathering to agriculture did not eliminate the former activity any more than the shift from agriculture from industry involved, or could involve, as elimination of agriculture, so the growing role of knowledge does not mean that purely intellectual activity will displace or replace material production, as post-industrialists believed. Rather, it means that material production will itself become much more knowledge intensive. As a result, there will come a time when the knowledge-related portion of many mass products will, so to say, begin to substantially outweigh the material portion (Bodrunov, 2018a).

Or, to put it in different words, while of course manufacturing remains a critical economic sector in developed countries ..., services dominate the contemporary economy. Production, including the production of goods, also takes on new, creative and cultural, forms (Freeman, 2008). While the number of workers primarily deploying creative, cognitive or knowledge skills has grown, practically all work now requires these skills to some extent (Bakshi, Desai, Freeman).

What does all this imply for the world, particularly, western economies and the impasse they face today? The 'Long Downturn' that set in around 1970s remained unresolved by the new neoliberal policy-paradigm. Growth remained slow (while also taking on, as we have seen, an environmentally even more destructive character). After 2008, it appeared to enter into an even more serious stagnation that has since been dubbed a 'New Normal'. For Bodrunov, though financialization and other neoliberal phenomena, such as rising inequality or insufficient effective demand may have played a role, the real problem is that *we have reached the limit of the existing development model's efficiency* .... Profound reforms are necessary' (Bodrunov, 2018b: 57). Neither the old model not its 'methods for overcoming crisis' work any longer. The results include: 'a global decline in investment, volatile demand and prices in the energy markets, volatility of unsecured currencies, lack of growth

in the revenue of the majority of the population of the developed countries
…, overall universal perplexity … market fluctuations, growing tensions and …
the appearance of seemingly unexpected leaders such as Donald Trump in the
United States' (Bodrunov, 2018b: 57–80).

What is needed is a transition to a new phase of the integration of knowledge in production, what Bodrunov, following John Kenneth Galbraith calls
the New Industrial Society 2.1. Once it is in place, we can look forward to
increasingly seamless integration of knowledge into production and increasingly friction-free forms of ever more efficient production that also eliminate
ecological destruction from the cycles of production and distribution.

One critical implication of this, more implicit than explicit, is that while
considerable progress towards it is already possible, it can only take limited
and distorted forms within the confines of capitalism, particularly in its current form of neoliberal, financialized capitalism and its tendency to subject
everything to narrow economic rationality. The sort of transition envisaged in
noonomy is only possible through extensive state intervention.

This is where geopolitical economy, with its emphasis on the 'materiality
of nations' comes in. It demonstrates that historically state intervention has
been critical to the development of the productive capacities of all societies
chiefly because the dynamic of capitalist international relations has con-
fronted them with the stark choice of developing them in this fashion or facing
subordination.

2   Geopolitical Economy

Geopolitical Economy (Desai, 2013a) is a new approach to understanding
world affairs. It places states at its centre by insisting on what may be called
the 'materiality of nations': the critical role states play in economies. Most
would consider it a statement of the obvious truth for all economies but the
capitalist. However, it is particularly true of capitalist ones. States have played
a central role not only in their foundation – something which liberals readily
recognise and even valorise in their celebration of the bourgeois revolutions
that brought them into being – but in their ongoing stability and development.

We can best appreciate the significance of geopolitical economy against
the background of reigning understandings of world affairs such as 'globalization' and US 'hegemony' or 'empire'. They all view the world economy in what
Friedrich List (List, 1856 [1841]) called 'cosmopolitan' terms in which states play
no roles, there are not national economies, and the world economy is a seam-
lessly unified whole. Its division into numerous states and national economies

is considered at best incidental and irrelevant and at worst it is entirely ignored. In the free trade and globalization paradigms, markets unify the world economy and no states matter. In the US hegemony or empire paradigms, a single world power unifies the world economy and only one state matters.

These approaches never gave an accurate account of the evolution of the world of capitalism or that of relations between its national states and economies. If they reigned, they did so as international ideologies, the international equivalent of 'ruling ideas'.

If the ruling ideas of any society are the ideas of the ruling classes, ideas that serve their interests and maintain their power, then the ruling ideas about the world order would understandably tend to be those of the dominant powers. They tend to be useful in perpetuating their dominance, in particular by mystifying the real sources of national wealth and power. Whichever form they take, their purpose is to perpetuate the dominance of already advanced countries.

By contrast, geopolitical economy points to realities that undermine that dominance and spread productive power around the world. Whereas they are, like their sister discipline of international relations, 'disciplines of Western Supremacy' (Van der Pijl, 2014), geopolitical economy is the discipline of multipolarity (Desai, 2015).

It argues, first and foremost that states play a critical role in the evolution of capitalist economies. As Marx understood from his study of Pre-capitalist Social Formations (Hobsbawm 1964), capitalist economies are very unnatural social formations, so much so that it has needed revolutions to establish them (Desai and Heller, 2020). Though the capitalist utopia (Polanyi 1985[1944]) is one of free markets unencumbered by states, particularly states that owe any scrap of their legitimacy to the non-capitalist working masses, in reality, capitalism has never been free of social and state regulation. For one thing, all capitalist societies emerge from non-capitalist milieus whose integument they never entirely shed. Just as important are capitalism's contradictions – both the horizontal ones arising from intra-capitalist class relations of competition and the vertical ones arising from the inter-class relations of exploitation and class struggle. They result in crises and instability, economic and political, and require state action to stabilise and reorganise capitalism regularly (Desai, 2010, 2020b). Such state actions take both domestic and international forms and the two are deeply interrelated.

The latter form of state action – the international – adds a final critical reason why states have had critical material roles in the capitalist world. It also explains why these roles have never permitted the utopia of a stateless or single state cosmopolitan world domain of capitalism to be realised. The explanation geopolitical economy provides goes thus.

Marx and Engels considered the world's division into nations as important as its division into classes. However, Marx's successors have faced considerable obstacles in the path to retrieving and developing this part of their legacy: the influence of neoclassical economics on Marxism (for further elaborations see Desai, 2010, 2016, 2017, 2020a; 2020d). It led to the implicit or explicit acceptance of the two Ricardian Fictions – Say's Law and Comparative Advantage – denying both capitalisms' contradictions and the imperialist imperatives that emerge from them – by most Marxists and led them to accept cosmopolitan understandings of the world economy and even extol Marx (falsely) as their precursor. While some notions of capitalist exploitation have persisted, largely in sociological and or political forms, most Marxist economists also question Marx's value analysis, claim that he never argued that capitalism tended to lack adequate demand and that he was wrong about the tendency of the rate of profits to fall. The result has been a contradiction-free and cosmopolitan conception of capitalism that attributes to it a Promethean productivity reminiscent more of Schumpeter than Marx.

In reality, not only have the manifold contradictions led capitalist societies to intervene more or less constantly to manage and stabilize capitalism, its international dynamics have added further weighty imperatives for state intervention in economies to develop their productive capacities.

These imperatives have their origin in the tendency of capitalist states to seek to externalise the consequences of the contradictions and crises and to compete with one another in inflecting them colonies and/or weaker states (semi-colonies). To develop the language of uneven and combined development (Trotsky, 1934), which Marx and Engels as well as many other Marxists shared (Desai, 2013a), dominant states seek to maintain the unevenness and *complementarity* that exists between their more productive and subordinate nations' less productive economies. Some countries are, however, able and willing to resist such subjection, imminent or actual, through state-directed development or combined development – using, *inter alia*, protection, state aid, channelling of credit, industrial policy and state investment in education, research and innovation – aimed at establishing *similarity* of productive structures. As a long line of developmental state theorists (for instance, Amsden, 1992, 2007; Wade, 1990; Chang, 2002) have pointed out, not all such attempts succeed but without them, there is not development of productive capacity.

Indeed, this dialectic of capitalist international relations between dominant and contender nations, not markets nor the imperial expansion of capitalism, has been solely responsible for spreading productive capacity around the world. By doing so, it had already made the world multipolar with the industrialization of the first challengers to UK original industrial and imperial supremacy, Germany, the US and Japan in the 1870s. The Russian Revolution introduced contender industrialization in a new, non-capitalist or 'socialist' form which has since spread to China and other countries. In the century and a half since the 1870s, therefore, multipolarity has only advanced further, including through the industrialization of the USSR, to the contemporary rise of China, the resurgence of post-Communist Russia and the emergence of other economies, including the BRIC economies, today.

Marx and Engels understood the economic role of states (Desai, 2017) though they did not get around to developing it further. Marx, in particularly, did not finish the planned volume of *Capital* where it would have. A second generation of Marxists would all emphasise how critical state's imperial activities were for capitalism in general (Rosa Luxemburg) or how critical it has become at the 'finance', 'national' or 'monopoly' stage of capitalism (Hilferding, Bukharin and Lenin). Hilferding also developed Marx's understanding that concentrated and cartelised capitalism that was just beginning to emerge in his time was setting the stage for socialism (Desai, 2021).

If this is not widely recognised even in Marxist circles, it is because a new 'Marxist economics' had emerged within a couple of decades of the emergence of neoclassical economics. Marxists who had been trained in the new discipline before coming to Marxism were simply unable to understand just how antithetical the two were. They could only understand Marxism through the lenses of neoclassical economics and could not comprehend Marx's critical political economy, with its emphasis on the necessarily contradictory processes of value production, the irrationality of capitalism and the coercive dynamics of uneven and combined development (Desai, 2010, 2016, 2017, 2020a, 2020b).

In this context, therefore, it fell largely to non-Marxists – particularly historical and institutionalist economists, and to John Maynard Keynes, to develop their understanding of the economic role of states. In the neoliberal era their torch was carried forward by the 'developmental state' theorists such as Alice Amsden, Ha-Joon Chang, Ilene Grabel, Robert Wade and others. None of them were Marxists and their understanding was never fully theorised. However, in these dark decades, they constituted the main front of intellectual opposition to neoliberalism.

They demonstrated that the doctrine of free markets and free trade is the only surefire recipe for economic backwardness and poverty (Reinert, 2007) and that the contender industrialization of all successful industrialiser, the 'early' industrialization of England included, has required the state to play a major role. States have had to manage trade, production, credit, on domestically and international flows of goods, capital and finance. Most recently, such writers have also shown how even innovation of all sorts, including in the information and communications technology sector, usually considered a paradigm of market-based innovation, has been state supported (Mazzucato, 2015; Block, 2008).

However, geopolitical economy develops an implication of this process that the developmental state theorists did not. It is this. As multipolarity spreads, and the more states have to manage even capitalist economies, all economies become more state managed and all economies therefore become susceptible to being run by the 'non-economic' criteria that Noonomy recommends. Multipolarity, with the spread of productive power, and by implication, coercive power, also deters more and more states (barring madmen in power, which remains all real possibility as the situation in the US demonstrates), from relating to one another with war and creatives incentives for international cooperation.

In conclusion, I would like to recall that Ernest Mandel reminded us that Marx and Engels understood that the capitalism of *Capital* never refers to any real system and that a "pure" capitalism existed nowhere. Indeed, as Engels even confidently predicted that it would not be allowed to since revolutionaries would not "let it come to that" (Mandel, 1978: 68). Notwithstanding Marx's strictures to German comrades – *de te fabula narratur* and all that in the introduction to the original German edition of *Capital* – it especially did not exist in England (Anderson, 1987). Everywhere capitalism has required state support, which only grows the more multipolarity spreads. This geopolitical economy of capitalism smooths the path to noo-production. Nothing is more urgent amid the current crisis of capitalism and the New Cold Wars it has launched (Desai, 2020f).

References

Amsden, A.H. (1992) *Asia's Next Giant: South Korea and Late Industrialization.* New York: Oxford University Press.

Amsden, A.H. (2007) *Escape from Empire: The Developing World's Journey through Heaven and Hell.* Cambridge, Mass: MIT Press.

Anderson, P. (1987) Figures of Descent. *New Left Review,* I/161.

Block, F. (2008) Swimming Against the Current: The Rise of a Hidden Developmental State in the United States. *Politics & Society* 36(2) (June): 169–206.

Bodrunov, S. (2018a) Noonomy and Marx. *The Free Economy Journal.* 30 June. Available (consulted 23 August, 2021) at: http://freeconomy.ru/english/noonomy-and-marx .html.

Bodrunov, S. (2018b) *Noonomy*. Special Edition as material to discuss at the Scientific Seminar, 'Marx in a high technology era: Globalization, capital and class'. Cambridge, 26–27 October.

Brenner, R. (1998) The Economics of Global Turbulence. *New Left Review* I/229, May-June: 1–265.

Brenner, R. (2009) *What is Good for Goldman Sachs is Good for America: The Origins of the Current Crisis*. Prologue to the Spanish edition of Brenner, R. Economics of Global Turbulence (Verso, 2006). Available (consulted 23 August, 2021) at: http://www.sscnet.ucla.edu/issr/cstch/papers/BrennerCrisisTodayOctober2009.pdf.

Chang, H-J. (2002) *Kicking Away the Ladder: Development Strategy in Historical Perspective*. London: Anthem.

Desai, R. (2010) Consumption Demand in Marx and in the Current Crisis. *Research in Political Economy* 26: 101–141.

Desai, R. (2011) The New Communists of the Commons: 21st Century Proudhonists. *International Critical Thought* 2: 204–223.

Desai, R. (2013a) *Geopolitical Economy: After US Hegemony, Globalization and Empire*. London: Pluto. Future of World Capitalism Series.

Desai, R. (2013b) Brics without mortar? *The Bricspost*, 23 March. Available (consulted 23 August, 2021) at: http://thebricspost.com/brics-without-mortar/#.UvdpVLTp_Oc.

Desai, R. (2015) *Geopolitical Economy: The Discipline of Multipolarity*, Valdai Club Paper #24, 22 July 2015. Available (consulted 23 August, 2021) at: http://valdaiclub.com/a/valdai-papers/valdai_paper_24_geopolitical_economy_the_discipline_of_multipolarity/.

Desai, R. (2016) The Value of History and the History of Value. In: Turan Subasat (ed) *The Great Meltdown of 2008: Systemic, Conjunctural or Policy-created?*, Cheltenham, UK and Northampton, MA, USA: Edward Elgar Publishing, 136–158.

Desai, R. (2017) Capital at 150. *Red Pepper*, September: 48–49.

Desai, R. (2020a) Consumption demand in Marx, his crisis theories and in the current crisis. Revised and updated version of 'Consumption Demand in Marx and in the Current Crisis' (2010), published at Exploring Economics. Available (consulted 23 August, 2021) at: https://www.exploring-economics.org/en/discover/consumption-demand-in-marx-his-crisis-theories-/.

Desai, R. (2020b) Marx's Critical Political Economy, 'Marxist Economics' and Actually Occurring Revolutions against Capitalism. *Third World Quarterly*. Special Issue on Revolutions edited by Radhika Desai and Henry Heller, 41(8): 1353–1370.

Desai, R. (2020c) Know your Enemy: The Dangerous Futility of Pseudo-Philanthropic Neoliberalism. *Canadian Dimension*, 18 June. Available (consulted 23 August, 2021) at: https://canadiandimension.com/articles/view/know-your-enemy-pseudo-philanthropic-neoliberalism.

Desai, R. (2020d) Political Hope in Search fo an Agent. *Canadian Dimension*, 20 May. Available (consulted 23 August, 2021) at: https://canadiandimension.com/articles/view/political-hope-in-search-of-an-agent.

Desai, R. (2020e) From Pandemic to Political Pandemonium. *Canadian Dimension*, 14 May. Available (consulted 23 August, 2021) at: https://canadiandimension.com/articles/view/from-pandemic-to-political-pandemonium.

Desai, R. (2020f) Political Hope Rises. *Canadian Dimension*, 6 May. Available (consulted 23 August, 2021) at: https://canadiandimension.com/articles/view/politi cal-hope-rises.

Desai, R. (2020g) Why Monetary Policy is No longer Enough. *Valdai Club*, 4 May. Available (consulted 23 August, 2021) at: https://valdaiclub.com/a/highlights/why -monetary-policy-is-no-longer-enough.

Desai, R. (2021) *Finance Capital* and Contemporary Financialization. In: Dellheim, J. and Wolf, F.O. (eds). *Hilferding*. London: Macmillan Palgrave.

Desai, R. and Heller, H. (2020) Introduction: Revolutions: a twenty-first-century perspective. *Third World Quarterly*. Special Issue on Revolutions edited by Radhika Desai and Henry Heller. 41(8): 1261–1271, DOI: 10.1080/01436597.2020.1779053.

Engels, F. (1970[1880]) *Socialism: Utopian and Scientific*. In: Marx-Engels Selected Works, Vol. 3, Moscow: Progress publishers, 95–151.

Financial Times Editorial Board (2020) A market rally built on shaky foundations'. *Financial Times*, 9 June. Available (consulted 23 August, 2021) at: https://www .ft.com/content/2f0c5f56-aa5a-11ea-a766-7c300513fe47.

Freeman, A. (2008) *Culture, Creativity and Innovation in the Internet Age*. MPRA Paper 9007, University Library of Munich.

Hobsbawm, E. (1964) Introduction. In: Marx, K. *Pre-capitalist Economic Formations*. London: Lawrence and Wishart.

Keynes, J.M. (1963[1930]) Economic Possibilities for our Grandchildren. In: Keynes, J.M. *Essays in Persuasion*. New York: Norton.

Kotz, D.M. (1997) *Revolution from Above: The Demise of the Soviet System*. London: Routledge.

List, F. (1856[1841]) *National System of Political Economy*. Philadelphia: J.B. Lippincott and Co.

Mandel, E. (1978) *Introduction. Karl Marx, Capital (Vol. II)*. London: Penguin.

Marx, K. (1867[1977]) *Capital (Vol. I)*. London: Penguin.

Mazzucato, M. (2015) *The Entreprenuerial State: Debunking Public vs Private Sector Myths*. London: Public Affairs.

O'Neill, J. (2001) Building Better Global Economic BRICs. *Global Economics Paper No 66* (30 November). New York: Goldman Sachs.

Polanyi, K. (1985[1944]) *The Great Transformation*. Boston: Beacon Press.

Reinert, E.S. (2007) *How Rich Countries Got Rich and Why Poor Countries Stay Poor*. London: Constable.

Trotsky, L. (1934) *The History of the Russian Revolution*. London: Gollancz.

Van der Pijl, K. (2014) *The Discipline of Western Supremacy*. London: Pluto.

Victor, P. (2008) *Managing Without Growth: Slower by Design, not Disaster*. Cheltenham: Edward Elgar.

Wade, R. (1990) *Governing the Market: Economic Theory and the Role of Government in East Asian Industrialization*. Princeton: Princeton University Press.

CHAPTER 9

Evolution of Political Economy Subject and Method at the Dawn of Digitalization

Anatoly A. Porokhovsky

1 Target Setting

Digitalization across its spectrum has become the major technological and socio-economic phenomenon as of late. But most of its influence it exerts on the infrastructure of the economy and society. Despite the rapid and large-scale development of artificial intelligence, the role of man increases rather than reduces. Economic relations between people, while preserving their nature, are taking new forms – rational, transformed, irrational. Let us consider the following issues in order to substantiate this scientific hypothesis:

- political economy as a consistent theory;
- essence of the evolution of political economy subject and method;
- economic sense of digitalization.

The huge number of new events and phenomena at the national and global levels puts pressure on many researchers to conduct their analysis using an interdisciplinary approach. This does not mean however, that objects and subjects of individual disciplines and theories wither away. The independent voice of political economy retains its significance in full.

2 Political Economy as a Consistent Theory

Abrupt changes in the development of human civilization associated with the collapse of the Soviet Union and the formation of the overall market globalization, supported by the ubiquity of the Internet under the leadership of the American economic model and economic science, have scaled down the interest in political economy in Russia and other countries. However, the global economic crisis of 2007–2009 and economic underperformance of Russian market reforms have again updated the scientific agenda with the issue of a comprehensive solution to the accumulated systemic problems. To the surprise of many experts, it is the very political economy that can suggest such solutions, as it is the only comprehensive system of economic theory. No other theory – neither institutionalism, nor economics, behavioral or evolutionary theory, other schools, programs or trends – hold the potential for a consistent approach, as they have only the tools to analyze their limited subject areas available.

Along with the first issue of the special journal "Problems of Political Economy" in 2015, there were monographic studies (Ryazanov, 2019) and textbooks devoted entirely to the current representation of political economy (Buzgalin, Kolganov and Barashkova, 2018) published. Moreover, the books of Russian scientist S. D. Bodrunov on the radical change in the economy itself in the digital era and the increasing role of man as the major creator are receiving publicity (Bodrunov, 2018). An unusual response to the 200th anniversary of Karl Marx's birth came from the employees of the Council of Economic Advisers of the United States. In October 2018, they released a report "Opportunity Costs of Socialism", which then became a separate eighth chapter in the book "Economic Report of the President" (Economic Report ..., 2019). The authors try to prove that in the USA, many elements of socialism have already been achieved better in terms of quality and scope, than in the EU countries and Europe as a whole (Economic Report ..., 2019: 381–426). This refers to economic and political freedoms, access to healthcare, education, housing and pensions. For the first time in recent decades, an official document of the US government describes certain advantages of the socialist structure of society in a positive way.

The information space of nowadays, although subject to manipulation by major players, allows citizens of all countries, especially those with developed economies, to keep track of current events in real time. The Americans compare their lives with the Europeans, and the Europeans – with the Americans. They show little interest in any economic theories. They see their country and the world around as is. And they want to be better off. This attitude of people puts pressure on the authorities to look for new theoretical approaches to tackle growing problems.

It is only political economy within the framework of general economic theory that is characterized by the systematic formation of its categories and laws. Therefore, the process of economic development serves actually as a process of development of the entire system of political economy, rather than that of a certain category, since all its categories are complementary and mutually dependent. Should the phenomena, new to the political economy, arise, they are evaluated and determined using the coordinate system of the political economy and they find their place in it. This is what makes political economy fundamental. Therefore, despite its 400-year history, political economy still remains of relevance in the third millennium.

The fourth industrial revolution shows how complex and diverse economy is becoming as a subject of study. Private, industry-specific and functional economic theories and disciplines do their part here. The number of such disciplines continues to grow. There number of branches and areas of economy is increasing, and the mechanism of its functioning is being modified. In the context of growing digitalization and uncertainty of the future, the role of such specific disciplines as information economics, financial theory, risk and insurance theory, investment theory and audit is increasing. Such theories consider individual segments of development, rather than the economy as a whole, which is the object of political economy.

Due to globalization however, national economies, including the Russian economy, are becoming interdependent. There are special trends in the development of the world economy at large. Despite the common generic features of market economy, we can't fail to see the features of both national economic models and the world economy. The reproduction process at the international level is strongly influenced by non-economic factors – military, political, and religious. For this reason, each country sets the optimal level of openness of its economy in order to safeguard its economic health. And political economy plays a dominant role in this process.

3   The Essence of the Evolution of Subject and Method

Political economy emerged as a discipline dealing with the laws of functioning and development of national market economy. Following the first industrial revolution, market development gained a long-term industrial underpinning, which allowed the full disclosure of generic features of market economy – private property, capital, hired labor, competition, various types of markets, value and market pricing. At those times, the development of classical political economy of the manufacturing period followed in two main directions – the consistent, or a Marxist one – based on the theory of labor value, and the neoclassical one – based on the theory of marginal utility, where land, capital, and labor were regarded as equivalent factors.

In the twentieth century, the service sector started to gain more and more significance. It also became an important factor in the development of material production. As a result, the economy of developed countries took the form of the so-called service economy, because the service sector accounted in average for 75% of GDP, and the production of goods – material production – for 25%. The employment structure was distributed somewhat accordingly. The economic significance of the production of goods and the production of services has become the same in the eyes of society, although material production still remains the primary basis of the reproduction process, since no branch of the service sector can function in the absence of the products of material production. The economy and society need both goods and services – tangible and intangible benefits. Many new services have appeared in the information age. All this has shaped the subject of political economy as economic relations between people about the production, exchange, distribution, and consumption of goods and services, or benefits.

The relative reduction in the share of material production did not cause a shrinkage in the subject of political economy, since the service sector is integrated into the overall reproduction process, and an aggregate employee includes those engaged in the production of goods and services. The input-output tables and the interindustry balance across the economies of developed countries proves the significant interaction between modern areas of the national economy. At the same time, the financialization of the service sector results in the fact that the essence of economic relations, including the nature of capital, labor, money and other phenomena, is reflected in everyday life in their transformed and irrational forms. One of the irrational forms, for example, are derivative financial instruments. Many transformed forms characterize the sector of employment – hired labor, physical and mental labor, self-employment. There is an irrational expression of intellectual property.

Since political economy deals with essential categories, its major method is the one of scientific abstraction, supplemented by dialectical interaction of quantity and quality, unity and struggle of opposites. Mathematical methods of analysis help to define quantitative parameters and proportions. In the context of today, political economy also widely uses digital technologies, which may be indispensable when working with big data, analyzing stock market transactions. Yet, whatever the case, it always considers economic relations between people, because market economy views all factors as personalized.

4   The Economic Rationale of Digitalization

Digitalization is penetrating into all areas of the economy and society at a torrid pace. Moreover, it has helped to create a global digital space that has become the basis of *globalization 4.0*. The visibility of access to almost any information to anyone who has access to the Internet creates many illusions about the almightiness of the virtual world, its dominance over the reality around us. The fetishism of digitalization will throw up in the air, if we get to the bottom of its economic meaning.

Analysts of the Organization for Economic Cooperation and Development (OECD) comprehensively review the process of digitalization and from time to time issue extensive research on its impact and development paths (OECD, 2019). Special attention is paid to artificial intelligence, which has not become a mere basis of the Internet of Things, but also claims to replace people in their working places in various sectors of economy. Despite the expectations, digitalization has not resulted in any significant increase in labor productivity in any national economy. Significant productivity growth rates are observed only in the sectors of the digital economy itself – the production of computers, smartphones, servers, other electronic devices, as well as software. So far, the growth rate of labor productivity in country terms at fourth industrial revolution is lower than that at each of the three previous industrial revolutions. Economically, this means that digitalization has most impact on the infrastructure of the economy, that is on the environment of its development, including the employment market.

It was as early as at the first industrial revolution, that such a form of employment as working from home appeared. It has begun to rapidly proliferate in the context of today. It may seem that a person becomes more independent of the employer (capital or the state) in case of remote employment and especially self-employment. But, in fact, such people and freelancers can hardly feel free when they do not get new contracts and orders and have to look for someone to temporarily work for. The area of economy with such type of employment is called *Gig Economy* (Schwab, 2019: 38, 45; Abraham et al., 2018). In this case, employees do not get any social guarantees from employers, they are protected by the state at the least possible level. The person assumes all the risks.

Thanks to robotics, artificial intelligence frees man from routine monotonous physical or mental labor. Nevertheless, the need for highly qualified labor is growing in the economy, and the role of man as the main creator of progress is increasing. It is only the state that has enough capacity and power to consider such opposite trends and to set society up to overcome their negative consequences. Therefore, the role of the state is increasing, rather than decreasing. This is what both, people and capital, need.

Artificial intelligence complements the human intellect as a tool to manipulate with the objects of labor. In the future, people may have more spare time for self-development. But so far, hired labor remains the key source of income for most citizens of developed countries. The vast majority of goods and services remains the result of hired labor. It is no coincidence that employment issues are the key points of election campaigns in both the USA and Europe.

5   Conclusions

The modification of political economy subject and method in the age of digitalization is due to changes in the economic relations between people in terms of the production, exchange, distribution and consumption of goods. Since the relationship between capital and labor has been essentially preserved, social contradictions have shifted towards state structures that define the model of national development. The common trends of the modern world are becoming increasingly manifest:

- the role of the state as a guarantor of modern "laws of the game" in the market system is increasing;
- new forms of monopolism, including those based on intellectual property, are emerging and expanding;
- the emergence of *Gig Economy* as a form of self-employment undermines social protection of employees;
- the area of creative labor expands the boundaries of an aggregate employee, but does not reduce unskilled labor;
- the fourth industrial revolution, digitalization and *globalization 4.0* do not reduce the intensity of competition between multinational corporations and countries for energy, raw material, water and human resources.

The application of political economy as a consistent theory can be instrumental in the search for responses to the challenges that civilization has produced for individual countries and for the whole of humanity.

References

Abraham, G., Haltiwanger, C., Sandusky, K., and Spletzer, R. (2018). *Measuring The Gig Economy: Current Knowledge and Open Issues. NBER Working Paper 24950.*

Bodrunov, S.D. (2018) *Noonomy.* Moscow: The Cultural Revolution Publishing House.

Buzgalin, A.V., Kolganov, A.I., and Barashkova, O.V. (2018) *Classical Political Economy: Modern Marxist Trend. Basic Level. Advanced level.* Moscow: LENAND.

Economic Report of the President, March 2019. Together with Annual Report of the Council of Economic Advisers (2019). Washington D.C.: U.S. Government Printing Office.

OECD (2019) *Measuring the Digital Transformation: A Roadmap for the Future.* Paris: OECD Publishing.

Ryazanov, V.T. (2019). *Modern Political Economy: Prospects of Neo-Marxist Synthesis.* Saint-Petersburg: Aletheia.

Schwab, K. (2019) *Technologies of the Fourth Industrial Revolution.* Moscow: Eksmo.

CHAPTER 10

Noonomy in the Transition to a Post-capitalist Society

Perspectives from the Global South

Leo Gabriel

"La Transición" (the transition) is the dictum that has dominated the discussions of left-wing intellectuals throughout Latin America since the outbreak of the pandemic. While Evangelicals indulge in doomsday scenarios and conspiracy theories, analysts critical of the system from Rio Bravo to Pantagonia agree that the neoliberalism that emerged in Chile in the 1970s has reached its dead end. Although the individual anti-capitalist schools of thought have the most diverse objectives depending on their political convictions, ranging from left-wing liberal neo-Keynesianism to geopolitical Stalinism, the authors agree that "after the pandemic" cannot be the same as "before the pandemic".

"La normalidad es la muerte" (normality is death), said the Peruvian economist Hugo Cabieses, who was briefly Environment Minister under Ollanta Humala until he resigned in protest against the construction of a gigantic gold and copper mine (the *Conga* case). In fact, the state of emergency that the majority of Latin American countries have now declared has in fact begun much earlier, leading to a large number of social protests as early as 2018/2019. The Italian philosopher Georgio Agambe even speaks of a century of state of emergency, which has always been present but has now been brought to light by the pandemic.

In this sense, Pope Francis, who just came out with a new encyclic under the title "Fratelli tutti" (to all brothers), distinguishes between the "small virus" and the big virus, the "virus of indifferent selfishness and injustice" that is currently spreading throughout the world. It is a fact that unemployment in Latin America has reached unprecedented levels and in not a few countries the collapse of their public finances is approaching slowly but consistently. This is not only indicated by the double-digit negative growth in many countries, but also by the fact that, unlike in Europe, the social security systems have virtually ceased to exist in the wake of the neoliberal turnaround.

1   The Second Wave Is Bringing the Economic System to Collapse

This is also the reason why in almost all countries of Latin America (perhaps with the exception of Uruguay and Cuba) the so-called "second wave" of the pandemic has become a nightmare – almost regardless of whether the governments had decreed a *shutdown* or followed a *laissez faire* policy. There is a race against time to avoid the collapse of the economic system, which most governments are losing just because the governments still refuse to look for alternatives to the free-market fundamentalism which has been and still is the main reference point for nearly all State-prone economists. Whilst in Europe the rapid rise of infection rates has led even the European Union (EU) to take at least verbally some distance from the dogmas of their austerity-policies the hardliners of the International Monetary Fund (IMF) and the World Trade Organization (WTO) still impose their murderous adjustment measures which provokes another pandemic: hunger.

Because at the difference to Europe where a majority of the people still can afford some months of unemployment with or without State-sponsoring, in Latin America it is the hardships of impoverished peasants and inhabitants of marginalized urban areas that prevent the population from taking protective measures. In most cities the last place to go with an infected person is a public hospital, because of the extremely high risk of infection there.

"No hay mal que por bien no venga" (There is nothing bad that does not have its good sides). This old Spanish proverb is immediately recalled when one cross-cuts the contemporary economic literature of Latin America. Even before the World Health Organization identified the COVID-19 as a global phenomenon, the publication of post-capitalist utopias has increased.

2   Alternatives in the Head

The multi-dimensional crisis as an opportunity for a paradigm shift is not new: "Change the system and not the climate" was the slogan that had inspired the environmental movement for several years. At the same time, the criticism developed against transnational financial institutions such as the IMF and the World Bank with its fixation on growth has become louder and more radical. There are many webinars putting forward *degrowth* as a worldwide concept and reference point which they say is now more necessary to stick to than ever. This theory, derived from the work of Ivan Illich (Illich, 1971), demystifies the purely quantitative approach to economy as a kind of substitute for religion, with which neoliberal economists from Friedrich Hayek to Milton Friedman subjugated the majority of the world's population.

On the other hand, the concept of *Buen Vivir* ("good life"), which derives from the cosmovision of the indigenous people in the Andean region and involves a unity of man and nature, has inspired not only many authors in Western Europe, but also big ecology movements like *Fridays for Future*. But also, the theories around the *commons*, which are public goods (like water, energy management, health and education) that should be withdrawn from private appropriation, have gained in relevance – just in a time when the pandemic has shown how life-threatening the privatization of sanitary services can be.

Closely linked to the *Buen Vivir* and the *commons* has developed throughout the last 30 years the theory and practice of the so-called *solidarity economics*. In a sharp contrast to the apologists of neoliberalism, who put self-interest first and subject the economy to a market mechanism based on competition, solidarity economics aims to a cooperation between communities based on an economic order, in which the cultural environment plays a leading role.

3   Noonomy – an Icebreaker for a New Economic Paradigm

It is in this extremely challenging context, also the concept of the Russian economist Sergey Bodrunov for reorganizing economy according to non-economic standards which he calls *Noonomy* is very important (Bodrunov, 2018). According to Bodrunov traditional economic concepts have failed to consider that economy by itself, which neoclassic economists have mainly reduced to material production, is a result of extra-economic factors like knowledge and culture. In *Noonomy* he has forwarded the thesis that with the development of the new digital technologies the classical dichotomy between capital and labour can be overcome.

At the same time, as human mankind can increasingly rely on the achievements of a rather complex knowledge society for the material production of goods, it also offers a space for cultural creativity which transcends the material production. This is particularly important for countries like the ones in Latin America which still rely on local, mostly agricultural production. Especially indigenous people often have a very ancient wisdom equivalent and sometimes even superior to knowledge in industrial and post-industrial societies.

Wherever it is applied *Noonomy* can serve as a structure for a globalized society on a world scale. The principle remains the same even if the cultures are very different. In a certain way the traditional communities whose cultures have not be distorted by the colonial and postcolonial traditions of enlightenment are able to understand and implement more easily to the virtues of a post-industrial knowledge society than industrial ones. Besides that, millions of communities are defending their *autonomies,* which is another keyword in the universe of *Noonomy.*

Also, one should bear in mind that many of the organisations of the so called "Third World" are more integrated in transnational networks than workers-organizations like trade unions. *Via Campesina* for instance, a peasant organisation created by the Brazilian landless movement disposes of a network of more than 50 million people. But also, the billions of so called "unemployed" who are living in the peripheries of the mega-cities could be activated easily, because being "unemployed" does not mean that they don't work.

By going beyond the classical distinction between "productive" and "unproductive" labour Bodrunov opens up a new world including those who have been suffering under the boots of industrial stakeholders. When Karl Marx had still written that he had "turned the state-supported concept of Friedrich Hegel and German idealism from the head to the feet", one could claim with Bodrunov that economy should go back to its very roots: *nature* and *life.*

It is clear that such a huge endeavour to create a new paradigm for a post-industrial political economics the State has to play a key-role – not only because of its ownership of important means of production and its control over the armed forces. The function of the (Nation-) State is to watch the mechanisms of redistribution of public and private wealth and to fulfil the role of a power-breaker between the old and the new economic world order by giving utmost importance to social security and a carefully elaborated plan of political action.

4   Strategies Waiting for Their Implementation

But isn't all of this an overly daring endeavor that falls more into the realm of utopia than into the ground of reality? Not at all, if one gets to the bottom of the manifold crises that threaten not only Latin America today, but the whole world. Because – as was unanimously expressed only recently at a virtual meeting of the International Council of the World Social Forum – the crisis does not originate from the virus, but has only become visible through the pandemic: extractivism, which destroys nature and people; the increase of authoritarian to dictatorial governments of different ideological origins; the rise of poverty and the associated migration flows, etc. All of this has now become visible in one swoop even to those media of the political mainstream which were previously busy with raising the sandy beaches of Copacabana and the mountain peaks of the Andes to the sky.

It is clear, then, that capitalism in its neoliberal form will no longer be able to destroy the "great virus" of which Pope Francis speaks and restore the status quo ante. But it is equally clear that there are already now more or less mature goals of a new world view. But what is still completely unclear is the way in which these goals can be achieved. At the moment it rather seems as if these ways are escape routes on which every single citizen and every single state tries to run away from the threatening disaster according to the principle "Save yourself, as much as you can".

5   The Second Wave of People's Movements

It is precisely in this respect that the American continent is once again a few steps ahead of Europe. While in this country people are still pecking at whether the prescribed mouth and nose protection is really as healthy as the health ministers claim, in Chile, Colombia, Brazil and above all in the USA crowds of people have joined forces to oppose the ruling power structures and – what is even more important – to change them. All these struggles are associated with great sacrifices of the persons, which have become victimized in a double sense: on the one hand, because their women and men are directly affected by the pandemic, and on the other hand, because they have to bear the full weight of police and many times even (para-) military repression.

Although all these social movements have partly very different objectives – such as the environmental and the peace movement, the anti-racist *Black Lives Matter* and the indigenous movements for autonomy, the movements for a new constitution and, last but not least, the international human rights and women's movement. They all have in common that they are not only critical of the system but also anti-systemic in the true sense of the word.

In this situation, which most authors refer to a as transition, the World Social Forum, founded almost exactly 20 years ago by Brazilian social networks under the lead of renowned intellectuals such as Noam Chomsky, Boaventura dos Santos, Alberto Acosta, Yanis Varufakis, Adolfo Perez Esquivel, etc., have developed a forum for the discussion of social and political issues:

"From an open space to a space of action" was the title of the first declaration, which can be read on the website www.foranewwsf.org (World, 2021), as much as other contributions. But there are also some comments on the slogan of the *Green New Deal* promoted by the EU. In a recent webinar, Yanis Varufakis, former Minister of Economy of the left-wing Tsipras government, said: "The Green New Deal is okay, but this alone is not enough to overcome the multidimensional crisis". Perhaps what it needs is *Noonomy* to find out the guidelines for the necessary transition.

References

Bodrunov, S.D. (2018) *Noonomy*. Moscow: Kul'turnaia revoliutsiia.
Illich, I. (1971). *Deschooling Society*. New York: Harper & Row.
World Social Forum. An official website. Available (consulted 23 August, 2021) at: https://www.foranewwsf.org.

Postscript

Alexander Buzgalin

The twenty-first century has become the period when history, which seemed to have ended with the fall of the USSR and the World Socialist System, has once again demonstrated its stern temper, intensifying challenges that have been facing humanity for a long time. The tragedy of poverty and social inequity; global rivalry, a tension not dissimilar to that of the eve of World War I; global challenges, which go well beyond the climate and the pandemic ... And all this against the background of increasing technological capabilities, which, however, are being implemented extremely slowly and unevenly: the futurists of the 1960s were sure that by 2000, industry, transport and most services would be fully automated, while the futurists of the 2020s are not sure that this will have happened even by the end of the 21st century ...

Now, these contexts make a conceptual understanding of the transformations that have been dragging on for almost a century extremely relevant again. Our world is on the verge of a new sort of technological and social existence, it takes a step forward and then two steps back. It rushes forward and retreats. It wobbles and is afraid finally to choose the high road of *development*. Reflecting this fear, a postmodern methodology even calls for the rejection of the 'grand narrative' of social progress, and proffers instead an 'ostrich-in-a-zoo-with-a-concrete-floor' strategy of deconstruction, deterritorialization, desubjectivization, and so on and so forth, and all this in the space of simulacra, in which we create ourselves.

Are there any alternative approaches? Yes, there are. But it would be better if some of them did not exist. Recently, the conservative trend has begun to gain more and more strength (especially in countries like Russia): back to great power statehood (or even autocracy), a feudal state and emphasis on power structures in everything from politics to economics, and not excluding culture.

Before that, the post-industrial discourse that *seemed* to inspire optimism, was very popular, which turned into deindustrialization, financialization, and two world crises.

In the marginal intellectual and political space, Marxism has been developing with its theory of the uneven leap in time and space from "the kingdom of necessity" to "the kingdom of freedom" (the author of these lines shares and develops this theory too). But there is a different search for different solutions.

The book you have read provides a vivid example of the reflections of the leading – I am not afraid of being accused of exaggeration – intellectuals of our time on the new theoretical concept proposed by Professor S. Bodrunov, the theory of noonomy. I will not supplement the reflections put forward in the book with my own vision of the challenge. I will allow myself to put something different in words, namely those provisions of the theory of noonomy, which, with numerous qualifications, are in fact accepted by the authors of this book. They are accepted to varying degrees, with the mandatory polemic (there is no science without this), with attempts to add to and develop them, but nevertheless they are accepted.

Firstly, there is the integration of the politico-economic and socio-philosophical approaches to the study of current fundamental transformations and trends leading to the future. Here, I would draw attention to the texts by A. Porokhovsky, who emphasizes the role of classical political economy, and ones by O. Smolin, who stresses the fundamental methodological and philosophical aspects of the theory of noonomy.

Secondly, there is the consideration of the theory of noonomy in the spatial aspect, in the context of the contradictions of globalization. These are the contributions from R. Desai, who offers her original vision for the integration of the theory of noonomy with her own geopolitical and economic approaches; from J. Galbraith, who points out straightforwardly that the theory of noonomy makes it possible to comprehend in a new way the deepest contradictions and global trends of economic and political confrontations, and global problems, including pandemics; and, finally, from S. Glazyev, who is focused on the search for spaces of overlap between the theory of noonomy and the theory of technological and world economic structures (I would emphasize that at the heart of Bodrunov's theory of noonomy is a thesis in which technological transformations play far from the decisive role).

Thirdly, I would specifically highlight the creative research of authors who demonstrate the potential of the theory of noonomy to solve a very wide range of problems that are very diverse and seem far from this theory, from the creative economy (A. Freeman) to the development strategies of countries as different as China (E. Cheng and S. Gao) and Cuba (J. Garcia Brigos). I would like to add to this A. Kolganov's contribution on the prognostic potential of the theory of noonomy, and the relations of this theory to L. Gabriel's attempts to find other models for a postcapitalist society. But all this is nothing more than just a flavour of the totality of the ideas contained in this book.

..

Perhaps, it would be a mistake not to emphasize specifically the short, but content-rich introduction to this book made by Professor Bodrunov, the author of the theory of noonomy. I will allow myself to give advice to the thoughtful reader: if you are interested in problems of noonomy (and I imagine you must be since you have reached the conclusion), then do not limit yourself to this one book. Bodrunov has written a whole series of works on this subject, including not the author's core texts, such as *The Coming New Industrial Society: Reloaded* and *Noonomy*, but also a number of later monographs, as well as numerous articles listed in the appendices to this book.

I would also like to note that preparation of this book took much time, which is understandable, given that the authors live in different continents (which, by the way, allows us to conclude that experts from many countries and various areas of socio-philosophical and economic thought have taken an interest in the ideas and theoretical foundations of noonomy), the book is supplemented with a list of the most significant works not only of the author of the theory of noonomy, but also with a small selection of those researchers acquaintance with whom will enable interested readers to develop a more complete understanding of the subject of this book and discover for themselves, in a combined fashion, an anthology both of the ideas of the theory of noonomy and its ontological foundations.

Index

www.ingramcontent.com/pod-product-compliance
Lightning Source LLC
Chambersburg PA
CBHW070104030426
42335CB00016B/2009